" *Or how to run a business...* *...while standing on your head!* **"**

THE COMPLETE GUIDE TO

UPSIDE
DOWN
MANAGEMENT

BY JOHN TIMPSON

First published 2002.

Second Edition Published 2005.

Written by John Timpson CBE, 2002.

© John Timpson CBE 2005.

ISBN 0-9547049-5-9

Produced by Timpson Limited.
Timpson House
Claverton Road
Wythenshawe
Manchester
M23 9TT

Telephone: 0161 946 6200
Website: www.timpson.com

Printed and bound in Great Britain by Butler & Tanner Ltd.

Contents

Introduction

We manage our business in an unusual way – this book should help you understand how and why it works. It describes our management culture in pictures.

I call it 'upside-down management' because the people who serve our customers run the business, everyone else is there to help.

Upside-down Management is such a simple concept you might wonder how it can fill a book. Turning your management upside down opens up a new world.

As we develop our business style more possibilities are revealed – this book sets our what we have learnt so far.

People matter most

I struggled to run a business for 20 years before discovering the importance of delegation. In the end, the concept arrived as a flash of the obvious. Our success depends on customers receiving an excellent service. We have over three hundred shops and I can only be in one at once and I am so ham fisted I can't repair shoes. I have no choice but to delegate.

When I change from retailer to a shopper and become a customer myself, I feel the frustration that comes from poor service. "This till is closing now love." "You can't have that it won't go through the computer." "You must see the manager and he's gone to the bank." "I am not allowed to do that."

These businesses don't trust employees. Their sales assistants are given lots of rules and no authority. You can't run a shop through regulations, every customer is different. Good service is about looking after unusual customers and dealing with complaints, not just handling routine sales according to the book.

Basic principles

There are some pretty stupid business sayings, like 'retail is detail,' (detail is useless if you are in the wrong market) and 'it's good to have healthy competition,' (it's a lot easier to have no competitor at all.) But there is truth in each phrase. You can't run a retail business sat behind a desk and strong competition sharpens the mind.

Four years ago, my main competitor, Mr Minit was acquired by the Swiss bank UBS. Having a rival with pots more money, made me uncomfortable. How could I compete? Fortunately throwing money at a problem is no guarantee of success. I adopted three objectives. First, to provide an excellent service, second to be the best at everything we do, from key cutting to watch repairs and third to be an excellent employer.

I was talking about this to my Deputy Chairman, Kit Green, whose passive wisdom has provided great benefit at most of our Company's defining moments. "Write it all down" he said, so I did, I wrote it in pictures rather than words and what follows is the result.

Chapter 1

Upside-down Management

Management style

Proof it works

Not long ago, James visited Julian Metcalfe the Chief Executive of Pret a Manger. "How did it go?" I said. "It's a great business" replied James. "They do lots of things very well, particularly training and customer service, no wonder they are so successful. But amazingly Julian Metcalfe is worried about failure. He is so terrified things will go wrong, he continues to strive for improvement."

I too worry about complacency, I fear every time we talk about success we risk pride before a fall. Despite this worry, I will still mention some achievements. I take that risk because success has come from managing in a way many people regard bizarre. I have been described as a 'Maverick.' We do things not found in the text book - but they work. Our ideas are not just theory they have been proved in practice.

Track record

During the last six years we have become the UK's market leader in shoe repairs, key cutting and engraving. In 1997 we introduced watch repairs which has become the fastest growing part of our business. While sales have been going up, labour turnover has fallen. In February 2001, we were fourth in the Sunday Times list of best companies to work for (the highest placed retailer, and the highest placed U.K. owned company.)

The thing I call "Upside-down Management" works. It has proved invaluable in securing an increase in profits while our industry has been in rapid decline. I hope I have already said enough to persuade you to read on.

Upside-down Management

Upside-down Management

Nearly all the best ideas are pinched from other people. You find them in the most unexpected places. In 1997 I was visiting New Zealand to see my daughter who was teaching in Auckland. I only read on holiday, for the rest of the year I don't get further than The Telegraph crossword. During a weekend at the Bay of Islands, north of Auckland, I read about Nordstrom, the successful American retail chain. In the book I found their management chart, with the customers and sales assistants at the top and the company president at the bottom.

I adapted their chart, called it "Upside-down Management" and have used the diagram to explain our philosophy ever since. At first glance it seems revolutionary but on closer inspection it is common sense.

Shop staff run our business

Football teams need good players on the pitch, the manager can't score a goal from the touchline and the chairman can't make a vital tackle in the directors' box. It's the same with us. If I am in Manchester, I can't help a customer who walks into our shop in Windsor. The shop staff run our business. I am there to help.

I don't plan to retire but intend to take an extra weeks holiday each year. I enjoy holidays. I know one Managing Director who never goes away for fear of letting his team loose in his absence. He misses a lot, I bet he never has time to read books and probably hasn't heard about Nordstrom.

Delegating authority

All our people have the authority to spend up to £500 to settle a complaint. Most outsiders think I am mad, but it shows we delegate to the people who meet our customers. I don't want customers thwarted with "I'm not allowed to do that." or "I must wait for the manager." I know how frustrating that can be.

Once, outside a pet food store, I lacked the £1 needed to obtain a trolley. I asked the cashier to change £5. "Can't do that love, I'm not allowed in the till." "Could I speak to the manager?" I asked. The cashier huffed grumpily and rang a bell. Four minutes later the manager arrived without a smile. "I'm not really allowed to do this" she said, suggesting I was the guilty party. It gave me poetic pleasure 12 months later when the store went bust.

I am wary of Electric Point Of Sale (EPOS) because I think you pay a big price for computer stock control. I started in retail before the computer age, when shop managers ordered from a central warehouse. They chose their own stock, and made sure they sold it. When computers started to issue merchandise, the shop managers had someone else to blame. Our managers order their own stock, the computer keeps score while people still run our business.

In Spring 2000 in Meadowhall, Sheffield, I met a watch repair competitor. "Tell me something?" he said "I can't understand your price list. Wherever we compete you beat us on price." I explained our price list is a guide, the final price is left to the person who serves the customer. He couldn't believe it. "How do you control the business?" he asked. "By visiting some shops every week" I replied.

You can't keep complete control and still give each customer an excellent service. Every watch repair job is different, only the person who takes in the watch can judge what needs to be done and what should be charged.

Don't think delegation lets you sit back and watch others do all the work. I spend one or two days each week visiting shops, asking questions, watching and listening. I need to discover where help is needed to make things better. Delegating authority changes the role of management but it doesn't take away the need for managers to manage.

To amaze or not to amaze

Amazing our customers

Recently I visited Lowestoft with our Area Manager, Dave Clark. I offered to buy lunch at a shop selling freshly made sandwiches. From an interesting menu both Dave and myself chose Waldorf salad on pitta bread. "They will be a couple of minutes" said the bearded man who served me. As we waited the two minutes stretched to ten and then fifteen while we watched other customers being served delicious looking food. We were on a tight schedule and could have done without the wait but I had paid the money and was determined to get my sandwiches. When they arrived, they were excellent but my clearest recollection is not of Waldorf salad but lousy service. Next time I'm in Lowestoft I will go back to Boots.

I want our shops to provide the best service on the High Street. We constantly look for ways to improve shop fitting and machinery but we know service mainly depends on the people who work in our shops.

Freedom to succeed

There is little I can do to help the customer who walks into Peterhead while I sit behind a desk in Manchester. But I can do something. I can give our branch staff freedom to do what they believe will amaze each customer.

The last sentence reveals two important principles. First, we must invest total authority in our shop staff to do what they think is best, no company rule must get in the way. Secondly, we should aim to amaze customers. We don't just look for good service, we want our service to be amazing. If you try to amaze every customer things start to change.

Our business does not advertise - no posters - no television - no press but we promote the business 250,000 times a week. Every time a customer visits a shop we advertise how good or bad we are. We want customers to be so amazed they tell their friends. That is the best form of advertising.

Our two rules

Golden rules

It took me 30 years to discover you can't run a business using a set of rules. Instructions from head office are seldom read and often ignored. I believe management should provide help not regulations.

But even our business has to have some rules. We have two, they cover things beyond question. 1) 'Act The Part.' 2) 'Be 100% Honest.'

People from outside the company wonder "Can you ensure the money goes in the till?" I run a constant anti-corruption campaign and now the majority of employees realise theft not only harms the company but costs them as individuals.

Our 100% honest rule goes beyond cash security, we expect everyone to be truthful. A business based on trust cannot condone lies.

The Timpson Tie

In 1979 our shops looked a shambles, untidy heel bars run by slovenly staff. Luckily I hit on an idea that made all the difference. I insisted everyone wore a tie. Since then, the Timpson tie has become a symbol setting our shops apart from other shoe repairers and key cutters. It is the visible sign of Rule 1, "Act The Part." I encourage everyone to produce ideas to improve the business, but common sense says you won't increase sales by turning up late, smoking in front of customers and looking scruffy.

Just two rules distinguish us from everyone else in our industry. Timpson people know if they are caught pinching money, they leave the Company, no excuses and no exceptions. The tie has set the Timpson standard.

Several years ago one of my main competitors asked "How do you stop your staff smoking in front of customers?" I didn't tell him the secret was to insist they wore a tie.

Our centres of excellence

Key Cutting

NIGEL HOBSON
MANAGER KEY
EXCELLENCE CENTRE
(SARSDEN)

IAN OAKES
KEY
PRODUCT MANAGER

Watch Repairs

GLENN EDWARDS
MANAGER WATCH
REPAIRS EXCELLENCE
CENTRE
(WOLVERHAMPTON)

JOHN PAYTON
WATCH REPAIRS
PRODUCT MANAGER

We aim to be the best at everything we do !

WE HAVE SET UP
FOUR STATE-OF-THE-ART
CENTRES OF EXCELLENCE TO PROVIDE
ADVICE AND CARRY OUT SOME OF THE
MORE TECHNICALLY SPECIALISED WORK.
IN ADDITION WE HAVE A PRODUCT
MANAGER DEDICATED TO DEVELOPING
THEIR OWN AREA OF BUSINESS.

Shoe Repairs

JIMMY CLARK
MANAGER
SHOE REPAIRS
EXCELLENCE
CENTRE (SARSDEN)

RICKY VASS
MANAGER
BRANDED SHOE
REPAIRS
EXCELLENCE
CENTRE (LUTON)

JOHN HIGGS
SHOE REPAIRS
PRODUCT
MANAGER

Engraving

MAL CHADWICK
MANAGER
ENGRAVING
EXCELLENCE CENTRE
(ST HELENS)

PHIL OSBORNE
ENGRAVING PRODUCT
MANAGER

Being the best

Thirty years ago shoe repairing produced 95% of our turnover. Every year since 1969, shoe repairs has declined, the market has fallen by 90%. Only one in ten cobblers has survived. Everyone who survived had to make a success of something else to compensate for the gap. Our future was secured by key cutting followed by engraving and now watch repairs.

In 1999 the Sunday Times featured us as a case study. Experts said we should look for yet more new services to help us grow. They suggested dry cleaning, jewellery repairs, repairs to spectacles and even servicing computers and mobile 'phones. I don't want to be Jack of All Trades but I rule nothing out, no one can forecast what a business will be doing in five years. In ten years half of the things that will be in common use have not yet been invented. We could do almost anything but I will only introduce a service if I believe Timpson can become the best.

For long-term success you need a competitive advantage. Our sort of business can't promote on price, the public doesn't trust a cut price service. The way to compete is to be the best.

We now cut one in eight of all replacement keys in the U.K. We have achieved that position by aiming to cut every key every time for every customer and making sure that it works. We have built up an £18m key cutting business simply by aiming to be the best at what we do.

Improving our service

> We can always get better !

Watch Repairs

In-branch mechanical watch repairing is widening the appeal of this fast developing service

Shoe Repairs

We are finding more ways to bring back the appeal of traditional, high quality footwear repairs

We are currently developing each main part of the business

Computer Engraving

By 2002 most engraving will be carried out on a while - you - wait service by computer engravers.

Key Cutting

New challenges such as developing the opportunities in transponder keys and the locksmith service mean our keycutting business still offers great potential.

Getting better

Whenever I visit one of our shops and find something wrong I think it's great. Every blemish gives us a chance to improve. If we know we have faults, there is a chance we can get better.

For 25 years I have had a list of problems. A collection of things that we can improve. Solving the problem improves the business. It is a continual process, each year reveals a new set of challenges and a further chance to progress. I like change, most people don't. But you have to change if you want to get better.

Each part of our business, shoe repairs, key cutting, watch repairs and engraving, has a product manager who aims to improve the quality of our service. In their quest for high standards, they established Excellence Centres - central workshops that set a standard of quality and expertise for everyone else to follow. Our workshops not only do the most difficult jobs they also provide the rest of the business with a telephone helpline.

I hope we never believe we are good enough. If we think we have cracked it we will stop wanting to get better. In five years time I hope we will look back in disbelief at how badly we do things today.

Creating the best

> We never stop trying to improve the business and keep updating our image - almost every shop will receive some kind of refit over the next two years.

Invest in the future

My first love was shoe retailing not shoe repairs. My Great Grandfather opened his first shop in 1865 and I was delighted when I achieved a management buyout to regain family ownership of the business 118 years later. It was a major wrench when I had to sell the shoe shops in 1987, but I had no choice. We couldn't justify opening another shop. The business was too difficult and the profits too low to support further investment. We couldn't even afford to keep our present shops up-to-date.

If you look at the High Street you see who is suffering. The signs of trouble at Marks & Spencer were seen in the threadbare carpets and dilapidated fascias well before poor figures were revealed in their annual results. Management can be seduced by new ideas, by growth and acquisitions and fail to invest in the core business that created the company's strong market position.

Don't stand still

Inertia is not a viable strategy. Companies can't decide to stand still, they either continue to progress or decline. You must invest to make progress, but the investment has to be wise, don't just pursue pet projects, find things that provide a payback within 18 months.

You may think 'Upside-down Management' gives the Chief Executive nothing to do. Don't believe it. The Chief Executive must find the money for investment. I have mortgaged my house twice to support the business and don't intend to do it again, so every year I must make sure trading produces a cash flow of at least £2$^{1}/_{2}$million.

Everyone helps

Everyone can help me run the business !!

Suggestion Scheme

Each year we receive over 300 suggestions from over 100 employees. Every suggestion published gets a cash award - the biggest award to date is £350.

Write to John Timpson

Everyone can write direct to John Timpson.

Introduce A Friend

Bring good people into the business and gain a special reward.

Annual Survey

Each year we carry out a detailed attitude survey and ensure that we are listening and acting on our own staffs' views.

Conscience Line

RING UP IF SOMEONE IS THREATENING YOUR BONUS

CONSCIENCE LINE

07887 561509 or
07979 595636

Everyone has a duty to ensure that company standards are maintained. If you spot a problem you must tell someone.

SHOP CLOSED	SCRUFFY	POOR SERVICE	MONEY PINCHED FROM TILL

Everyone runs the business

I can't repair shoes and I can't cut a key. That is not quite true, I did cut one key following a full day's training from Stephen Davenport our main key blank supplier. The key worked first time, so I decided not to risk cutting any more.

Early in 2001 I was in London on the day of a tube strike, I met Lee Nichols our Area Manager in Victoria at 7.45.am. He and his ADM team already had everything organised. All shops were open, anyone who couldn't get transport to their own branch had arrived somewhere else. I stood back in admiration watching them manage a tricky situation. It made me realise how much more our people know about my business than I do.

It's a mistake for a boss to think he knows better than everyone else. A good boss does a lot of listening. His job is to find the right strategy, pick the right people and invest in the right projects. For a manager to make those decisions, he needs to listen to the people who know best, the people who work for him.

How to be heard

The listening can take many forms, like a suggestion scheme, an attitude survey, our "Introduce A Friend" recruitment scheme, or calls to our conscience line. The best managers listen as part of their day-to-day life. At Timpson that means lots of shop visits and discussion groups which give everyone a chance to have their say.

There is a wealth of knowledge in our company, loads of good ideas just waiting to be found. When a manager finds a gem and it works, he should always thank the person who gave him the idea.

Give credit to the people who really run the business, you can't do without them.

Telling everyone, everything

We believe in telling everyone everything about our business

Weekly Sales

LAST WEEKS % ON LAST YEAR		
+9%	+2%	Repairs
	+6%	Keys
	+11%	Engraving
	+29%	Watch Repairs
	+6%	Merchandise
Best Area: Lee Nicholls +17% (cumulative)		

Branch Results

		872 Swindon
BRANCH CONTRIBUTION		
Total	24,718	23,693
% of Turnover	19.2%	19.9%
STAFF COSTS TO TURNOVER %	30.1%	24.9%
MATERIAL USAGE	7.5%	8.6%

Regular Video Updates

TIMPSON VIDEO

Annual Profits

Martin Tragen
Finance Director

Martin Tragen, Finance Director is very pleased with current trading. "In sharp contrast to the difficulties seen by many fashion trade retailers, our turnover remains consistently good."

Martin goes on "The benefits coming from our investment in watch repair Super Centres, computer engraving branches, refits, new sites and practical skills training are seen in another year of record profits. This is as well as new business from contracts obtained by the branches and from our Excellence Centres.

Already this year we appear to be on target for making another record and this means we can confidently plough even more investment back into the business for the benefit of all our employees.

Company Magazines

TIMPSON WEEKLY NEWS
Recognition
Sunday Times puts Timpson in Top 5
"Best companies to work for in UK"

THE SUNDAY TIMES
50 BEST COMPANIES TO WORK FOR 2001
See page 6

TIMPSON NEWS
AMAZING!!

An open book

I don't understand why people keep their business a secret. They hide things of interest in a file labelled "Strictly Confidential". They probably think competitors might pinch their ideas, or staff will sense success and ask for a wage increase, or see poor results and jump ship to work elsewhere. Often files marked "Strictly Confidential" are part of a political power game and some senior executives believe no one below a certain level should know what is going on.

This secrecy loses the advantage of telling everyone everything. Never mind about prying competitors, if the figures are good, they won't believe them. If the figures are bad all they do is gloat.

Most businesses don't copy ideas, they prefer to pursue projects developed in their own backyard. So forget secrecy and take advantage of open communication. Let everyone know what is going on, and broadcast everyone's achievement, it will do the business nothing but good.

If you keep quiet, people fear the worst and formulate a rumour. When you tell the truth, you develop an atmosphere of trust. You can't disclose absolutely everything, some things must be marked "Confidential," - they concern individuals whose privacy you should respect.

We are not fettered by Stock Exchange rules, but reveal all our figures. The only time I can be accused of keeping our people in the dark is when I don't know what is going on myself.

Every call to Timpson House will get a helpful response

WE PROMISE TO RESPOND TO EVERY REQUEST WE GET FROM A TIMPSON BRANCH

BOARD OF DIRECTORS

JOHN TIMPSON — CHAIRMAN & CHIEF EXECUTIVE
JAMES TIMPSON — MANAGING DIRECTOR
PARESH MAJITHIA — FINANCE DIRECTOR
PATRICK FARMER — NON - EXECUTIVE DIRECTOR
ROGER LANE-SMITH — NON - EXECUTIVE DIRECTOR

ASSOCIATE DIRECTORS

PERRY WATKINS — SALES
BILL TAYLOR — OPERATIONS
TRICIA DAVIS — PROPERTY CONTROLLER
HELEN THOMPSON — HEAD OF FINANCE

SWITCHBOARD

DORYS PARKINSON

SECRETARIES

BARBARA MASON — SECRETARY TO JOHN TIMPSON
MARTINE TEMPEST-MITCHELL — SECRETARY TO JAMES TIMPSON
DOREEN BARNES — SECRETARY TO SALES & OPERATIONS ASSOCIATE DIRECTORS
KAREN CARTER-LEAY — PA TO PARESH MAJITHIA

HEALTH & SAFETY

KEN BARKER — MANAGER
MICHELLE STYAN — ASSISTANT

PEOPLE SUPPORT

GOUY HAMILTON-FISHER — HEAD OF PEOPLE SUPPORT
CHARLOTTE HIPKISS — DEPUTY HEAD OF PEOPLE SUPPORT
BILL PLATT — PEOPLE PERSON

PRODUCT MANAGERS

IAN OAKES — KEYS/SHOE REPAIRS
JOHN PAYTON — WATCH REPAIRS/ENGRAVING
GLENN EDWARDS — TECHNICAL MANAGER WATCH/JEWELLERY REPAIRS

CUSTOMER SERVICE

MIKE DONOGHUE — CUSTOMER SERVICE CONTROLLER
MANDY KAY-BLACKWOOD — ADVISOR
JOAN BYFORD — ADVISOR

EXCELLENCE CENTRES

STEPHEN MARSH — NATIONAL WORKSHOP MANAGER
TRICIA HARPER — NATIONAL WORKSHOP ADMINISTRATOR

TRAINING

PETER HARRIS — TRAINING CONTROLLER
CYNTHIA HAMMOND — TRAINING ASSISTANT
NATALIE VALLANCE — TRAINING ASSISTANT

PENSIONS

ROSEMARY WHITEHEAD — PENSIONS

HOUSE NAME PLATE

BRIAN THOMPSON

FINANCE DEPARTMENT

KARINA KENNA — FINANCE MANAGER
GAIL COBB — PAYROLL MANAGER
JANET LEIGHTON — FINANCE MANAGER

I.T.

ANDY BAUGH — I.T. MANAGER

BUYING DEPT.

PHILIP TINKER — BUYING CONTROLLER
HELEN KERRIDGE — BUYING OFFICE MANAGER

HERE ARE THE FACES OF THE PEOPLE IN TIMPSON HOUSE AND THE WAREHOUSE WITH WHOM YOU MAY NEED TO SPEAK FROM TIME TO TIME.

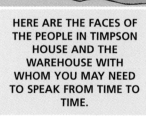

WAREHOUSE

JOHN QUANTRILL — WAREHOUSE MANAGER
DAVE BENTHAM — WAREHOUSE SUPERVISOR
EMMA WALKER — PA TO JOHN QUANTRILL

NEWSLETTER

CLAIRE HOLLINGSWORTH — NEWSLETTER EDITOR

WEBMASTER

RUSS SANDERS — WEBSITE/ARCHIVES

DEVELOPMENT DEPARTMENT

ANTHONY HORSFIELD — DEVELOPMENT CONTROLLER
JOHN MONKS — SHOPFITTING MANAGER
SARA HONEY — MACHINERY MANAGER/HELPDESK SUPERVISOR
PETER BODEN — DISPLAY MANAGER

LOCKERS & KEYSDIRECT

CLIVE STIRLING

POSTROOM

STEVE RODGER — MANAGER
STUART DONOHUE — ASSISTANT MANAGER

LOCKSMITHS

MARK TALBOT — MANAGER

One big helpline

We have just put stickers on the 'phones in our office. "The person on the other end has a customer waiting." A reminder that branch staff have the most important job.

For years people believed all power should be at Head Office. In Autumn 2000, I was in Scotland for an Area Dinner. I flew up in the morning to visit some branches and was surprised to see a notice on the shop door at Kilmarnock. "We close early tonight and reopen at 10 o'clock tomorrow." "Why 10 o'clock?" I asked the Manager. "I want to open at 8.30am as usual but the notice came from Head Office." was his reply. "Why 10 o'clock?" I asked the Area Manager. "I thought it was company policy." he responded.

Head Office

It's hard to shake off the idea that Head Office runs the business. Everyone at Timpson House has an important job, but they are no more important than anyone else. When it comes to day-to-day management, that's done in the shops. People at the office can't run the business. They can't repair shoes or cut keys and they are not in the shops to serve customers and put the money in the till.

In the last five years things have changed dramatically. Everyone at Timpson House recognises they play a vital part, but they don't send instructions that might get in the way. Customers are more important than memos. The office role is to help, when a shop rings up, the perfect answer is "Yes, no problem, I can help, I will do it straight away."

Sports, social and charity

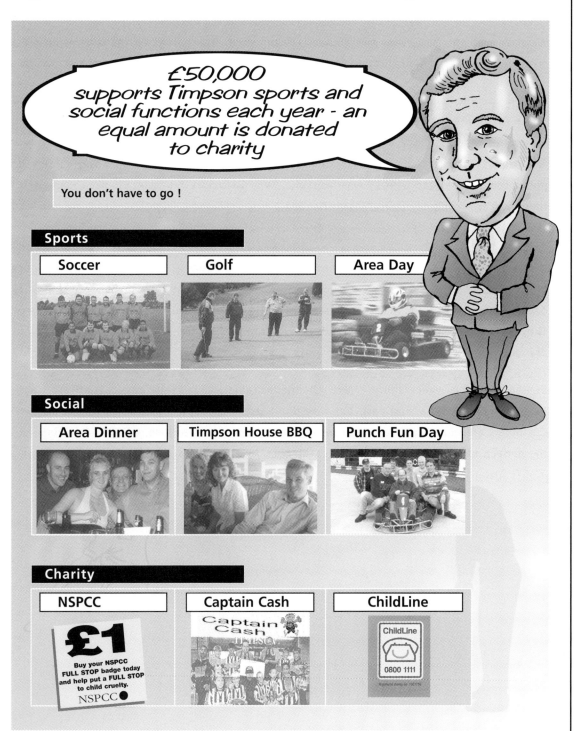

£50,000 supports Timpson sports and social functions each year - an equal amount is donated to charity

You don't have to go !

Sports

Soccer

Golf

Area Day

Social

Area Dinner

Timpson House BBQ

Punch Fun Day

Charity

NSPCC

Captain Cash

ChildLine

Fun and fellowship

Business life is not just about business, we must make room for fun and friendship. No one has to join the Timpson social scene but it's there for anyone who wants it. Company and area functions give us a chance to relax and say 'thank you,' not only to the people who work with us but also their partners who give unpaid support.

We have a growing sporting programme, golf and football are particularly popular. Our annual football tournament draws a large crowd who witness the strength of team rivalry between areas. Once a year we try and find a novel activity for Area Managers. Clay pigeon shooting, paint balling, go carting and an evening at the races. Business is pretty serious. You don't make money unless you work hard but leisure is equally important. Business can be tough but there is no reason why it can't be fun.

Good causes

I believe we should have a social conscience, we show it in our annual charity campaign. Charity is not just about writing a cheque to the Chairman's favourite fund, but something that involves the whole company, not just giving money but also time and commitment for a worthwhile cause. The £300,000 that we raised for children's charities (NSPCC and ChildLine) in less than two and a half years did more than provide money, fundraising gave everyone the chance to do something worthwhile and in the process improved our stature with customers.

We have buildings, machinery, materials and stock but the company is mainly made up of people. The Timpson social programme says a lot about the business.

The superstars

To be successful we must have good people. Nowadays there's not much point in advertising for qualified cobblers and key cutters, the best already work for us.

When we changed our job advert and asked people to apply to the business that came fourth in the Sunday Times list of the best companies to work for, we got a great response. But it is one thing getting replies to an advert, it's another picking the people who will be a success.

Mr Men

Three years ago I was wondering how I could help Area Managers select candidates who fit into the Timpson culture. On a train from Crewe to London, I came up with the answer, my 'Mr Men.' I realised we wanted people with the right character, ambitious, friendly, faithful, skilful people, not the careless and grumpy, slow and dull. I turned this thought into cartoons and we have been using the 'Mr Men' chart for selecting people ever since.

You can waste a lot of time training people who are never going to be any good. Find the right people and ask them to bring their personality to work, supply the training and you will make them into a success.

Businesses used to talk about synergy, I never really understood what the word meant but I think it is something like 2+2 = 5. If you put good people together that's what you get.

Recognising achievements

> ## We try to recognise every special achievement

Long Service

All staff who complete 25 and 45 years with Timpson have a presentation at a special lunch held at John Timpson's home. We also recognise from 10 years of service with special awards.

Chairmans Award

Up to £500 has been awarded by John Timpson for action "beyond the call of duty".

Customer Compliments

When a customer sends in a special letter of praise it is sent to the member of staff being complimented.

Area Prizewinners

Every area has a Company Dinner every 18 months. Everybody who works in the branches are invited with their partners. Prizes are awarded for:

- Young employee of the year
- Most improved branch
- Manager of the year.

Regular Competitions

We hold regular competitions to encourage staff and maintain standards.

A Simple Letter

John Timpson sends out up to 30 letters each month to shops that have achieved special results.

Well done

Every day someone in our business does something fantastic which is never even noticed by default. We fail to say "thank you" and "well done" to people that really deserve it.

Even though we miss a lot of good things, we try hard to discover the heroes. We recognise long service with a cheque every 5 years and a special event after 25. We have shops of the week, shops of the month and an annual quality competition. Customer care winners have been given a free holiday. For action beyond the call of duty there is a special Chairman's Award. I send a cheque direct to the winner's home with a handwritten letter to say "Thank you."

Pepper with praise

We should praise people ten times as much as we criticise. We need lots of reasons to say "well done." Every week about 100 people are mentioned in our newsletter. Many win a cash prize but people don't always need money to feel valued. Each year I send over 200 personal letters in my almost unreadable handwriting, simply to say "Well Done" to people I feel deserve it. There isn't a cheque inside but the letter still seems welcome. Praise is important, it is nice to be appreciated.

Pay in line with success

Share in success

I don't believe in equality, the best people should be paid more than the worst. People who like bonus schemes are good for the business. We want to encourage everyone to be involved in our success.

For years our shop staff have been motivated by the Timpson bonus. It works because it is simple to understand and is paid out weekly. We distribute 15% on all sales over the turnover target. The target isn't set by a faceless executive, but by the wage bill. The week's wages are multiplied by 4.5 to set the target for every shop every week. If someone is sick their wages are excluded from the calculation, those left to do the work get the extra bonus they deserve.

No limit

This weekly scheme has been in operation for 25 years. We tweek the calculation occasionally but only after consultation and a full trial and always in a way that increases the bonus. There is no limit on earnings. Recently, Dean Tugman in St Albans got an order for 2500 keys, he cut them all in a week, produced a record shop turnover of £7,385 and collected a personal bonus of £912.

There is no point in capping a bonus scheme, the more our people earn, the more I like it.

Occasionally, employees suggest we should scrap the bonus and have a bigger basic wage. I disagree. The bonus is not always fair, but it's the best we have found. It's worked so well, I wish I could discover something as good for people at Timpson House.

Training

Everyone is responsible for their own training

We have a manual to help develop every skill

GUIDE TO KEY CUTTING

GUIDE TO WATCH REPAIRS

GUIDE TO ENGRAVING

CUSTOMER CARE MANUAL

GUIDE TO EXPERT SHOE REPAIRS

Each manual contains a detailed practice pack

You are surrounded by people who can help develop your skills

Qualified Trainer

Area Manager

Area Development Manager

The training secret

Five years ago, I thought training cost a lot of money and didn't do much to develop the business. I had the impression people were bored by training courses, and qualifications were assessed by ticking boxes on a Government approved form. I now understand where we were going wrong. The training needed 'Upside-down Management'. Training is only effective if the trainee wants to learn. That's why we made every individual responsible for their own training. Our job is to encourage them to learn.

Self taught

We try to make training fun, using illustrated manuals and providing self practice packs. Timpson people can teach themselves, the manuals set out everything they need to know in words and pictures. If they can't learn from the book, there are plenty of people to help. Each area has its training development manager and a team of in-branch trainers qualified to teach a range of skills from apprentice to expert cobbler. By giving everyone responsibility for their own training, we have created a culture where people are keen to learn.

It's taken four years to develop our training scheme, now Timpson people ask for help with their own training.

Qualifications

> *Qualifications and improved skills bring increased pay*

Skill Bonus

- 1 Point for each level 1.
  Shoe Repairs, Keys, Engraving

- 1 Point for Manager's Diploma

- 1 Point for Watch Repairs Level 1.

- 1 Point for each Level 2
  Shoe Repairs, Keys, Engraving

Further points will be awarded in the future for higher skill levels.

Trainer Bonus

- £5 Trainer Bonus for every day of training by a qualified In - Branch Trainer,
  £25 Trainer Bonus for every week of training by a qualified Apprentice Training Manager.

It's worth paying for experts

Training is not just a question of going on courses. We want people to get real qualifications, to be better at shoe repairing, key cutting, engraving, watch repairs and providing customer care. Our training should create a better service for our customers.

We measure success with a set of diplomas, levels one to four in each of our main skills. The diplomas are not just judged by ticking boxes, candidates have to pass a practical test. They must show they can provide a quality job for customers.

Cash for skills

To encourage people to learn, each diploma attracts an extra bonus. The thought of spending more money on wages put a worried look on the face of Martin Tragen, our Finance Director. "We already pay them to repair shoes and cut keys, they don't need an extra bonus to do a proper job". But people don't do everything for nothing. If it takes an extra bonus to produce a bit more effort, then it's well worth the money. I want everyone to be in favour of training.

Peter Harris our Training manager agreed the bonus payment was a good idea. He suggested a one off special payment for every diploma, but I wanted something more permanent. The diploma should be more than just a certificate like GCSE which stays in a drawer long after you have forgotten what you revised for the exam. Our diplomas are like a golf handicap that is kept up-to-date, indicating everyone's current expertise. We link the diplomas to the weekly bonus scheme. More skilful individuals get a bigger share of the bonus. We introduced the scheme on June 1st 2001, it changed our culture, overnight everyone took full responsibility for their own training.

Help at hand

We help staff negotiate financial problems

Hardship Fund

BANK STATEMENT

FINAL DEMAND

£739

ACCESS

GAS BILL

Up to £2000 loans available to cope with short term financial help

Personal Loans

After 12 months employment you may be considered for personal loans to assist with a major purchase.

Convenient Payment of Wages

Choose the most suitable method of payment, cash, cheque, weekly, monthly.

NAT WEST

CASH   BANK ACCOUNT   SAVING SCHEME

Pension Fund

All employees can apply, usually after 2 years service.

TIMPSON LTD PENSION FUND

Mortgage Guarantee

Established employees, (generally after 5 years with the company) can apply for help with a home purchase.

Financial disaster

We aim to pay people as well as possible and reward success. But financial help is not confined to basic pay and bonuses. Employees should have the chance of using the company's financial muscle, not just with pensions but other things like life insurance and company loans.

We don't want to pry into people's personal finances, but we are available to share their financial worries. The shoe repair business has a bad track record for dishonesty. Staff found it easy to solve their money problems by taking cash from the till. Given this background it's in everyone's interest for the company to give financial help rather than waiting for staff to help themselves.

Sometimes we are told it's our fault people pinch money, they claim we put them in a fix because of travelling costs, a drop in bonus, or because they are overlooked for promotion to a higher paid job. We should already know if there is a problem but on the other hand they should tell us first.

Give us a call

Most Timpson employees now realise its best to talk about their problems. Between 10 and 20 people take out a Timpson company loan every month. Our hardship fund really works. Most people get confused in a complicated world of credit cards, mortgages, tax and standing orders. Cobblers and key cutters are no different to anyone else. From time to time they need some financial assistance. If the company can help, then that's what we should do.

Promoting from within

> We always aim to promote from within

INDUCTION

All new recruits to Timpson undergo an induction programme that usually takes about 3 months.

SHOE REPAIRER / KEYCUTTER

Following induction, qualified employees take on day to day responsibilities reporting to a branch manager.

MANAGEMENT EXPERIENCE

As part of their development all members of staff are trained in the book work and if possible will have the opportunity to run their branch on the managers day off.

RELIEF MANAGEMENT

Joining the relief staff is a major step bringing the chance to manage a branch and see a lot of different Timpson stores.

BRANCH MANAGEMENT

Timpson believe in True Delegation, and the Timpson manager (with the support of HQ) really does take responsibility for the running of this branch.

BIGGER BRANCHES

The Timpson chain includes the biggest shoe repair and key cutting shops in the UK. There is considerable scope for advancement in the management role.

SPECIAL ASSIGNMENTS

Some branch managers take added responsibility visiting other shops playing a leading role in our training programme.

AREA MANAGER

The focal point of our field team. The Area Managers have prime responsibility for the day to day running of the business.

REGIONAL MANAGER

The most senior field role has a significant influence on the company's present and future success.

Home grown

In 14 years our only outside appointments have been people connected with property, finance or computers. All our Area Managers started as apprentices. We promote from within because it works. New Football Managers change the team and change the tactics. Outsiders coming into a business also bring change and in the process can upset a lot of people.

I don't want a dramatic upheaval, I believe in progressive improvement, evolution not revolution. Experience shows we already have the talent, our current team knows so much about our business any outsider would spend a year getting up to speed.

No stigma

The business must train existing people to form the next generation of management. We give future managers special assignments, which provide a chance to assess their potential. We look kindly when we make a mistake and promote someone too far. There is no stigma attached to going back to a job at the right level.

Many companies fail to recognise the quality of their own people, they are tempted to bring a superstar from outside and 12 months later discover the change was a disaster. Home grown Timpson people have developed our business extremely well for 14 years, I see no reason to change.

Confidential advice

A problem shared

I have seen it so many times, if a good manager starts to do badly, there is usually a reason behind it. Initially all we see is a business problem. The figures are down, customers are complaining, the shop looks a mess.

It's often nothing to do with work, it might be a marriage problem, bereavement, an illness or debt. It could be drink, drugs or gambling. We need to tackle the real problem and help the person through their personal difficulty.

Speak up

We can't solve problems until our people talk about them. They don't have to tell us, they could confide in a colleague but they must start talking, it helps a lot when someone listens. The company is sympathetic to someone who wants to help themselves. We may be able to help just by listening, but often can arrange time off or a move to a different job. It's well worth our time and effort to help employees who are going through a difficult period, once their problem is resolved they nearly always return better people.

Chapter 2

The people who matter most

The people who matter most

Too many businesses are screwed up by managers who think they are more important than anyone else in the organisation. The scenario is only too familiar, an accountant, a merchant banker or someone else who has learned management out of books, sweeps into the Board Room in the belief they are bound to do better. They see an easy way to improve profits by cutting out costs. Cutting costs means culling people, not at Head Office and certainly not the Finance Department, but out in the field by tightening the wage percentage and cutting out a level of line management. A pay freeze and a reduction in bonuses brings in a substantial saving in salaries, but this arrogant management approach assumes budget sales will be achieved. When front line troops get turned off, there is every chance sales will fall. This set back is met by further rounds of cost cutting until senior management politics takes over and the Chief Executive fires the Managing Director or the Chairman fires the Chief Executive and another professional manager is given a high salary and big share options to repeat the process until the Receiver arrives.

Amaze our people

There is no point in talking about 'Upside-down Management' if you don't believe that people matter. It seems such an obvious principle, the better we look after our people, the better they will look after our customers. But I still find people who raise their eyes when I say our aim is to look after the people who work in our business, by increasing their pay. We haven't adopted these principles because I have left-wing ideals, I am not paranoid about being politically correct, nor am I nervous of falling foul in the forest of employment legislation, I want to look after my people because I think it's good for the business. In fact, I will go further, I say we should aim to amaze our people, we should look after their interests so well they are amazed at what we do on their behalf.

A difficult concept

Some time ago, I decided the way to improve customer care was to ask our people to amaze customers. If we amaze the people who work for us, they are more likely to give our customers great service. "They won't believe you" said Kit. "Why not?" I replied, "it's obvious, a business that looks after its people is bound to do better." "You might think that" said Kit "But you won't find it easy to persuade others to believe in your idea."

Pay increase

When I started to write the manual, I realised what he was saying. You can't look after people without turning some well established management principles on their head. There is no better example than our attitude towards pay. We don't believe in making profits by keeping pay down, our aim is to increase pay. But we don't want a pay structure, rigid salary schemes ensure the worst people are paid as well as the best. We want to pay the best people better. It is right that the business shares its success with the people who deliver the improvements.

Everyone runs the business

Better pay is not the only way to amaze employees, we should also promote praise rather than criticism. Congratulate people on their initiative rather than criticise them for not toeing the line. 'Professional' managers who run businesses into the ground by a series of cost cutting and redundancies, see people as a cost centre they can manipulate. In the process they ignore their greatest asset. Employees are the best source of ideas, they are the people who have their ear to the ground, not the market researchers or the consultants, why ask outsiders what to do, when there are plenty of insiders who know the score. Too often people are not involved in the running of their own business. Managers not only fail to ask them for advice, but they starve them of information. Executives will happily brag at the bar of the golf club, revealing their latest management accounts, but fail to show the same figures to their fellow workers. I believe in telling our employees everything, that puts them in a better position to help me run the business.

After hours

Amazing your workforce can extend beyond the business itself. We have the resources to help when they have a problem. We can help with financial and marriage difficulties, bereavement and drugs, but the Company should not force itself into an employee's home, we are only there if help is requested. Nor does an employee have to be involved in the Company's community work. Company Dinners are optional, and commitment to the Company's charitable causes is very much on a voluntary basis.

Promotion

Management won't do things that amaze its workforce unless it trusts them. The whole thing works even better if the workforce trust each other, that is why I emphasise promotion from within. Not just because it's a nice thing to do, but because it works brilliantly for our business. The only time we look at outside appointments is for specialist skills that don't exist within the business, usually accounting or computing.

Proof it works

When I first showed the draft manual about amazing people to our area managers early in 2000, I was in for a surprise. They thought some proposals were revolutionary, but agreed with them. None more so than Don who had been the most dictatorial. He was so taken with the idea of amazing people to improve the business, he took my notes away with him. The change he has made in the atmosphere, his sales and his profit has been nothing short of remarkable. He proved you make more money by looking after people than by cutting the wage bill.

Amaze your people

Stun the troops

It only takes one minute of logic to work out why people are so important at Timpson.

Q. What does the company do?
A. Repair shoes, cut keys, repairs watches and engraves.

Q. Who does all these things?
A. The people who work in the shops.

Q. What single thing do you need to be successful?
A. Satisfied customers.

Q. Who serves the customers?
A. The people who work in the shops. You had better look after them.

Every day we want someone in Timpson to tell a friend "I work for a great business." We ask our managers to amaze their people. We can only amaze if we do things they don't expect, things that other employers don't do. You don't amaze people by writing a set of rules. However good the pay, the praise and the fringe benefits, if they are part of company policy, they can be good but they won't be amazing. 'Upside-down Management' gives area managers the chance to amaze, they have the freedom to do what they like. I want them to do something special for their people, because we want our staff in turn to do something special for our customers.

We aim to pay people according to their ability

The rate for the job

Most pay structures are unfair, good people are paid the same as passengers, I want our best people to get more money, that's why there is no limit to our bonus scheme and why there is such a big difference between the lowest and highest paid managers.

Unequal pay

Every year I hear the same complaint. "Why can't you pay your managers the same basic rate?" the reply is simple. Managers are not the same, what incentive is there for a superstar if he is paid the same as a pedestrian. Our salary bands are so wide that our highest paid managers can get more than their area manager. I don't see a problem with that, if all the area manager wants is more money, he could go back to management. But he would never be able to earn as much as the best paid area manager, that's the way our system works.

People who work to rule might not like our pay scheme, but the people we want in our business think it's entirely fair.

Pay according to ability

ANNIVERSARY REVIEW CONTENTS

Everyone has their basic salary reviewed annually, usually on the anniversary of their joining the company.

BIG INCREASE

BETTER THAN AVERAGE

A STUDY THE FACTS
1. Current pay v Company average / Area average.
2. Average pay increase.
3. Current performance.

AM **MUST** DECIDE

AVERAGE

B MAKE YOUR DECISION

C TELL EMPLOYEE
- How much.
- Why.

MODEST

NO INCREASE

EXPLAIN TO YOUR STAFF THAT THEY HAVE A RIGHT OF APPEAL

APPEAL

- NO STIGMA... REPLY GUARANTEED
(No pay system can be totally fair!)

APPEAL TO:
A.D.M | A.M | R.M | JAMES | KIT | J.T. | GOUY

NOTE

LONG SERVICE COUNTS
We value experience
PENSION FUND / ANNIVERSARY / LONG SERVICE / BONUS

The pay review

It's easy to give everyone the same annual salary increase every year, but it isn't fair. We helped to develop an individual approach to pay by reviewing everyone's salary on the anniversary of the date they joined the company. It's not my idea, it was introduced by Kit Green's predecessor, Michael Frank in the 1970's and it's worked very well ever since.

Happy anniversary

This separate annual review date makes the managers think about each individual - should it be more or less than the current company increase. If someone's increase is below average, they must be told why they have been held back and given an opportunity to register an appeal (with no worry of retribution.) Individuals should have the chance to complain about their salary, no system can be totally fair.

Our policy of rewarding people according to ability takes account of management skills, craftsmanship and length of service. We like loyal employees. There is a range of ability amongst the people who work for Timpson, I hope it is reflected in their pay.

Our aim is to use company success to increase individual pay

BONUS SCHEME

TOTAL OF ALL WAGES
PAID IN THE BRANCH
X 4.50
= BRANCH TARGET
ACTUAL SALES - TARGET X 15%
= <u>BONUS PAID</u>

NEW

POINTS ALLOCATED

POINTS	SKILLS PASSED	
1	SHOE REPAIRS	1
1	SHOE REPAIRS	2
1	KEY CUTTING	1
1	KEY CUTTING	2
1	ENGRAVING	1
1	ENGRAVING	2
1	WATCH REPAIRS	
1	MANAGERS DIPLOMA	
2	MANAGER	

MANAGER — Maximum 10 Points
No.2 — Maximum 8 Points
PART-TIME — Pro-rata

LEVEL 3 will qualify for bonus in due course

NEW

SICKNESS RULES   A TYPICAL EXAMPLE

MISS 1 DAY	LOSE 1 point
MISS 2 DAYS	LOSE 3 points
MISS 3 DAYS	LOSE all branch bonus
MISS WEEK	LOSE all branch bonus
MISS SATURDAY	LOSE 3 points
MISS SAT & 1 DAY	LOSE all branch bonus

NEW

ADM BONUS

55% OF AREA MANAGER BONUS - WHICH IS LINKED TO AREA CONTRIBUTION INCREASES.

AREA MANAGER

▶ **YOU'RE IN CHARGE**

ALL BONUSES IN TIMPSON LIMITED & TIMPSON GROUP ARE SUBJECT TO CANCELLATION OR AMENDMENT AT ANY TIME.

Happy to pay

Can it be true that we are really keen to increase individual levels of pay? Of course it is, we must look after our people, if the business does better, the people who create that success should benefit.

Business is not a game, but it should be fun, so why not introduce a competitive edge in the form of incentives? Footballers get a win bonus, why can't keycutters. I like incentive schemes because they work. Some people say "Why pay incentives, you are already paying people to do the job?" But people come to work for the money, if you give them a chance of earning extra, they will be more motivated.

We have used the same basic bonus scheme for 30 years, whenever we change it we make sure the pay out increases and the bonus is always unlimited. However high your bonus, you get paid on Thursday the following week.

Everyone who works in our business has the right to ask "What's in it for me." Everyone should get a fair reward and if the business does well (and I do well,) everyone who helps create success, should feel the benefit.

We provide the security of guaranteed minimum pay

GUARANTEE

We guarantee that your overall annual pay* will be the largest of the following calculations

* Subject to a good disciplinary record (nothing above oral warning) and a good attendance record (below the Company's average index)

1 BASIC GUARANTEE

90% OF LAST YEARS TOTAL EARNINGS.

2 MANAGERS GUARANTEE

BRANCH TURNOVER	MINIMUM GUARANTEE
UP TO - £1,000	£12,500
£1,000 - £2,000	£14,500
£2,000 - £3,000	£15,500
£3,000 - £4,000	£17,000
£4,000 - £5,000	£19,000
£5,000 - £6,000	£20,000
£6,000 - £8,000	£21,500
over £8,000	£23,000

YOUR PAY

BONUS LINKED TO SKILLS

90% GUARANTEE

MANAGER'S GUARANTEE

YEAR TO APRIL 5

APPEAL

APPEAL TO:

A.M.   R.M.   JAMES   KIT   J.T.   GOUY

IF THEY DISAGREE WITH THE CALCULATION – THEY CAN APPEAL.

Safety net

We want job security to mean exactly what it says. Our policy of giving big bonus earnings makes pay fluctuate from one year to the next. We have a guaranteed minimum to create stability. Everyone is assured their pay will be at least 90% of the previous year.

No one forgotten

In most companies there is someone who suffers through neglect, I want to make sure no one is put in a side water on low levels of pay. Our guaranteed minimum pay system makes sure that doesn't happen. Everyone is assured of a minimum rate according to their skills and, if they are a manager, the size of their turnover.

Just in case my minimum guarantee isn't foolproof, there is the opportunity to appeal. It's important to protect the rights of the individual. By working for us, they put their faith in the company, in turn, we have a duty to them and their family.

We aim to be the best payers in the industry

WARNING → **THERE IS ALWAYS SOMEONE WHO MAY PAY MORE**

ADVISE THE EMPLOYEE TO LOOK FOR THE HIDDEN PITFALLS

DESPERATE COBBLER CO.

Payments in cash.

No Pension Fund.

Management Style.

3 Months Only.

No chance of promotion.

Poor Working Environment.

Long hours.

TIMPSON PAY SURVEY

AVERAGE PAY IN	TIMPSON BRANCHES	- £14,200
	NEAREST COMPETITOR	- £10,640
	OTHER HIGH STREET SHOPS	- £11,420

ATTITUDE SURVEY 2000

We keep listening to the comments on pay.

	STRONGLY AGREE	AGREE	OK	DISAGREE	STRONGLY DISAGREE
18. I am better rewarded in pay and benefits than others doing a similar job in our industry.	12	26	31	17	14

Top of the pay league

If we say we pay as well as possible, we must be willing to undergo the supreme test. How do we compare with our competition? A comparison of our levels of pay is an important measurement.

The best businesses nearly always pay the best wages. They may not always have the best talent, but their training makes them the best, that's a secret of success. It always pays to be in a winning team.

Our pay rates are not just compared with other shoe repairers, we look at everyone else on the High Street. It should reassure our staff to know we are so keen to be top of the pay scale, but I don't want people to only look at our pay. We aim to be a great place to work.

Praise

Pat on the back

Lots of people do something amazing every week. They should be congratulated, but bosses seldom say "Well Done," they worry that people take advantage of praise.

The right idea

For a time James carried £50 notes in his pocket, to give to branches doing something exceptional. At first I thought, the gesture was too dramatic, but it worked, people got the message that James was looking for excellence and was willing to give spontaneous praise. But our area managers were not so pleased. They asked James to keep his £50 notes to himself and, he reluctantly agreed.

Praise pays

We all like to be appreciated, but praise has almost disappeared from the vocabulary. When I started in business, most executives responded to a salary increase with a "Thank You" letter. After a Company Dinner, we got loads of letters. Very few write today. Praise may be old fashioned but it's still important.

Personal tip

When my father visited shops in the 1960's, there was no McDonalds, he lunched in café's - meat and two veg at the top of a staircase in the middle of the High Street. The cost for two people was about 7/6d (less than 40p.) Father always gave a tip, usually a shilling (5p!) he gave it to the waitress personally. Praise means much more when it's given face-to-face.

Unsung hero

I worry about the people who deserve praise and never get it, all the good things that happen in our business that we never hear about - people who say to themselves, "I don't know why I bother, nobody notices."

We should praise ten times as much as we criticise. It shows you care about the most important people, the people who serve our customers.

Who do you praise

The superstars

Praise as many people as possible, you will find lots of good reasons. A complimentary letter from a customer, or a good week, passing a skill test or a particularly big sale. You can't praise unless you know what is going on. Keep up-to-date with the business gossip. Make a habit of giving out praise every week - it helps you keep your eyes open. One way I issue praise is through hand-written letters to people who have done well. 12 years ago, I made this letter writing a regular routine, but I wasn't particularly well organised. When I went to Canterbury, the manager, Derek Reyes, (now an area manager,) had ten letters pinned on the wall, all sent within the previous six months. That taught me a lesson, I now try and spread my praise round the business. I keep a list to make sure I praise as many people as possible each year.

No favouritism

Don't just praise the manager, a lot of the good things are done by his team. It's important to praise the right people. When a Manager Of The Year is announced at an Area Dinner, you know whether you have picked the right name, the audience tells you. People know who deserves the accolades, its your job to be in tune with public opinion. Any sign of favouritism will quickly be exposed.

Make is special

Make your praise personal. A circular letter congratulating a number of branches is a waste of time. Ring up specially, visit the shop or write a personal letter. Make praise memorable with something special like tickets for a show, or three days off to visit a girlfriend in Ireland. There are loads of ways to praise and they all pay off.

What deserves praise...

...anything special!

Ways to give praise...

1. AWARD A TROPHY
2. CREATE A CERTIFICATE

   This is to certify that
   Julie Harrison
   has successfully completed her
   first year at Timpson with
   exceptional skill and dedication

3. RING THEIR MUM OR DAD
4. AREA NEWSLETTER
5. ADD % TO THE BONUS
6. GIVE A REST DAY PAYMENT
7. AREA DINNER AWARD
8. LEND YOUR CAR

The big question

HOW MUCH DO YOU KNOW ABOUT YOUR PEOPLE?

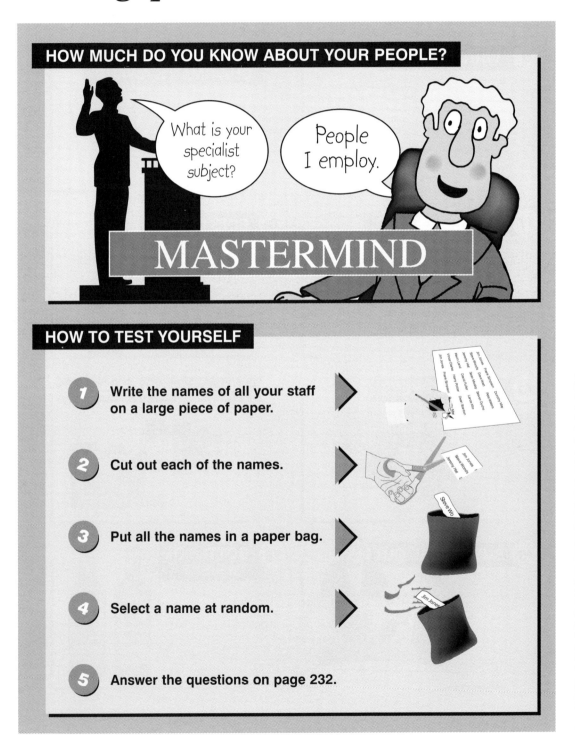

MASTERMIND

What is your specialist subject?

People I employ.

HOW TO TEST YOURSELF

1 Write the names of all your staff on a large piece of paper.

2 Cut out each of the names.

3 Put all the names in a paper bag.

4 Select a name at random.

5 Answer the questions on page 232.

The critical test

Recently our 14 year old son Henry started part time work under the guidance of Wayne Pheasant our manager in Northwich. Every term Henry's school report told us that he found learning quite difficult. Wayne had no problem. Henry took his apprentice manual home and was discovered reading it at 6.30 in the morning. He learned more about key cutting in a week than his school taught him about history during a whole year. He learned quickly because he was interested in the subject.

To be a good manager you have to be interested in people. 'Upside-down Management' gives your team the freedom to do what they think is best, but don't leave them alone. You must know your people well, not just their work but also their personalities. Check how well you know your people by taking the test on the next few pages. If you pass, you are equipped to be a good manager. You can give help where help is needed. You will amaze them with your interest in their lives and, most of all, you will be able to talk to them. The test is easy. Have a go and see if you pass.

The test paper

DO YOU KNOW YOUR PEOPLE?

SUBJECT...(put randomly selected name here)

All the questions relate to your chosen subject

	POINTS AVAILABLE
AGE	5
ADDRESS	5
PARTNER	10
CHILDREN'S NAMES/AGES/SCHOOLS	20
LAST HOLIDAY	10
NEXT HOLIDAY	5
MAIN HOBBIES	10
PARTNER'S HOBBIES	5
CAREER HISTORY	10
SKILL DIPLOMAS	5
HEALTH RECORD	5
MAKE OF CAR	5
PARENTS	5

Score out of 100

More than 70

⟶ You are a people person.

Less than 70

⟶ Get to know your staff before taking the test again.

What you can do with your knowledge

The area agenda creates BUZZ

SUCCESSFUL AREA MANAGERS HAVE SHOWN LEADERSHIP THROUGH...

...Newsletters

...Evenings out

...Area meetings

...Competitions

REMEMBER **YOU ARE IN CHARGE!**

EACH AREA REFLECTS THE CHARACTER OF THE AREA MANAGER.

YOUR LEADERSHIP WILL SET THE STYLE FOR THE AREA

Creating buzz

You need to go to Oban to see how isolated a shop can be. It's a one man unit, 50 miles away from the nearest shoe repairer down the road in Helensburgh. To create an area team spirit, you want every branch to relate to each other. Not so easy when people work on their own and the shops are so widespread.

Team spirit

Somehow you must create the feeling of community. You want them to be rivals, but also colleagues who help each other out. An area newsletter plays a big part in creating that atmosphere. It helps promote competition between branches. Meetings get people together but don't make them boring and don't have meetings which only talk business.

Who presses the buzz button?

As we open more outlets, we make slight changes to the area boundaries. Some shops like Peterborough and Derby are often moved from one area to another. Branches that have seen a number of area managers are best placed to know how one area style differs from another. It's the people who make the team but area managers supply the leadership that gives business life a bit of buzz.

Area newsletter

YOUR BEST WAY IS COMMUNICATION

HOW IT LOOKS MATTERS

People read the big words and pictures.

IT IS WORTH LEARNING DESK TOP PUBLISHING

TIPS

DELEGATE PRODUCTION OF YOUR NEWSLETTER TO AN ADM MANAGER OR SALES ASSISTANT WHO IS CAPABLE.

TIPS

PRODUCE A NEWSLETTER EVERY WEEK.

TIPS

DON'T WORRY IF IT TAKES 3 SHEETS OF PAPER.

Hot off the press

People from many other businesses think our newsletter is amazing. They can't understand how we produce 25 pages every week. The Company newsletter has been a great success, because it is written by everyone in the business. Area manager's should pinch the good ideas that work for the Company and produce a newsletter that amazes their team.

Make it readable

Mention lots of names. The first thing your readers look for is news about themselves. Use Good News notes to gather information. It's the simplest way to get people to contribute.

Take pictures, always have a camera with you. People like reading pictures more than words. Produce your newsletter every week. Once in a while is not good enough. Every so often change the format, it's easy to get stuck in a rut.

Clip art

Before long you will need to become a computer expert, word processing will help the look of your newsletter. That may not be your thing, so why not delegate production to an ADM or branch manager who is a computer wizard.

Use big headlines, to get your important ideas across. Don't waste this wonderful opportunity to spread your message.

Ideas for your newsletter

How to get the news

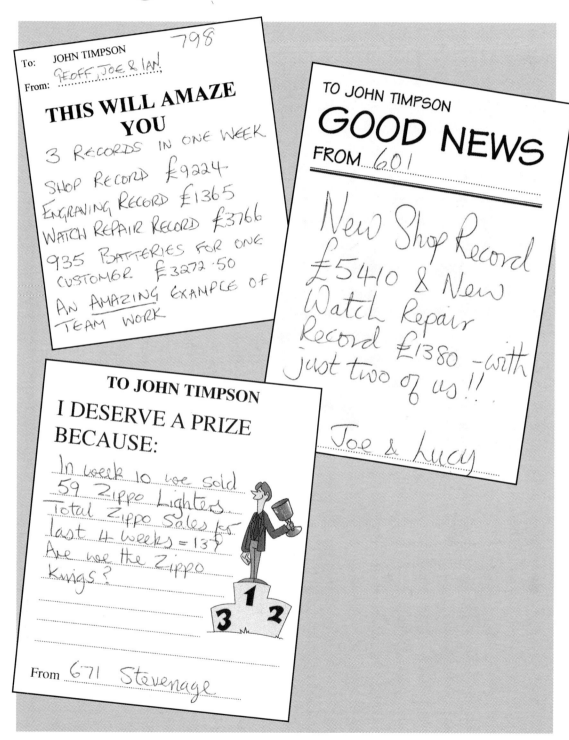

To: JOHN TIMPSON

From: GEOFF, JOE & IAN!

798

THIS WILL AMAZE YOU

3 RECORDS IN ONE WEEK

SHOP RECORD £9224

ENGRAVING RECORD £1365

WATCH REPAIR RECORD £3766

935 BATTERIES FOR ONE CUSTOMER £3272·50

AN <u>AMAZING</u> EXAMPLE OF TEAM WORK

TO JOHN TIMPSON

GOOD NEWS

FROM 601

New Shop Record £5410 & New Watch Repair Record £1380 — with just two of us!!

Joe & Lucy

TO JOHN TIMPSON

I DESERVE A PRIZE BECAUSE:

In week 10 we sold 59 Zippo Lighters. Total Zippo Sales for last 4 weeks = 137 Are we the Zippo Kings?

From 671 Stevenage

Social events

Playtime

An area manager is not only the area leader, he is also the social secretary, who should organise an attractive social calendar. Don't penny pinch. Spend enough money to make sure everyone enjoys their day or evening out. If everyone has a good time, it will be money well spent.

But don't pay for everything. Everyone who goes should pay a bit towards the function. They appreciate it more if they make a contribution.

Be bizarre

Make your social function special. The most bizarre occasions are often the best. Don't choose what you want, think what everyone else enjoys. Don't do anything to do with the business.

You want everyone to enjoy themselves, so they will come again. Turn up early to make sure everything works well. You will have to keep alert but there is no reason why you shouldn't enjoy it.

Meetings

65% OF ALL MEETINGS ARE BORING

BEFORE HOLDING A MEETING
1. Know what the meeting is for.
2. Plan in detail.

WARNING

3 GOOD REASONS FOR A MEETING

1. TO LAUNCH A NEW IDEA.

2. TO CARRY OUT TRAINING.

I'M NEXT FOR ROLE PLAY

3. TO LISTEN & LEARN.

NOTE **ALL PAGERS AND MOBILES OFF.**

Bored meeting

I am wary of meetings, they can do more harm than good. They are particularly annoying when I 'phone and I find "He's in a meeting." This often happens when businesses are in trouble.

Before our acquisition of Automagic, every time I rang their Head Office, they were in a meeting. I am sure there have been a lot of meetings at Marks & Spencers over the past two years.

Think first

Meetings have a role, but think before you meet. Think what you want to achieve. Is the meeting for training? Are you spreading some important news? Are you just there to listen?

Plan your meeting in detail. Start on time and finish early. Rehearse your part carefully. Don't be fooled by the accomplished impromptu speaker, he probably spent hours preparing his talk.

The purpose

Think what you want everyone to take away from the meeting. Are they going to think "that was useful" or "thank goodness it's over." Get some feed back, ask people what they thought, or use a questionnaire. If you make your meetings popular, you will have accomplished a rare achievement, but don't be tempted to hold too many. Have a good reason before you call a meeting.

Run lots of competitions

Timpson Olympics

It's not British to brag about business. Big salaries are criticised in the press and many schools have cut out competitive games. But in the United States it's ok to celebrate success. The captains of industry are celebrities. Life is a competition which you can't win by being average. You can't make your way in life by being mediocre, so I say let's have lots of competitions - they make a difference to our performance.

Lots of ways to win

Don't just award prizes to the people with the best turnover, vary the type of competition. During a pet tag window display competition, the sales of pet tags increased 38%. We solved the housekeeping problem at Timpson House with a tidy office competition at Christmas.

Lots of prizes

Occasionally, award a big prize, but usually lots of little prizes work well. Meals out, and time off are particularly popular. There is no need to give a 'Round The World Cruise!'

Make a fuss

If in doubt, give cash, but don't just add it to the wage packet, present it separately or send a cheque, addressed to the winner's home and always add enough to the next month's salary to cover the tax to be paid on the prize. Whenever you can, make a fuss of the prize giving. Mention it in the newsletter, or at one of your meetings. Write a personal letter, or feature the award in the shop window. Customers like to be served by prize winners.

Put a £1 in the box

Sweet charity

With our charity donations everyone is a winner. We now collect money for jobs we did for nothing and the charity gets the cash. Customers are pleased to see us supporting a local charity and, our branch staff are keen to give the causes their support.

Charity choice

In recent years we adopted a national charity. First the NSPCC, now Childline. The charity is chosen after company wide debate. We only support one cause and want to make sure it's the one everyone wants. But you don't have to follow the company's lead. Currently, Derek Reyes' area is successfully supporting Cystic Fibrosis, raising money for a new unit in Liverpool.

Alan Key at Stafford was keen to raise money for the local hospice, so the four Pottery branches have done so and raised £1000 in the first four months.

I like areas to adopt their own charity, it creates commitment. We raise more money if the area manager takes the lead.

Fundraising champ

We don't just ask customers to put a pound in the box, over the years Timpson people have created some amazingly successful fund raising events. Keith Dutton from Cheadle has cycled to Blackpool and raised £400 and Bob Northover from Taunton raised £3000 by having his chest waxed.

Adopt the cause

Take an interest in the charity you are supporting. Visit ChildLine Centres to see how their system works. It takes determination and effort to raise money, but it's worth the trouble when everyone is a winner.

Who are we looking for

Talent spotting

We don't just want shoe repairers, we want personalities. If you can find people with the right attitude, you can teach them the job. For years our job adverts asked for experienced shoe repairers/key cutters and we got very few replies. Not surprising when you think about it, there are less than 15,000 shoe repairers in the whole country and many of those are people we have already found unsuitable.

Our new job advert "Come to the Top British Company to work for, listed by the Sunday Times," gave us lots to choose from. We don't look for relevant skills, it's not qualifications we want but the right attitude. Superstars come in all shapes and sizes. Men, women, Asian, African, Australian, engineers, teachers, bus drivers and computer salesmen, 17 years old or 57, they can all be winners as long as they have the personality.

We like training people who want to be a success.

Recruitment

Chief scout

Dave Twigg our area manager in the South of England, is fully staffed but recruits all the time. Whenever he has a vacancy, there is someone waiting to fill it. Every week we lose some employees. Most are trainees that fail to reach our standards, but there are always a few surprises. You never know who might decide to make a career change. Good recruitment is vital. We make money selling a service, that service depends on the people we employ.

Shoe repairing is not the most sought after career, so we have to sell the business. We want to attract people who 10 years ago would never have thought of working for us.

Better image

We advertise on our record as one of the 50 best companies to work for, and send applicants more than just a letter. We provide a video and a booklet, discussing our Company history and the way we do business. They are sent to the applicant's home, we often have to convince mum, dad or a partner that we provide a good career.

Set up the interview quickly, 40% of applicants never turn up. Many get another job while they are waiting for a reply.

No worries

I recently heard an area manager complaining he had too many applicants. "That's a worry you can handle," I told him. "Remember when we were looking for shoe repairers and hardly had a reply."

What the candidate receives

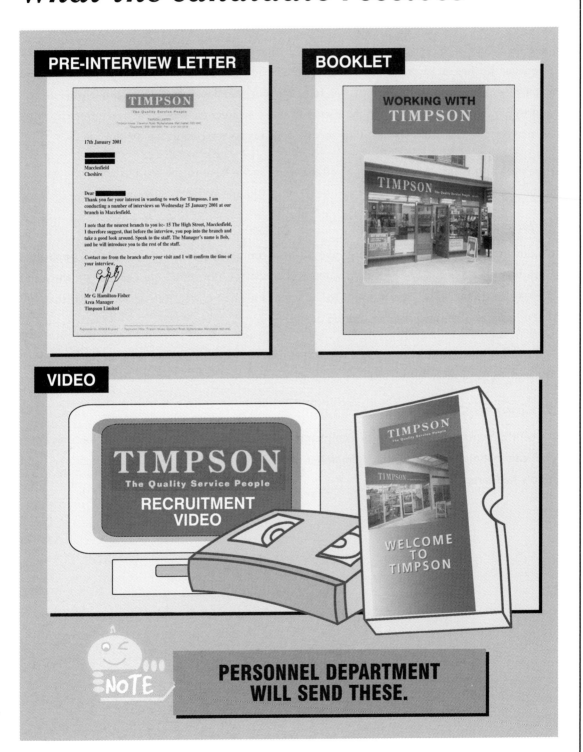

Simplify the selection

Picking the right people is one of the most difficult business decisions. Look at the number of times you get it wrong. People who appear superstars at an interview can become a disaster when they turn up for work. Make life easy for yourself. Persuade candidates to spend a day working in a branch, they will learn a lot about us and, we will learn a lot about them. Your branch staff do most of the interviewing for you. If your team have a strong impression of 'thumbs up' or 'thumbs down' they will almost always be right.

Part time trial

In the 1970's most of the Saturday staff in our shoe shops, were pupils in their last year at school. It gave us a good chance to assess them. Several became full time employees and because of the part-time experience we knew who we were getting.

Look for clues

It's more difficult if you rely solely on an interview. Use all the clues available. Study their application form carefully, don't just read the words look at the handwriting. If possible have someone else with you during the interview, a second opinion helps a lot.

Look the part

Remember interviews are two-sided, you are finding out about them while they are checking out the business. You don't want interruptions, switch off your mobile and choose a quiet location. Don't meet in McDonalds. Be ready to start on time even though candidates often turn up late. Look smart, you could be about to meet the next Timpson Superstar.

Setting up the interview

1 TELEPHONE THE APPLICANT

Once you have the candidates
interest, set up interview quickly,
before interest wanes.
If you are not available delegate.

**2 LINE UP PRE-
INTERVIEW TASTER**

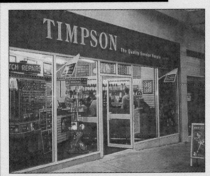

Get applicants to look
around the branch.

**3 BRANCH STAFF
CAN ENCOURAGE
APPLICANTS TO TALK**

Is he a winner?

4 CHECK BRANCH STAFFS IMPRESSION

Question time

The questions don't matter, nor do the answers, rely on your gut instinct.

In the 1980's, as Chairman of Governors at a local secondary school, I had to interview for a new Head. There were strict rules laid down by Manchester City Council. I had to judge everybody purely on their experience and qualifications with everything else excluded from my mind. I could not ask about their home life or hobbies - - nor could I ask their age or years in the job. You can't pick people like that.

Probe the personality

We need to know what sort of person is applying. Will they fit into the company? Will they work hard? Are they our sort of person? Their past experience is not as important as whether they can make a conversation and look you in the eye. Think who else they remind you of, that will provide a key to their personality.

For months I tried to find a way to explain the importance of personality. I found the answer while sitting on a train to London I invented my 'Mr Men.'

To the point

An extreme example of interview technique was demonstrated by an eccentric ex secretary of my Golf Club. A prospective new member went to see him in the Secretary's office. The candidate brought 20 letters of support from personal and business colleagues. The Secretary took one look at them, and threw them into a waste paper basket, "Those don't tell me whether you are a sxxx" said the Secretary, "Let's go out, play golf then I will know what you are really like."

First impressions do count, but you have to rely on instinct, you are never sure you have made the right choice until they start work.

Pointers for your interviews

YOU ARE REPRESENTING THE COMPANY

Present a smart, professional image.

TWO HEADS ARE BETTER THAN ONE

Get someone to join you.

IF INTERVIEWING FOR THE DAY PASS YOUR PAGER ON TO YOUR ADM OR SENIOR MANAGER

READ THE APPLICATION FORMS

ARRIVE ON TIME!

Timpson assessment form

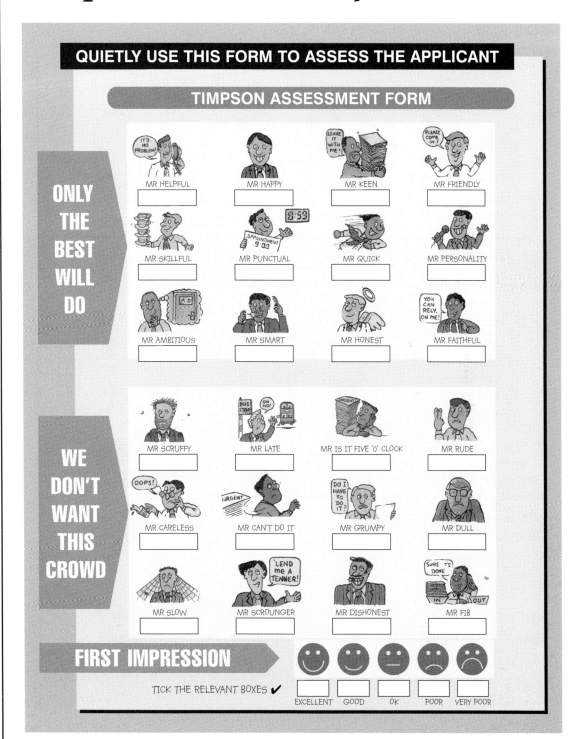

QUIETLY USE THIS FORM TO ASSESS THE APPLICANT

TIMPSON ASSESSMENT FORM

ONLY THE BEST WILL DO

MR HELPFUL
MR HAPPY
MR KEEN
MR FRIENDLY

MR SKILLFUL
MR PUNCTUAL
MR QUICK
MR PERSONALITY

MR AMBITIOUS
MR SMART
MR HONEST
MR FAITHFUL

WE DON'T WANT THIS CROWD

MR SCRUFFY
MR LATE
MR IS IT FIVE 'O' CLOCK
MR RUDE

MR CARELESS
MR CAN'T DO IT
MR GRUMPY
MR DULL

MR SLOW
MR SCROUNGER
MR DISHONEST
MR FIB

FIRST IMPRESSION

TICK THE RELEVANT BOXES ✔

EXCELLENT   GOOD   OK   POOR   VERY POOR

Promoting from within

Keep it in the family

During the last 15 years a few finance, property and computer people have come from outside, but every other management role has been filled from within Timpson. All our Area and Regional Managers have grown with the business. We appoint from inside, because it works. Ours is an ideal business for internal recruitment.

Special skills

We have unique skills, shoe repairs, engraving, key cutting and watch repairs, and the technique of running a multiple service business. There is no one else like us on the High Street, Johnsons, Klick and Supasnap, are similar but not the same. Outsiders find it difficult to adapt to a shoe repair business, and it takes time to become accustomed to 'Upside-down Management.'

Sketchleys successfully developed a shoe repair business in the 1980's with a specialist team of shoe repair area managers. When profits dropped during a period of recession, they saved money by putting the whole business under one area management team. The dry cleaners didn't like shoe repairs which quickly withered and nearly died.

Plenty of scope

Our future depends on how we develop our own people. Not everyone has to be a superstar, there is a role for anyone who works hard and plays a part in our team. But for the ambitious, there is plenty of opportunity, our job is to find the talent and nurture it.

How does the area team develop individuals?

HELP YOUR STAFF TO HELP THEMSELVES

ONE WAY APPRAISALS   A FORMAL TALK EVERY 6 MONTHS

Why 'one way'?
YOU LISTEN, THEY TALK!

You want people to tell you what they really think
- ENCOURAGE CRITICISM!!

QUESTIONS TO ASK

HINTS

GIVE OUT THE QUESTIONS BEFORE THE MEETING.

How do you get on with your colleagues and me?

How can the company do better?

How can you do better?

What are your ambitions?

What would you change about your job?

Do you need any training?

VITAL TIPS

LISTEN CAREFULLY. DON'T MAKE FALSE PROMISES. MAKE NOTES.

Developing talent

Everyone is in charge of their own training and that includes management development. Our job is to help them go as far as possible. Appraisals swept through most businesses in the 1980's, but often did more harm than good. Bosses thought they were sitting in judgement on their team. Weak leaders made false promises while the tough unnecessarily upset their employees.

Employees talk - boss listens

In 'Upside-down Management,' it's the employees who appraise their boss. We believe in appraisals where the employee does the talking, we want them to tell us how they are doing, what they want to do and how much help they need. The bosses' job is to listen, not to make snap decisions or build up false hopes. In the end, each individual will determine how far he can go. The boss should help them reach their potential.

How does the area team develop individuals?

Career guidance

Michael Frank, who was Timpson Shoe Repairs General Manager for 20 years, often told me, "Good people attract work to themselves." He was absolutely right. Good managers have a habit of rising to the top. But, senior management must spot the winners and help them develop.

Pace yourself

Young ambitious people need to gather responsibility at the right speed. If their development is too slow, they get bored and perform badly. If they are pushed too far too fast, they will fall down. We can put them back in their old job without any stigma, but the trainee will have been set back for years.

Set goals

You can't develop management unless you know your people. Keep talking, maturing is a gradual process, management heavyweights do not appear overnight like pop stars. Help people set their personal goals. Good people want a challenge, they need to be stretched. Suggest valuable experiences. Job swaps, sabbaticals, a day out with an area manager, or even helping to write one of the Company manuals. There is no greater job satisfaction for a manager than seeing a member of his team develop into a superstar.

How does the area team develop individuals?

HELP THEM TO SET THEIR OWN GOALS

APPRENTICE

ASSISTANT MANAGER

MANAGER

3 x level 1 by Christmas.

Shop manager before
I am 20 years old.

BRANCH MANAGER

ADM

Training ADM.

Product Manager?
Area Manager?
Introduce a new system
for computer engraving?

NOTE

**LET INDIVIDUALS SET THEIR OWN GOALS –
YOUR JOB IS TO HELP THEM SET
A REALISTIC AGENDA AND TIMETABLE.**

Selecting superstars

It's easy to promote someone, but demotion is difficult. Picking the right team is one of the biggest decisions a manager makes. If in doubt, don't make any changes. So often people are promoted for the wrong reason. Because the candidate lives near the new shop - or simply was the only person who asked for the job.

Use the evidence

Be wary of having favourites, you can get disappointments when you promote your blue-eyed boy. Even the best managers can be deceived by a good talker. Don't ignore the obvious clues, the sales figures often distinguish the good from the bad. One manager who is no longer with us, was able to trade well for about six weeks then his performance fell away. He deceived his area manager who only noticed the six weeks of excellence and the manager was promoted to bigger and bigger branches.

Probation

If you don't spot the winners and losers, you can be certain the rest of your people in the area will. You will gain the respect of everybody if you pick the right person.

It's a good idea to have a trial period, but it's best to get the choice right straight away. Take time making your decision, if you are wrong, you will ruin the individual's career and cause a lot of work for yourself. If you get it right, you will be amazed how much the whole of your business improves.

Who deserves promotion

Who deserves promotion

Chapter 3

Helping our managers manage

Helping our managers manage

Sales can change dramatically when we appoint a new manager. I have seen turnover go up or down by as much as 50% within a week of a new manager taking charge. For ten years Kit Green has been asking me the same question. "How do you define a good manager?"

The best sales don't come from the best shoe repairer, they are more likely to be achieved by someone who is good with customers. But I always give Kit the same reply. "You've got to look at the figures. The sales show the quality of your manager." But for Kit that wasn't good enough. "If we are going to improve" he said, "We must train people to be good managers. We can't do it without knowing the elements that create success." So I wrote another manual, The Manager's Guide – How to Run a Shop.

New guidelines

It was a useful exercise, I brought together all the nitty bits you need to know from opening the shop in the morning, to shutting at night. It covered housekeeping and how to increase sales, dealing with cash and filling in paperwork. All the information had previously been issued in a file of instructions labelled "Standing Order for Timpson Shoe Repair Factories." The old system owed much to the military regime that ran the business in the 1960's. By turning instructions into guidelines and words into pictures, our new Manager's Guide made life easier and didn't put obstacles in the way.

As I listed the contents for this Manager's Guide, I started to realise the hidden quality I was looking for. It wasn't just a question of paperwork and housekeeping, good managers have a special talent - their enthusiasm influences everyone who works with them. I tried to recreate it in the section 'Managing People' which is reproduced in this chapter. It covers the training of recruits, tips on dealing with trouble and how to develop teamwork. Well run shops operate 'Upside-down Management'.

Culture of freedom

Ordinary managers like to have a set of rules, it gives them something to blame when things go wrong. There is no need to use their initiative, they don't even need to think. Their objective is to stick to the rules rather than find ways to maximise turnover. Good managers look at things differently. They achieve extraordinary results by looking after the people who work with them. They create a culture of freedom, allowing individuals to show their initiative. The Company rules are purely a guideline not an end in themselves. Good managers achieve superb results by looking after their customers rather than keeping to the rules. They would like to pass every inspection when the Area Manager calls but their real objective is to improve customer care and increase turnover. The Manager's Guide recognised that 'Upside-down Management' already existed in our most successful shops. To prove the point I delegated the job of writing the manual to one of our most successful managers.

Team work

1 A <u>success</u>ful branch has all staff working as a team

I'VE A BIG KEY ORDER HERE

WE'LL HELP YOU CUT THEM

2 A <u>poor</u> branch has no team spirit

FIVE OF EACH, I'LL BE HERE ALL DAY

YAKETY YAK

The customer will have to wait a lot longer here !

A. WHAT MAKES A TEAM ?

1 *MORNING BOB, SUE. I'M JUST MAKING THE TEA, WANT ONE ?*

Relaxed, friendly atmosphere

2 *SHALL WE HAVE AN IN-STORE COMPETITION ?*

OK, TODAY I'D LIKE TO DO £1,500

Talking and **listening** to each other

3 *WE GOT A LOT OF MORTICE BACK YESTERDAY*

LET ME CHECK THE LANCER AGAIN

Problems discussed

4 Share and discuss information

Winning teams

It might seem odd talking about team work in a business that has only two or three people working in each shop, but it's even more important for us than a company with much bigger branches.

Right atmosphere

Some years ago I was spending a day with another multiple visiting their shops. In one town we were walking past our branch so I popped my head through the door and immediately realised something was wrong. The manager pulled me to one side and told me about his troubles. His marriage was going through difficulties and he was living on a temporary basis with the other member of staff, the arrangement was not working. I knew there was a problem because I sensed the atmosphere as I walked through the door. You could cut it with a knife. If I could sense it a customer would notice as well.

Behind the desk

A manager can't run a branch on his own, he needs a team. As the leader he is the catalyst who creates the group's personality Our managers not only lead but are important team members. It's not like the old days. When I started working in our shoe shops, every branch had its office where managers spent too much time behind a desk.

If you rang the branch the manager would answer the telephone immediately because the 'phone was sitting on his desk. Today I hope the telephone isn't answered, that means we are busy.

The High Street has no place for the floor walker depicted in "Are You Being Served?" Today's managers serve as many customers as the rest of the team. They set an example, and in the process, do as many dirty jobs as everyone else. A good manager is generous, both with his personality and his time. A dictatorial approach won't get the best results. Successful managers are good at helping their team get better.

Team work

A. WHAT MAKES A TEAM ? continued

You are the manager **and** part of the team

Set a good example - always arrive first and leave last

Clean up as often as everyone else

You can delegate the daily book work - but you must check and sign

Always be honest with your staff

and listen to their ideas

Demarcation dispute

In the 1970's many of our shoe shops had separate shoe repair counters. These counters were inside the branch but had entirely different management. If a customer approached the girl behind the shoe repair counter, she would only help with shoe repairs. She wasn't allowed to sell shoes. Likewise shoe shop staff had nothing to do with shoe repairs.

No secrets

Today, our most successful shops rely on team work. They maximise turnover by helping each other and take advantage of our group bonus scheme. Good team work goes beyond the day-to-day business of cutting keys and repairing shoes. To be successful, team members must be honest with each other and admit their mistakes. They should always be able to talk, share information and listen to each other's problems. You can't maintain a healthy atmosphere if you keep secrets from colleagues.

Team work

Upside down shops

To people outside the business our shops probably look the same, but to me they are all different. Their individual character is created by the people. Our 'Upside-down Management' style encourages individuality. No company rule gets in the way of what is best for the business. There is plenty of scope for each team to introduce their own ideas. They can change displays, after the price list and run their own in branch competitions. I don't want all our shops to be the same, I want each to aim to be better than the rest by being ahead of the game.

Setting an example

Every year we have a golf match between the staff in Scotland and a team from England. In 2000 I was playing against Andy Robertson who, at that time, was running our shop in Dundee. We had a good game and I thought he was concentrating on the golf, but as soon as we finished, he contacted his shop on his mobile. During our round I told him his was Shop of the Week in our newsletter, he couldn't wait to tell his team. He was delighted to discover his shop was still trading well while he was on the golf course.

Delegating is not telling people what to do it's about helping, training, encouraging, giving freedom to have initiative and most important giving out praise. Dictators don't delegate. They are too detached. A good delegator checks on results, not to criticise but to find ways to help people get better. Andy was right to ring his shop, as a manager he shouldn't be taking the credit, he should give out praise.

Here to help

Each shop team is full of personalities, the more they know each other the better the team works. The Manager should remember they not only have record weeks but they also have illnesses, holidays and birthdays. He should show an interest in all sides of their life. 'Upside-down Management' is not just the way we run the business, it's also the way a good manager runs his shop.

You must be firm but fair

Toe the line

You may wonder why we need rules when I talk so much about 'Upside-down Management.' But every business needs some regulations. I try to have as few rules as possible. They are there to maintain common sense standards. Every shop should look the part, follow health and safety guidelines and have a strict code of honesty. There is no place for irrelevant rules. When I first went to boarding school, new boys had to carry their books with a straight arm, goodness knows why, it was extremely difficult to do, but we were fined if seen carrying books with a bent elbow. Silly rules gain no respect.

Respect for the rules

Although we keep our rules to a minimum, some think some of those are silly, particularly when we insist everyone wears a tie. But we don't issue a rule without explaining why it's important. I introduced ties because customers think they look smart. It's important to see the business through a customer's eyes.

With a small number of rules we can make sure they are seldom broken. That's important, if standards slip, people loose respect for discipline. The strength of a rule diminishes every time a manager walks past a problem without taking action. It's as bad as the manager breaking the rules himself. If a rule isn't respected, it won't work.

Ties matter

Despite the criticism I receive about ties, I know the rule commands respect. Every time I produce my camera to take a picture, anyone not wearing a tie begs me to wait until they are properly dressed. Ties will continue to be important. If dress standards are allowed to slip, other evidence of slackness will quickly follow. It's important to look the part.

You must be firm but fair

B. WHAT DO I DO IF SOMEONE IS NOT RESPONDING ?

NOTE YOU MUST KEEP YOUR AREA MANAGER INFORMED EVERY STEP OF THE WAY

Find out if the employee understands what they are doing is wrong

Clearly explain all procedures. Ensure staff sign to say they have read the policies

Explain that any further deviation may lead to disciplinary procedures. Make a mental note of the offense

If the employee re-offends ....

On guard

I sometimes wonder whether I get a fair picture when I visit branches. If I am with an Area Manager, shop staff are primed to be on their best behaviour. If I visit unannounced, I only visit one shop before all the others in the area have been warned I am around. I get a better insight when I visit shops with Alex. Sometimes she goes in as an advance guard. As Alex is seldom recognised, she can tell me exactly what is going on. Once we called at High Wycombe, Alex didn't fancy walking from the car park so I dropped her outside the shop. The branch was a tip, the manager was smoking a cigarette and reading the newspaper while chatting to a female friend. Alex simply said, "I am going to do you a favour, I am John Timpson's wife and he will be here in five minutes." Things were pretty perfect by the time I arrived.

Whistle blowers

We don't visit shops to catch people out, 'Upside-down Management' is based on trust. We still find dishonesty, but not as often as we used to. For years we have campaigned to cut down theft. The people who work in our branches have played a big part in reducing dishonesty. They realise that money taken from the till affects their own bonus, it is in their interest to cut out pilferage so they are willing to blow the whistle.

Refreshing honesty

Some employees think it is smart to cheat the company, they play a game to see what they can get away with. In Timpson we respect honesty, I will give you an example. Several years ago while visiting Brixton, I was talking to our manager, Michael Wynter. The shop was having a tough time, Michael had done extremely well over the previous two years, but now turnover was falling. I asked him what was wrong. "It's me," he replied with refreshing honesty. "I have lost the plot a bit, got bored with the job." We discussed it and decided he needed a change. He moved to Ilford and did a wonderful job. It's so much easier to work in an environment where people give honest answers when asked about problems instead of producing a range of excuses.

You must be firm but fair

Tell the employee
that you have made a note
of the offense

Explain that you have
informed your Area Manager
and a further deviation will
lead to disciplinary procedure

C. WARNINGS

If the employee continues to break the rules then the following disciplinary procedure is likely to be actioned by your Area Manager

A re-repeat of an offense

A further repeat

Following a further repeat

If the employee repeats the offence
again it will result in dismissal

Legislation

Confrontation between the boss and his employees has been encouraged by recent employment legislation. Rightly the element of doubt is given in favour of the employee but I don't like the way some use employment legislation to blackmail their boss. It's often cheaper to settle out of court than to go to an industrial tribunal even though you know the employee is bound to lose.

We try to follow employment legislation to the letter, but it's in the company's interest to go further. We want to be fair to our employees, indeed we want to be so good they are amazed. In the process we must be fair to everyone we employ. People who push employment legislation to the limit, can get an unfair advantage and receive compensation even though they are in the wrong. We will take cases to an industrial tribunal whenever we feel it's in the interests of the company regardless of the cost.

Be consistent

Timpson only has a few rules. We allow our people more scope to use initiative than any other shop on the High Street. Running a business is not the same as playing a game. The company must be consistent and maintain standards, if discipline goes, and employees lose interest, the company's fortunes can slide very quickly.

You must be firm but fair

D. THE PUNISHMENT FITS THE CRIME

These offenses are considered to be gross misconduct and are likely to result in instant dismissal

Theft

Breach of cash security policy

Fraud

Violence / Fighting (actual & threats of)

Harassment on sexual, racial, religious, nationality or disability

Negligent of responsibility

Housekeeping

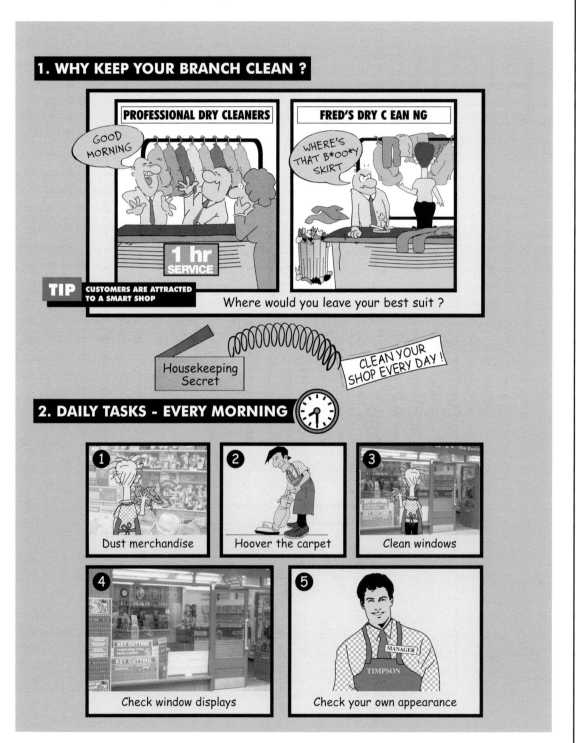

1. WHY KEEP YOUR BRANCH CLEAN ?

PROFESSIONAL DRY CLEANERS

GOOD MORNING

1 hr SERVICE

FRED'S DRY C EAN NG

WHERE'S THAT B*OO*Y SKIRT

TIP CUSTOMERS ARE ATTRACTED TO A SMART SHOP

Where would you leave your best suit ?

Housekeeping Secret

CLEAN YOUR SHOP EVERY DAY !

2. DAILY TASKS - EVERY MORNING

1 Dust merchandise

2 Hoover the carpet

3 Clean windows

4 Check window displays

5 Check your own appearance

Clean & tidy

You may wonder why we are so keen on good housekeeping. Some people say it doesn't matter if they work in a scruffy shop as long as they maximise the turnover.

New customers don't know how good we are, but housekeeping gives them an indication. If we can't look after our shops, why should they think we can look after their shoes.

Tatty tradition

Tattiness has become a tradition amongst shoe repairers. Despite our training, people who leave us to start a business of their own often forget to keep the place tidy. When we took over the Automagic shops in 1995, they were filthy and no one cared. Housekeeping wasn't part of the daily routine. One of the first shops to be refitted was in Cheapside, London. Within six weeks standards deteriorated so much we had to refit it again.

We must keep up-to-date. Shops that display Christmas posters in February don't deserve to do good business. We all need gentle reminders about tidiness to maintain standards. Every shop needs a spring clean.

Don't assume everyone knows how to dust a shelf. Our housekeeping guidelines deliberately go into great detail, but they are guidelines not rules, anyone who follows the illustrations should finish up with a tidy shop but if they know a better way, that's fine by us. It's the look of the shop that matters not how it was achieved.

Simple guidelines

All our training guidelines start from first principles. We assume the reader knows nothing about the subject. On the rare occasion when I have come home with a DIY flatpack to build a chair or a barbecue, I am quickly covered in sweat and confusion bemused by the instructions. Our training guidelines are designed to be as simple as possible.

Customers are attracted to a smart shop. There is truth in the expression "cleanliness is next to godliness," and "a tidy shop shows a tidy mind". If you want an insight into someone's character, look at the state of their office, or their back garden, but please don't look in my car!

Housekeeping

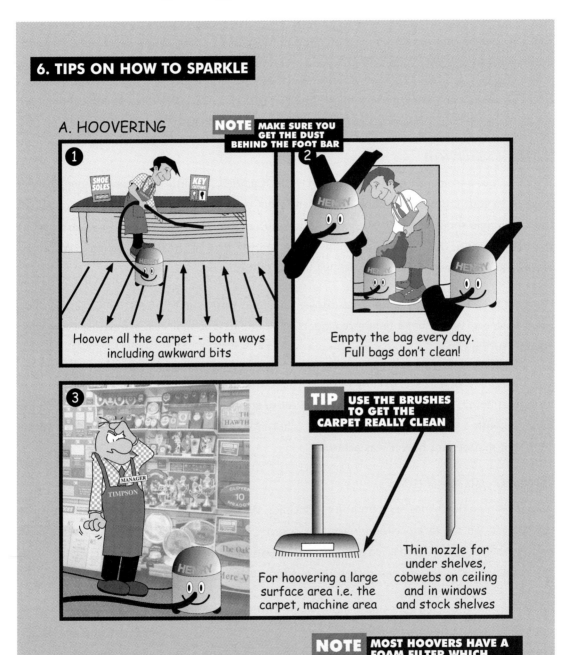

B. THE TOILET

Which one do your customers want to use ?

ONLY FIVE MINUTES EACH DAY

Bleach loo all over, remember under rim

Bleach block into cistern

Whilst mopping behind the counter - mop the loo floor !

Have air freshener handy

Check your toilet roll supply

Don't forget the window & window frame

133

Daily administration

FILLING IN A TICKET

ST HELENS ORDER

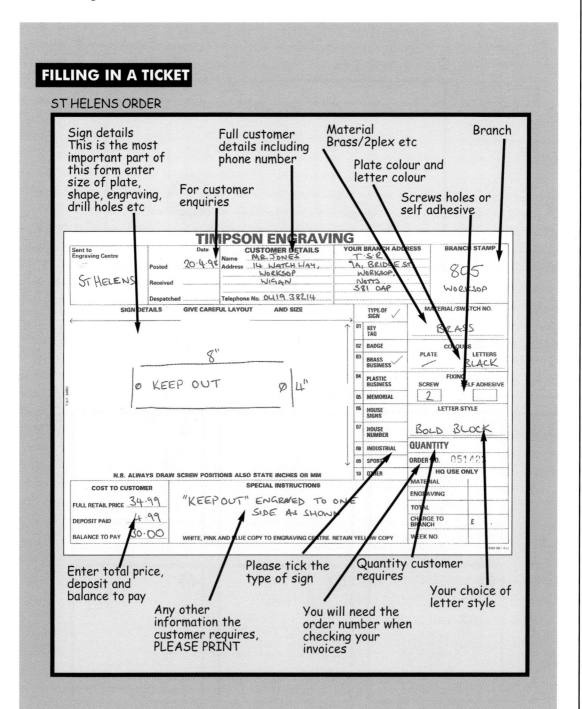

Sign details
This is the most important part of this form enter size of plate, shape, engraving, drill holes etc

For customer enquiries

Full customer details including phone number

Material
Brass/2plex etc

Plate colour and letter colour

Screws holes or self adhesive

Branch

Enter total price, deposit and balance to pay

Any other information the customer requires, PLEASE PRINT

Please tick the type of sign

You will need the order number when checking your invoices

Quantity customer requires

Your choice of letter style

Bloody paperwork

I hate administration, forms fill me with horror. I dread tax returns and credit card applications. I would love to cut down the amount of paper in the business. We have an office full of filing cabinets and shop staff that spend time filling in forms. It's difficult to cut out administration, if you are not careful, a campaign to cut out paperwork succeeds in creating more paper than you started with.

Bin it!

Everyone in the business has my personal permission to throw any paper into the wastepaper basket, but administration is here to stay. Everyone is keen to complete the form that claims their bonus.

We try to ease the burden by explaining every form in fine detail. The simpler the system the better. 35 years ago, our shoe repair factories started to hang their most important paperwork on hooks in the back office, this simple filing system has served us well.

Cut our complications

We can't avoid paperwork but we can cut out the complications. Things have got better. When I was a shop assistant, the manager spent half his time doing the books, hidden in a private office. Some managers still consider bookwork confidential. Robin Nicholson who ran our branch in Lancaster, took all the paperwork home on his day off. He didn't let his team see the figures. I am happy for anyone to look at the books and keen for everyone to do the bookwork. It's an important part of their training. Three years ago I met a bright young trainee in Banbury. I asked her whether she knew the bookwork "I am not allowed to do it, the Manager keeps that to himself." My immediate suspicions were well founded, he had good reasons for keeping the books a secret.

We are one of the few High Street retailers that doesn't have EPOS (Electronic Point of Sale.) As a service business, we don't need a computer stock control system. It's an advantage to be more 'hands on'. People become more aware of figures if they have to write them down rather than rely on a computer.

Daily administration

METHODS OF PAYMENT

CREDIT CARD PAYMENT

1. All customers may pay by credit card
2. However small the amount
3. Some branches have electronic terminals
4. Others use imprinters
5. All have a retailer instruction booklet issued by natwest; make sure it's kept safe otherwise contact Adrian Baldwin at Timpson House
6. We only accept these credit cards
7. When accepting a credit card, you need to make the following checks

ACCEPTING A CREDIT CARD

8. Make sure the signature matches the one on the voucher and check the signature strip has not been tampered with
9. Check the embossed characters are the same size, height and style

Get priorities right

It's not the paperwork that matters but the end result. Some managers think that as soon as they have issued a memo, the job has been done. Wise executives check the message has been received and understood.

No one should let paper get in the way of good service. If administrators are allowed to rule silly things can happen "I can't sell you that we are stocktaking." "The rejects are not for sale, until our area manager puts through a mark-down."

To emphasise sales are more important than administration, we accept credit cards for a purchase as low as 50p. I want customers to buy 50p items by credit card, so they can experience our amazing service.

Mental arithmetic

A lot of young people can't add up, they need a calculator to work out £3.50 plus £4.25. I was brought up in the days before calculators when we worked in £.s.d. We had to be good at mental arithmetic, soon only pensioners will be able to add up, everyone else will use a computer, but they will still need people to run their business.

Good customer care

The customer is king

Tracy Green in Ashford, told me something I have heard from many managers in the last two of years. I asked her why we trade better than our competitors. "Customer service." was her reply. "That seems too simple Tracy. Why is your service so good?" "Oh, that's easy," she said. "You let us get on with it."

I can get quite angry when I go shopping, served by assistants who aren't allowed to give me good service.

Security guards

In the early 1990's I met the Chief Executive of B & Q, who had recently decided to emphasise customer care. "Why have you made the change?" I asked. "We had to" he replied. "Until a few months ago, the culture of this business was based on security. No one cared about sales figures we were only interested in stock losses. The staff spent their time making sure customers didn't pinch the stock. They were security guards, not salesmen. Customers had to stick to the rules."

Free advertising

We don't pay for publicity in the papers or on television but we advertise at least 250,000 times a week - every time we serve a customer. Good service is the perfect advert, it encourages customers to spread good news about the business. I don't aim to be the biggest retailer on the High Street, my dream is to be known as the shop that gives the best service.

I have always believed in customer care. 25 years ago when I was running shoe shops, I launched a big service campaign, but went about it the wrong way. I launched the idea by telling the area managers to make sure their shops gave a better service. We didn't improve. The service only got better when we spelt out customer care in detail. A vague intention to serve customers better is not good enough. You have to say what you mean by good service.

Good customer care

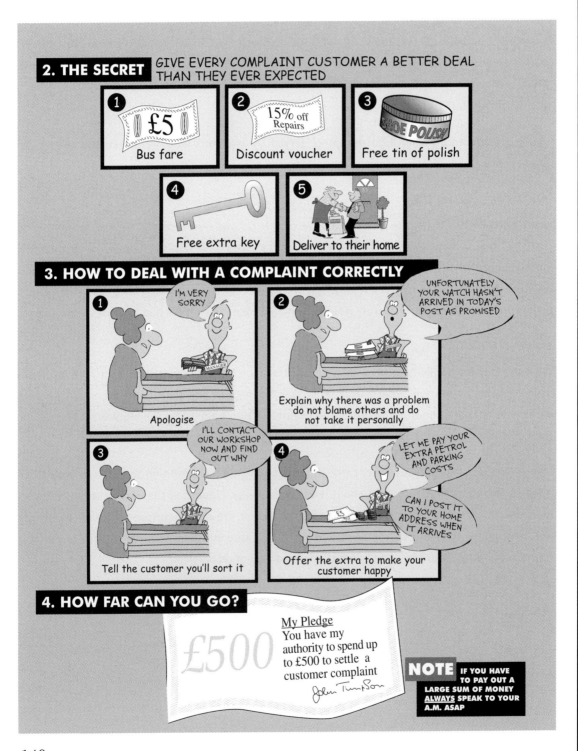

Natural talent

Some people have a talent for looking after customers. James is a born salesman and has always been keen to try out new ideas. When he worked in Cannon Street he started giving away sweets. He was the first to suggest customers without enough cash to pay the price should take the item now and call back to pay later.

I wrote the Customer Care manual after listening to people like James, the best salesmen in the business. It's a collection of practical ideas that work. Customer Care courses have succeeded in putting service at the centre of our agenda. But there is no room for complacency when it comes to looking after customers. We should aim to amaze the next customer that comes through the door. The manual provides the guidelines, but 'Upside-down Management' gives everyone the freedom to do what they think will best amaze their customers.

Good news

I think complaints are good news, they are an opportunity to give amazing service. 3% of our keys don't work, that's 5,000 a week that could come back as a complaint. Our method for handling complaints is quite simple. We always say "sorry" and never blame anyone else. We can deal with the problem straight away because everyone has the authority to spend up to £500 and give the customer more than they ever expected. Follow those guidelines and often the complaint creates a customer for life. It's not easy to be nice to every customer, most people have a bad day once in a while. But whatever happens at home, the best sales assistants still smile at customers.

Mystery shoppers

We check our service standards by regular mystery shopping. This isn't big brother spying on shops but a genuine way of measuring the level of service. If we get a poor report, we see whether training will improve the service. Good reports bring a special bonus for everyone in the shop.

Good customer care

Satisfied customers

Most weeks someone says to me "I was in one of your shops the other day..." They nearly always go on to compliment our staff. It shows how much they appreciate good service. Receiving those personal comments is one of the best parts of my job. Customer care is the most effective advertising campaign ever.

The plain truth!

TOP TEN EXCUSES

①

The weather

②

Road works/
bus route changed

③

The new one way system is
taking trade away from
this part of town

④

New supermarket

⑤

Cheaper prices elsewhere

⑥

Trade is bad

⑦

Saturdays are quiet

⑧

Cup Final

⑨ BANK OF ENGLAND

Interest Rates

OUR BEST MANAGERS LOOK FOR WAYS TO IMPROVE TRADE - THEY DON'T LOOK FOR EXCUSES !

⑩
Everyone's on holiday

The buck stops here

I have kept several old Automagic annual accounts. The Chairman's report is full of excuses. Poor trading was due to the weather, a tube strike or the economy. Each year had its new set of disasters. Nothing ever seems to be right for cobblers, it's either too hot, too cold, too wet or too dry. Poor shop managers are very good at finding the reason why things are going wrong. But they never blame themselves. Good managers believe they can create success. Jim Malcolm is an example. He ran Selfridges our biggest branch, but then we moved him around and he made a difference wherever he went. Some are suspicious about Jim's methods, especially when he puts 25% on the turnover. They claim he uses pressure salesmanship and inflates the prices. But there is no hidden agenda, Jim simply makes the most out of every sale.

Not my fault gov!

Mediocre managers never think they are to blame, the outside world determines their level of business. They don't think they have any influence on results. Good managers don't look for excuses, they search for ways to develop the business. We used to take £1000 a week in Arbroath, it became almost £2000 because Tony Stevendale went out in the evenings to look for contracts. Even when trade gets difficult, good managers find a way to improve business. If, on Thursday morning they are still well behind last year, smart staff get on the 'phone to persuade customers to pick up jobs waiting collection. Managers who always look for ways to increase business, achieve the best sales and get the biggest bonus. Running a shop isn't just a question of opening the door and waiting for customers to come in, there is a lot you can do to create business. It's an important part of 'Upside-down Management.'

Set your own targets

1. HOLD DAILY AND WEEKLY COMPETITIONS

1

TODAY'S TARGET £560

STRIKE RATE COMPETITION
BOB ME SUE

2

THRU SOLES
ME SUE BOB

	ME	SUE	BOB
MON	///	D/O	//// ////
TUES	///	//// ////	//
WED	D/O	//// ////	//
THUR	//// //// ////	//	
FRI	//// ////	//	
SAT	//// ///	////	D/O

OFFER PRIZES

YOUR A.M. WILL ARRANGE THESE FOR YOU

Extra Time off

Cash

Favourite tipple

2. CAN YOU BEAT THE TIMPSON RECORDS ?

FEAT	RECORD	HOLDER
Fund-raising - Chest Waxed for NSPCC	£3,006	Bob Northover, 774 - Taunton
Highest Turnover in one week	£14,300	520 - Selfridges
Most shop visits in 5 days	128	John Timpson, shop tour for NSPCC August 2000
Most keys cut for one customer	3,000 keys for P & O Ferries	490 - Liverpool, Central Station
Most long sole repairs in one week	48 Pairs	629 - Fish Street Hill
Highest price watch repair	£450	485 - Brent Cross
Highest lighter sale to one customer	£420 of Zippos	793 - Birmingham, Martineau Way
Highest umbrella sales in one week	£2,650	640 - Cannon Street, London

Be ambitious

People achieve more if they know what they are aiming for. Everyone does better with a target. I still set myself objectives every day, they are lists of all the things I need to do. On a good day I do everything on the list. Successful branches not only have a weekly target, they break it down day-by-day and person by person. This helps create the positive atmosphere that goes with a successful shop. I like shops where everyone knows the sales so far this week and how they stand against last year. They even know exactly how much money has been taken during that day.

Competition

We run Company competitions which help highlight different parts of the business, but area competitions work even better. The number of shops is small enough to give everyone a good chance of winning. It helps to know all the people you have to beat.

Buzz

It's a dull life in a shop if people don't have a goal. If all they are only interested in is surviving until they can go home at five-thirty, there isn't much job satisfaction. The buzz in retail comes from achievement. Setting new records, getting better skills and winning craft competitions all help to make the job worthwhile. 'Upside-down Management' allows each branch to create its own buzz and invent it's own competitions in the knowledge that the company will pay for the prizes. Individual endeavour creates a better business, it's one of the biggest benefits of 'Upside-down Management.'

Ideas that work

DISPLAYS

A: SANDWICH BOARD

❶ MANAGERS SPECIAL

❷ BORROW A WATCH WHILE WE REPAIR YOURS

❸ £50 CASH BACK AVAILABLE FOR BIG CLUB TROPHY ORDERS

NOTE TRY NEW IDEAS AND SEND THEM IN !

B: COUNTER DISPLAY

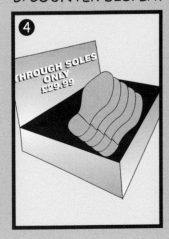

❹ THROUGH SOLES ONLY £29.99

❺ SAVE £1
2 BRUSHES ONLY £2.50

C: BADGES

❻ I HAVE JUST PASSED MY KEY SKILL TEST LEVEL 2

❼ I GOT 95% FOR CUSTOMER SERVICE

Brain waves

You don't get many good ideas sitting behind a desk. In our business nearly every successful wheeze starts in a shop. That's why I spend so much time visiting branches. I go round the country not to catch people out but to discover the people who do things better than anyone else.

Free to experiment

Shortly after we took over Automagic, I was in the Metro Centre in Gateshead. They had a new display on the counter for shoe care, I thought it looked good. They were serving customers so without saying a word I took a photograph of the display. The manager stopped serving his customer and turned to me. "I am sorry," he apologised, "I will take it off straight away." "No, don't, I took a picture because it is good." "You mean you don't mind me putting on my own displays?" "Certainly not," I replied. "You can do anything you want as long as it improves the business." There should be no embargo on new ideas, anyone can have a go at anything. If it works tell us about it, perhaps through the suggestion scheme and claim an award. If it fails simply stop it and keep quiet.

Helping us grow

Shoe repairs is a difficult business, a large chunk of the market has disappeared. As a result, we have changed from shoe repairer to multi-service shop. It's been a long process. Inside today's shop hundreds of small ideas have been brought together to make an excellent business. Today's ideas develop our future. It's the freedom of 'Upside-down Management' that lets everyone have a go and helps the business grow.

Training

BEFORE YOUR "NEW STARTER" STARTS

1. PREPARE YOURSELF

Be sure of your own skills

Ask your Area Manager to re-assess you, many new ideas come along, you may have missed some good tips

If you need to ask for training, your Area Manager/ADM or Training Manager will be happy to help

SO NOW YOU'RE READY

Trials of training

Some managers dread the thought of looking after young trainees. They see them as useless upstarts who get in the way. A few recruits are undesirable, they turn up late and aren't willing to learn. But most apprentices are enthusiastic, their success depends on the quality of their training and the personality of the manager who guides them through the first few weeks.

The ability to train is an important skill that should be recognised. We run courses to train our Trainers. We test training skills before an individual is let loose on a raw recruit. We reward qualified trainers' with a special bonus.

Good teachers

We need people who find training a challenge. To be effective trainers need to keep their own skills up-to-date. Successful tutors work out how to get the best out of trainees. They develop a bond of trust but become brutally honest when appraising skills.

It isn't a game, to gain our skill diplomas the trainees really needs to know their subject. Today's new recruits will make a major contribution to the future success of the business. Training is the company's most important investment.

Training

BEFORE YOUR "NEW STARTER" STARTS continued

2. PREPARATION

Check with the warehouse that the uniform is on the next delivery. It is automatically ordered when the application form is sent to personnel, but it is always worth checking.

If there is a problem - telephone your trainee and advise what to wear

Invite your new starter to come and look around

Chapter 4

The big barrier

The big barrier

Delegating authority to the people who serve your customers won't work unless middle management is on your side. For us that means winning over our area managers. I'd hate to be an area manager. I wouldn't be any good at the job, working from home looking after twenty shops, dealing with the problems of seventy staff, while hoping to keep a regional manager and Head Office happy. It's a lonely role and you don't get much thanks for it. When things are good the Chief Executive praises a few shops and takes the rest of the credit himself. When things turn bad he blames the area manager. But middle management people are vital, we can't run the business without them, we rely on them to make 'Upside-down Management' work.

Safer to issue orders

The natural tendency for an Area Manager is to do things himself. Why risk someone else doing a job if you get the blame when things go wrong? It's much safer to issue orders than give your team initiative. But to be a real success an area manager must learn to delegate.

"You'll have to explain the whole thing in detail." Said Kit. "And that means explaining every part of the area manager's job, then they will see where your upside-down idea fits in." So I went back to the drawing board and wrote a manual to describe an area manager's job. He is the leader, the thinker, the representative, the communicator, he builds the team and he becomes their agony aunt and he can't achieve anything unless he also becomes the delegator.

The main tasks

The most difficult job

When a shopkeeper opens a second unit life becomes more difficult than he ever imagined. If he can master running two places at once, the transition from two shops to twenty isn't too bad. It's when you get over twenty the real test comes. You can't control all the shops yourself, you have to appoint an area manager.

The most difficult job

Shop managers think their area manager has little to do. But area managers have so much on their plate they don't know where to turn. It's the most difficult job in the business. Area managers have more influence on our success than anyone realises, including the Chairman! Area managers protect standards, create the buzz and most of all pick our people and look after them.

Good managers in every shop

Ten years ago I invited Dean Butler, who introduced the Vision Express business to the UK, to talk at our area managers conference. He was a down to earth businessman who had the finger on the pulse of what makes a multiple tick. He talked about the chain of shops he used to have in Canada, where one year he set the objective of having a good manager in every shop. It worked, with good people running each of his businesses he had a record year. The same applies to us, a good team of area managers is the vital ingredient of success, especially if they employ a good manager in every branch.

Centre of everything

Being an area manager can be the worst job in the business, I certainly wouldn't do it. But in many ways it's the best, you are at the centre of everything. There is so much to do the only way to cope is to pick the right people and trust them.

The way to be a successful area manager is to operate 'Upside-down Management'.

Your authority

You're in charge

In the old days area managers had to stick to the rules. Just before we took over Automagic some of their area managers had to ring Head Office as soon as they arrived at their first shop, to prove they started work on time. Even in Timpson area managers had to follow Head Office orders. They spend their time stocktaking, supervising refits, bringing old machines back to Head Office and installing new displays.

Head Office ran the company and area managers did as they were told. Sometimes this made their life impossible. But it also gave them an excuse. "I did what Head Office wanted."

Power of delegation

We now recognise the benefits of delegating to area managers. They know their shops better than anyone at Head Office and should have the authority to develop the business as they see fit.

When we introduced a bonus linked to profits, area managers seized the initiative and quickly found short term cost reductions that increased their profit. But even area managers have to have some rules, they can't cut too many corners. They must keep company standards of customer service and housekeeping.

The more freedom we give area managers, the greater chance we have of improving our business. It's important that the area managers understand 'Upside-down Management'.

The thinker

FIRST ☛ FIND OUT THE FACTS

You can't start to think
without information

10% COMES FROM FIGURES

90% COMES FROM WALKING ABOUT AND OBSERVING AND LISTENING

Walk the business

A new whiz kid from outside the company, can make some big mistakes, especially if he jumps in and makes changes without knowing the facts. It's not just a question of looking at sales figures and knowing the profit – you must know why those sales have occurred.

A printout of our Watch Repair sales shows the best shop takes over £3000 a week and the worst about £30. The figures tell you who's doing well and who's doing badly, but you need to know why. Go to the shop that's taking £3000 and see what's happening.

Find out yourself

Every good manager knows his business, he doesn't rely on a computer to tell him what's going on, he finds out for himself. Be naturally suspicious of figures, they don't always tell the truth. Instead of having reports delivered to your desk go and find the truth at first hand.

When I visit shops I don't have an agenda, I just wander around. I never know what I'm going to find. I discovered our pilaster board display outside a competitor's shop in Oswestry. Our shop in Norwich has great window promotions. Our current shop layout, with its separate watch department, came out of a conversation I had with our manager in Stretford.

If you're too close to present problems you can miss the best ideas. Walk about with an open mind, a camera and a notebook. The better you know the business the more you can think about the future.

Where to look for inspiration

Where ideas are hidden

Ideas are all around you, you just need to keep your eyes and ears open, and have an open mind. You'll miss a lot if you're arrogant. If you think you can't get better you won't spot ideas that help improvement. If you think you're better than your competitor you won't learn from what they do.

Around 1970 I was a shoe buyer. Every year we spent a week visiting Italy looking at other shoe shops. We based our business on other people's ideas. The Italians were better at design and fortunately were a year ahead of the game. All we had to do was to watch the fashions in Florence and copy them faithfully for our customers the following year.

Open mind

Good managers don't have to think up their own ideas but they need to know where to find them. Arrogant people think they know the lot, but no one knows everything. Managers with an open mind get others to spill out their knowledge, and unashamedly pinch the ideas.

A management style which concentrates on rules and routine stifles initiative. You make money by being different. If you want to find new ideas, put yourself into new situations, meet up with competitors, swap jobs with someone else and have discussion groups with a wide range of people. The new surroundings help you see things with a different eye. That's why you find so many good ideas on holiday.

An open mind doesn't bring with it a good memory. Make notes or take a picture, most good ideas are forgotten before they are put into practice.

Problems and ideas

Not a problem

In a business with 325 shops things go wrong every day. Some branches open late, others are short of stock, every day someone is rude to a customer.

There is a positive side, every time you spot a problem, you've found a way to improve the business. Be pleased whenever you find a fault, you have discovered a way to make the business better. Every business has its problems, but many ignore them. They know things are wrong but haven't time to put them right.

Pick up the phone

When I was first buying ladies' shoes, I shared an office with Tom Hardman, whose wisdom came from years of experience. I trusted his judgement and often asked his advice.

One day I had a real problem. I had spent a lot of time developing a new range of shoes with one of our suppliers, but the delivery was over 3 weeks late and liable to miss the selling season. What should I do? I knew what to do in my mind but hadn't the courage to cancel the order. Tom knew the answer, but he didn't' tell me what to do, he just took the 'phone off the hook and handed it to me. "You know the answer. Why not ring him now?" I cancelled the order and probably saved the business about £50,000.

Do it now

If you don't sort out a problem – it won't go away, things usually get worse. Beware of the excuses you give yourself. "I'll do it next week." "I'll wait to see if it gets better." "I'll do it as soon as I can." When you know there is a problem and you have the solution, there is only one way to tackle it. Do it now !

Problems and ideas

KEEP LOOKING FOR PROBLEMS AND IDEAS

THINK GLOBAL

If there is a problem in one shop can it be happening in the whole of my area?

PROBLEM LIST

If you don't know the answer…

PUT IT ON A LIST

What no problem

- Engraving is worse than the company average
- Management at Southampton
- Not wearing ties
- Poor at securing contracts
- Dull window displays
- High telephone bills
- Lack of support for Area Dinner
- 8 managers can't use a stitcher

TIP

MOST PROBLEMS ARE TO DO WITH PEOPLE

The big picture

An area manager must think in terms of 20 shops instead of one. Some situations are unique to a branch, like personal problems or road works, but most are common to the whole area. Don't just think of the shop where you are, consider everywhere else at the same time. If a good idea works in one place it probably works everywhere. The same applies to problems. If one branch gets it wrong, it's likely other shops are doing the same thing.

Spread the word

If putting coloured keys on a pilaster board outside the shop increases sales in one shop, do it in the whole area as soon as possible. If a shop is displaying a Christmas poster halfway through January, assume others have made the same mistake and mention it in your weekly newsletter.

An open mind will find loads of ideas and problems every week. Write them down. Keep your list on an A4 pad or a laptop. Once you have a list of problems you're well on the way to finding solutions that influence the business.

What's the problem

Over the past few years nearly everyone in retail formed their own theory about Marks & Spencer. What was the Marks & Spencer problem? Was it poor buying, customer service, lack of investment or simply poor public relations? They appear to have found a solution and I bet they discovered their problems were mainly to do with people.

Collect ideas

Ideas for the picking

'Upside-down Management' gives the freedom to do things better. With very few rules we are all free to find ideas that work. Some people write to the Suggestion Scheme but most keep their ideas to themselves. Brilliant wheezes lie waiting to be harvested.

Ideas that work

I wouldn't know why Kettering does so well with house signs, if I hadn't visited the shop. Their idea is simple, they wheeled the internal free-standing display onto the pavement and sales doubled.

Within a year of starting Watch Repairs the team in Dundee became star performers. They took £1500 a week, while others took only £50. I watched them in action and discovered how they talked to customers. As a result we designed our 'Watch Wizards' training course to spread the Dundee technique throughout the business.

Ideas can cover cost cutting as well as sales. Throughout the country there are Timpson people who have found a better way of doing business. The team at Thurrock don't just use their computer for engraving they have adapted it to do their shop administration.

Bob Crombie in Inverness organises his shop life around a diary, a simple system which keeps track of customer orders. Darren Brown in Lancashire has shown us how to develop contract sales with local businesses.

Look for inspiration

But it's not just people within the business who provide ideas, look at our competitors. Coloured keys came from Mr. Minit. Our projecting signs were first seen in Dixons.

You find ideas all over the place, but you don't find many sat behind a desk. If you want inspiration you've got to go out and look for it.

Think

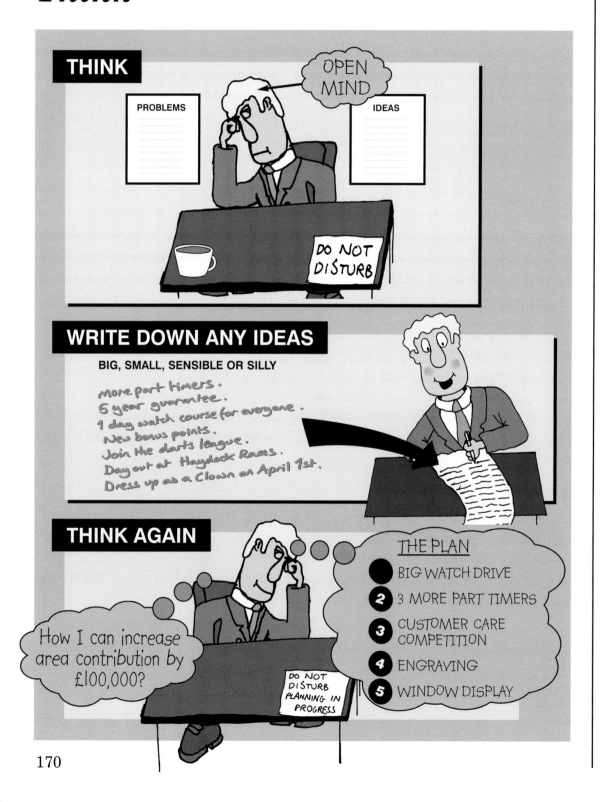

Time to think

It's easy to get too close to your business. When things go wrong, managers are accused of not seeing the wood for the trees. If you don't set aside time to think you may miss the big picture.

Despite today's time saving devices we have little time to think. It's easy to be swept up in the rush of modern living, and wonder where all the time goes. It's probably been soaked up by inventions like television, the Internet, traffic jams and mobile phones.

Flash of the obvious

Everyone needs a period of constructive thinking. No mobile phones, no computers, just a blank A4 pad and an open mind. If you can detach yourself far enough from the business to allow prejudice to give way to experience, you may have a flash of the obvious, something that's been staring you in the face for months suddenly coming to the forefront of your mind. That's why I enjoy working on holiday.

Once, in the Caribbean, I suddenly realised the importance of training. I'd seen training as a waste of time, but sitting on the beach with the Atlantic waves breaking on the shore I saw the error of my previous judgement. In a service business training is vital, it's the only way to improve the quality of our product.

Day in the office

We used to complain if area managers spent time at home, with some justification. Several years ago, one area manager claimed to work at home 3 mornings a week. When we checked, he spent those 3 days as a green-keeper at the local golf course.

Things are different now. I don't worry how area managers spend their time, it's the end result that matters. To do their best they need time to think.

Talk about your ideas

Making it happen

First identify the problems, then find ideas that provide a solution, and finally make sure the ideas work.

'Ah But'

There will be plenty of obstacles in your way - "not invented here" people who block their minds to new ideas. A current budget that prevents money being allocated to a new project. And, most of all, people who know why your latest ideas won't work.

Persuade doubters by demonstrating success. Test a theory in the place where it's most likely to work. Don't be tempted by 'if it works there, it'll work anywhere.' Go the safe route, try an idea where it's most likely to succeed.

Don't give up

A compelling reason to abandon a new idea is "we tried it before, and it didn't work then." That is not always valid advice.

We planned to introduce Watch Repairs in Tonbridge 12 years ago, but couldn't find a watch repairer. For 7 years watch repairs was something we couldn't do. We now realise we never needed a watch repairer, we train our own people to be the experts.

When testing an idea, don't trust the results. Figures may not be what they seem, a hearsay comment can be tinged with prejudice. Go and see for yourself.

Consult

Ideas only work if they have the backing of your people. Take time to listen to everyone's view. And when you've done a full round of consultation, ask everyone again. If you talk enough, some original critics will claim that it was their idea. The biggest obstacle you have to overcome is yourself - it takes determination to make ideas work. It's easy to find reasons to put things off, but in the end you must go for it.

Agony aunt

People can't help bringing their problem to work…

…you need to know what is on their mind.

MAKE IT EASY TO CONTACT YOU

Confidential Note
to Area Manager

Confidential

AM HELPLINE
0456 512334
24 HOURS

TALK TO EVERYONE DURING A SHOP VISIT

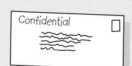

How's
it going

Are
things ok
now

Any
Problems

TALK OUT OF EVERYONE ELSE'S HEARING

Social service

An area manager's job is to help his people, and that includes anything on their mind. It's in his interest to help. Personal worries can affect the business, whether it's money, marriage or any other part of someone's lifestyle. We shouldn't pry or interfere, but we should make it easy for employees to talk. They must be confident that we will treat their personal life as confidential. That's why we provide everyone with access to a free confidential helpline which is independent of the company.

Easy to talk to

To command a position of trust, an area manager must be discreet. It helps to be "someone I can talk to." Make it easy by giving everyone your home and mobile telephone numbers. Remember we have a changing community. New employees join us each week and don't know of the confidential helpline. Occasionally send a personal note emphasising the help you have to offer.

Speak to everyone every time you visit a shop. Give them a chance to talk confidentially. They may find it difficult to broach an important subject, make it easy by starting the conversation. If you already know there is a problem, ask a direct question, "Is there anything on your mind?"

Your job is to help. The most important issues in our business are seldom to do with key cutting and shoe repairs, they are to do with people.

Agony aunt

Listening post

Personal problems are bad enough, but people make things even worse by keeping concerns bottled up in their mind. You can help a lot without being an expert. You can make a difference just by listening. It doesn't take much to listen, except time, patience and understanding. You can't listen if you are in a hurry. If someone says "Can I just have a word?" they may want a minute, or they may want an hour. You must make the time. You're response should be, "No problem, take as long as you like."

Listen but also ask a few questions, "How long has it been going on?" "Is there anything I can do?" Don't rush into a solution, you probably don't have the answer yourself. Keep asking questions and let the person with the problem talk it through.

Keep your promises

Talking might be enough on its own, but if you see an obvious way to help, act straight away. Always promise to talk again, one conversation often isn't enough. If you make that promise - keep it !

Helping people with personal problems is one of the most satisfying parts of the job. We've helped people through all kinds of difficulties, drugs, violence at home, bankruptcy and many more.

We can often find an expert to help. At the Area Managers' Conference we've had talks from the Citizens' Advice Bureau and from drug and debt counsellors. We have information about several agencies that provide help to people in need.

You may wonder what being an 'Agony Aunt' has to do with business. Our business is about people, if we look after them, they in turn will look after our customers.

The delegator

Use the team

It's not surprising people are reluctant to delegate. They worry that putting faith in their team, can land them in trouble. The boss is responsible for all the mistakes. On the other hand, if things go well, one of the team could become a superstar and get the top job. These are good reasons to be suspicious but unless you trust your team you can't delegate.

When we bought Automagic, we found no one had freedom. They were positively prevented from developing their key cutting business. The shop managers could see Timpson were doing well with keys so, when management wasn't looking, they increased key displays and promoted low key prices outside the shop. Disobeying company orders led to trouble, they could get a written warning for trying to increase turnover.

Give people space

You can't delegate unless you let go of authority. You have to give people space to get on with it. You don't delegate by giving out a list.

Managers who find delegatation difficult, are the first to complain about their workload. They don't have enough time and often suffer from stress. These are not false complaints. It's difficult doing a job all by yourself. No area manager can cut every key or do every stocktaking, or even deal with every personal problem. They can only be in one shop at once. They must delegate to create time to do their job and one of the most important parts of their job is to delegate.

The leader

Role model

The boss can make a big difference just by being himself. People follow his example. If he looks after customers well, so will they, but if he doesn't care about his business, nor will the team.

Bad influence

Several years ago we caught a corrupt area manager in Scotland. He regularly took money from the till as he travelled round his shops. We caught him by chance but already knew there was something wrong because his sales figures were so poor. When we looked in detail, it was not only the area manager that was on the fiddle, a number of shop managers followed his example. Leaders can be a bad influence.

Lead by example

Our regional manager, Brian Elliott has shown the benefit of leading by example. As an area manager, he was the first to recognise the potential of key cutting and his keenness was infectious. It spread throughout his area and created the biggest key cutting business in the country.

A leader, must set the agenda, decide the vital elements of success and show the team what is most important.

Our Scottish branches have always produced individual window displays, constantly trying new ideas. When one works, it's quickly spread throughout Scotland. My regular trips north of the border often produce new display techniques for England and Wales.

Stay in touch

The Leader picks the agenda but makes sure he is in tune with popular opinion. Things work better with everyone's agreement. Leadership isn't about giving orders, it's persuading people to excel.

The leader

High standards

The Timpson standard of tidiness varies from one area to another. This reflects each area manager's passion for housekeeping. We produce guidelines but area managers set the standards. They decide where to draw the line and when to turn a blind eye. I liken the management of our business to keeping plates spinning on sticks, if you don't keep watching your shops, standards will slip.

Figures help

The best way to keep in touch is to visit branches, but figures help, they show where you have a problem. I look at the company cash position every day. The bank account is my best business barometer. But it's no good just looking at figures, you have to act on them. If I see the cash has suddenly fallen, I want to know why.

Be on their side

To be a good manager you must command respect, that's why it's so important to be honest with the people you employ. Admit your mistakes and say sorry when you get things wrong. But if someone in your team causes a problem, you still have to carry the can. Good leaders care about their people, they fight for them in the same way they would support a child in trouble at school. Our people may need help with a company loan or a problem with payroll. It's important to support the team – you are looking after the people who look after your customers.

The representative
FIGHT FOR YOUR AREA

CAPITAL EXPENDITURE

Equipment   Stock   Display   Refits

GET RECOGNITION

SHOP OF THE WEEK

GET HELP

DISPLAY   TRAINING   KEYS

SHOE REPAIRS   WATCH REPAIRS   ENGRAVING

What no problem

You're the one who clears
away the obstacles

FIGHT LOCAL BATTLES

Spokesman

An area manager is like a Member of Parliament, he is elected to look after the interests of his constituents. He must fight for his area and that means standing up for his people - opening doors and clearing the obstacles that get in the way of success. Good managers spend as much time chasing people on behalf of their staff as they spend chasing the staff themselves. In his representative role, an area manager must be resilient. Many requests to head office are rebuffed by a range of excuses. "You will have to take your turn." "All the investment money has been allocated." You don't care about anyone else. Fight for your department and jump the queue whenever you can.

Right for recognition

You must admire the way Scotsmen get what they want. It's a joy going to Scotland, the road system is brilliant, an example of how Scots have more than their fair share of investment. They have done the same in Timpson. Scotland has a higher proportion of shop refits and computer engravers than the rest of the company.

You don't just represent the commercial interests of your area, you also represent individuals. Involvement may go as far as accompanying an employee to the Citizens' Advice Bureau to solve sticky situations such as debt or housing.

As well as seeking personal solutions, fight for recognition. Nominate your people for special company awards in the knowledge that praise can work wonders, whether it's first prize in a quality competition or a personal letter from the Chairman. A pat on the back can do as much for turnover as a refit.

Within 'Upside-down Management' the boss is there to help and represent the interests of his employees.

The communicator

NO SECRETS

Give everyone access to all your information

▼

THE EXCEPTION
Personal and Confidential papers

OPEN DOOR

Don't keep it all to yourself

HIGHLIGHT YOUR MESSAGE

Watch repairs are a goldmine

Sounds good to me, I'll go for it!

Shop Visits

NEWSLETTER

AREA NEWS

WATCH REPAIRS - a goldmine

AREA +23 %

WATCH REPAIRS ARE A GOLDMINE

MEETINGS

EDIT YOUR NEWSLETTER

AREA +23 %

BE THE AREA PR AGENT

Is that the weekly Gazette

Watch out! It's another prize for Kelvin

Good news

Good managers don't keep things to themselves, but a lot of businessmen like stamping documents 'Private and Confidential.' There is no need to be secretive. If a matter is personal, then keep it quiet, but everyone has the right to know about the business in which they work. Tell everyone as much as you can, the more they know, the more they can help you run the business and the more they will trust you. Trust comes from an open style of management.

No Secrets

I believe in showing everybody our branch profit figures but others think I am foolish, they worry the information will lead to unreasonable wage demands, but that never happens. Telling people what's going on seldom creates trouble. It's lack of information that causes problems.

Last year I visited our shop in The Eagle Centre, Derby, they were worried whether we were closing down. A rumour was being spread by the shopping centre management and they were understandably concerned. There was no truth in the story and I quickly put their minds at rest.

If anyone wants to know what's going on in our business, give me a ring, if I know what's going on, I will tell them.

Spin doctor

You can't make ideas work on your own, you have to sell the message to turn your idea into reality. You can't change the business unless you communicate. You are a 'Spin Doctor,' spreading news as you visit shops, and writing newsletters. You can even become your own PR agent ensuring that company news gets into the local paper. The people who serve customers run the business, you communicate.

Team builder

YOUR SUCCESS DEPENDS ON YOUR TEAM
BUILDING THE TEAM IS YOUR JOB

PICK GOOD ADM'S

CHECK LIST

(1) **Look at what an ADM does**
(NOTE: Don't just go for the best branch manager.)

(2) **Will He / She gain respect?**

(3) **Will you be happy to delegate?**

LOOK AT THE WEAKEST LINK

ACTION
1. Help and training
2. Be firm but fair

2 CHOICES
1. Get better
2. Get out!

Squad training

We have discovered an area manager can't cover 20 shops on his own. The area needs the help of at least two good Area Development Managers (ADMs) to be successful. The best branch manager doesn't always make the best ADM, different qualities are required for different roles. An ADM must understand our business philosophy. 'Upside-down Management' should come to him naturally. You must have confidence in his ability, you are putting a lot of trust in his performance. Most of all you must be sure he has the respect of the shop staff.

Good people in every shop

In 1995, we recognised that people make our business and adopted the objective of having good people in every shop. Nothing has changed, we will never stop looking for good people. We do a lot to help employees but we are not a soft touch. We can't afford poor performers, we have to weed out the weak links because passengers let down the team.

Back biting

Here is an interesting fact. 15% of work time in the UK is spent complaining about fellow employees. Sounds plausible doesn't it? I invented the fact but it is probably true. Maintaining the quality of your team is a continuous task, you must know your people well and meet them regularly. Listen for the first signs that things are going wrong. A good team is like a garden every year it will improve - if you look after it.

Career consultant

People are not pawns on a chessboard, notice their personality and how they progress. Think ahead, one thing is certain, your team will change. Plan everyone's career – how they will fit into the team of the future. You need to know who can do what and, who gets on with who. If you genuinely try to develop your people, you may win the greatest accolade, a waiting list of people wanting to work for you.

Team builder

KEEP IN TOUCH

Q1 Have you met everyone in your area in the the last two months?

Q2 Can you pass the Mastermind test? (see People Section)

Q3 How soon do you meet new recruits?

THINK AHEAD

Q1 What other jobs could he/she do?

Q2 What jobs will need doing?

Q3 What changes should I make?

Q4 When should I make the changes?

REMEMBER — **YOU NEED A GOOD MANAGER IN EVERY BRANCH!**

THE GREATEST ACCOLADE

Be the Area Manager good people want to work for!

PLEASE CAN I COME AND WORK FOR YOU?

STAR

? DO YOU HAVE A WAITING LIST

The art of management

'Upside-down Management' makes formal structures almost irrelevant. What matters is having people who work as a team. Mould the organisation to your people rather than change people to fit the business. Management is an art not a science, you can't run a business according to a set of rules.

At university I learned the need for clear lines of communication and to have no more than seven reporting to an individual. But Nordstrom (one of America's best retailers), break all the rules, the only structure they publish shows that management has been turned 'Upside-down.'

Structures that look fine on a piece of paper often don't work. We once had two managers who were both doing extremely well in small shops. We put them together as a team in a large branch. It was a disaster, they didn't like each other and as a result our turnover suffered.

There is no short cut to team building. Major management reshuffles are seldom successful, they are more likely to upset the organisation than strengthen it. Finding people the right job is a continuous process, you never stop building a team.

Manage your time

TIME SAVING TIP → **DO IT NOW**

MAKE LISTS

Put it in your Notebook → Transfer to A4 Pad or Laptop → Weekly Review → New Pad for a new week

WEEKLY REVIEW

Notes from previous meeting:

Visit every shop every 5 weeks. Work in a shop every fortnight. Spend a day in Timpson House. Visit 2 other areas. Join a Computer Engraving Course. 3 spare days a month. Go to Wolverhampton

SALES FORCAST

For notetaking on the move keep a tape recorder in your car.

TIME SAVING TIP → **LEISURE TIME IS A PRIORITY**

SET YOUR OBJECTIVES

THINK

Allocate Time to Think →

FOR EXAMPLE:
Visit every shop every 5 weeks
Work in a shop every fortnight
Spend a day in Timpson House
Visit 2 other areas
Join a Computer Engraving Course
Keep 3 days spare a month
Go to Wolverhampton

ALL WORK NO PLAY

TOP TIME SAVING TIP → **DON'T TRY AND DO TOO MUCH**

Time to think

Time goes by much quicker than you think and it gets worse as you get older. Everyone else seems to be so efficient, it makes you feel inadequate. My weekends were ruined every Friday night on the way home when I saw a man who had finished mowing his lawn and was already cutting the hedge at 5.30. He seemed to have his life totally organised.

It's easy to think others are super efficient but they are not. If they are effective for 25% of the time, they are doing well. We don't help ourselves when it comes to time management. "Don't worry I'll remember." "I'll do it tomorrow." We never do it tomorrow, because we have lousy memories. Life needs to be structured.

Life of lists

My life is ruled by lists, I won't go anywhere without a notebook. Whenever I find an idea or a problem I write it down. At the end of each day I add new items to the master list on my A4 pad. Lists help as long as you don't forget where you left the list. Every Sunday I check what has been done and create a new list for the next 7 days. That weekly session is my form of strategic planning. You need a regular big think to keep the business on track, it gives you confidence that you know what you are doing.

Skeleton plan

My 'Upside-down Management' style gives everyone lots of freedom, so the job is less structured. It helps to invent some personal objectives. I plan to visit every shop every year, meet a discussion group every month, attend monthly Board Meetings and, of course, fit in holidays. These objectives set the framework but you need a detailed agenda.

Have a personal planning session every three months. Fill in your holidays first, they are the most important and leave plenty of spare time to think.

Manage your time

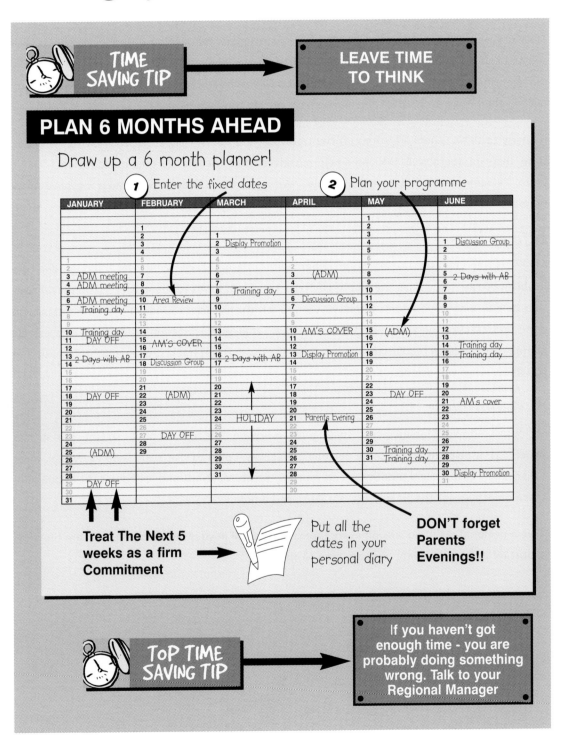

Whenever I plan the diary, I give myself too much to do. Don't be too ambitious, leave two free days every week, nearer the time you will find a use for them.

Be flexible

The best time saving tip is "Do it now." Whatever you plan, be flexible, no programme is written in stone, you have to react to emergencies. But don't cancel appointments just because you have found a better offer.

Whenever I fill in the diary, Alex says I am wishing time away. Planning nine months ahead does seem to make time race by, but you will achieve much more and life will be more enjoyable.

Do some dirty work

CLEAN THE LOO

GAIN RESPECT BY TAKING YOUR JACKET OFF AND
DOING THE JOBS, THAT NO ONE WANTS TO DO.

1. Bleach the loo all over, remember under the rim!
2. Put bleach block into the cistern.
3. Whilst mopping behind the counter - mop the loo floor!
4. Have air freshener handy.
5. Check your toilet roll supply.
6. And don't forget the window and window frame!

HOOVER THE CARPET

1. Hoover all the carpet - both ways including all the awkward bits!
2. Empty the bag every day. Full bags don't clean!

MAKE THE TEA

1. Switch the kettle on
2. Put the teabag in the cup!
3. Pour in the water.
4. Then add milk and sugar

VITAL

**DO AT LEAST ONE DIRTY JOB EVERY WEEK!
EARN RESPECT!**

Back to the floor

When I visited the Arndale in Manchester one Christmas, they were so busy I was sure I was getting in the way. "Just who we need." said Denise the manager, who knew I couldn't repair shoes. "You can make us a cup of tea." So I did. When the boss does the junior's job it sends a lot of good messages. It shows he is willing to play his part in the team without pulling rank. It also shows the small jobs are important. Any boss who is willing to help is showing his commitment to 'Upside-down Management.' All that can be achieved just by making a cup of tea.

Get your coat off

Little things make a difference. If the shop has a problem that needs help from Head Office, don't tell them to ring, make the 'phone call yourself. Your willingness to do dirty work will colour your reputation. At a discussion group in the North East, I asked how they were getting on with their new area manager. "I like Andy" they said "he doesn't mind getting his coat off." If you gain the respect of your team, it makes your job a lot easier.

Area meetings

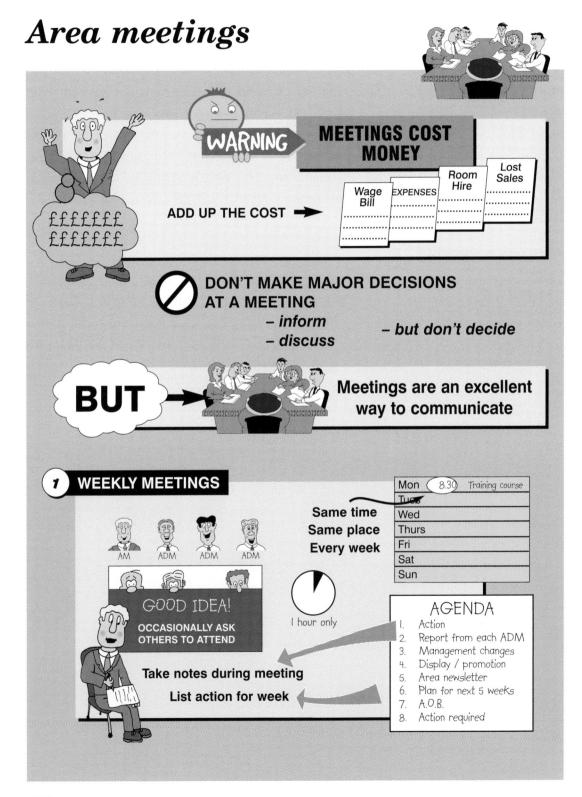

WARNING **MEETINGS COST MONEY**

£££££££
£££££££

ADD UP THE COST ➡

Wage Bill | EXPENSES | Room Hire | Lost Sales

🚫 **DON'T MAKE MAJOR DECISIONS AT A MEETING**
- *inform*
- *discuss*
- *but don't decide*

BUT ➡ **Meetings are an excellent way to communicate**

1 WEEKLY MEETINGS

AM   ADM   ADM   ADM

GOOD IDEA!
OCCASIONALLY ASK OTHERS TO ATTEND

Take notes during meeting

List action for week

Same time
Same place
Every week

I hour only

Mon	8.30	Training course
Tues		
Wed		
Thurs		
Fri		
Sat		
Sun		

AGENDA
1. Action
2. Report from each ADM
3. Management changes
4. Display / promotion
5. Area newsletter
6. Plan for next 5 weeks
7. A.O.B.
8. Action required

In conference

It's very annoying if you can't speak to someone because he's in a meeting, meetings get in the way of communication. If everyone else's meetings are a pain, are yours important?

Once I sat on the committee developing NVQ's for the shoe repair business. About 14 people turned up for each meeting. Fortunately, we met in my office so I didn't waste time travelling, but at least four people came from London by train. Some never said a word, others said too much, but we seldom made a decision, deferring discussion of the important items to the next meeting.

Some meeting tips

I don't like meetings, they take time and money but they do have a place. They involve everybody in decision making and let people know what is going on. Never make a decision at a meeting, use them to communicate what you have already decided. Short meetings are the most effective. Most people can discuss all they have to say in under an hour. It helps to have a firm finishing time, especially if someone cannot stay beyond the appointed hour. Our non-executive director, Roger Lane-Smith seldom stays at a Board Meeting longer than an hour and a half so we make sure the important items are discussed while he is still there. Don't waste time going over the same points again and again, I did on a Government Quango, the National Economic Development Committee looking after footwear. We met every eight weeks and had exactly the same discussion each time.

Write the agenda carefully, (you don't always need the same list of topics) and make sure someone takes minutes - you might have to do them yourself. Minutes do not need to be long, don't camouflage the truth with waffle, make it abundantly clear what was agreed and what action everyone should take.

Area meetings

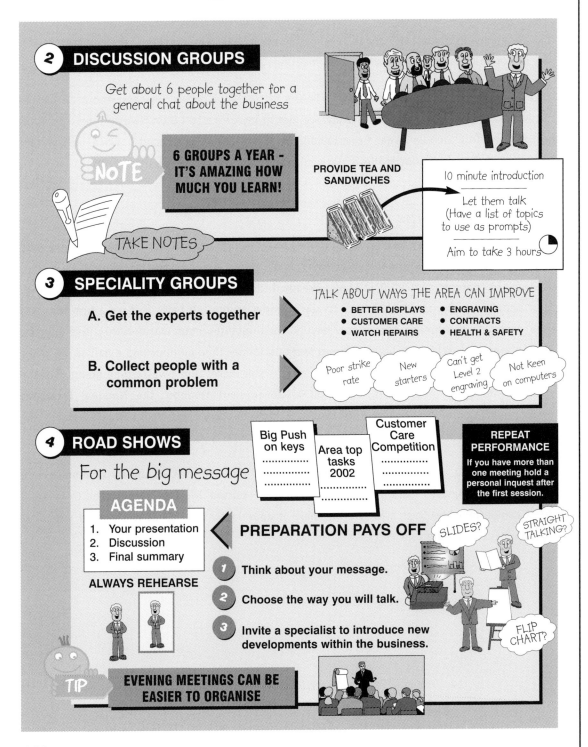

2 DISCUSSION GROUPS

Get about 6 people together for a general chat about the business

NOTE

6 GROUPS A YEAR - IT'S AMAZING HOW MUCH YOU LEARN!

TAKE NOTES

PROVIDE TEA AND SANDWICHES

10 minute introduction

Let them talk
(Have a list of topics
to use as prompts)

Aim to take 3 hours

3 SPECIALITY GROUPS

A. Get the experts together

B. Collect people with a common problem

TALK ABOUT WAYS THE AREA CAN IMPROVE

- BETTER DISPLAYS
- CUSTOMER CARE
- WATCH REPAIRS
- ENGRAVING
- CONTRACTS
- HEALTH & SAFETY

Poor strike rate

New starters

Can't get Level 2 engraving

Not keen on computers

4 ROAD SHOWS

For the big message

Big Push on keys
....
....
....

Area top tasks 2002

Customer Care Competition
....
....
....

REPEAT PERFORMANCE

If you have more than one meeting hold a personal inquest after the first session.

AGENDA

1. Your presentation
2. Discussion
3. Final summary

ALWAYS REHEARSE

PREPARATION PAYS OFF

SLIDES?

STRAIGHT TALKING?

FLIP CHART?

1 Think about your message.

2 Choose the way you will talk.

3 Invite a specialist to introduce new developments within the business.

TIP

EVENING MEETINGS CAN BE EASIER TO ORGANISE

Discussion groups

The best meetings have no agenda, they are discussion groups, people getting together simply to talk about the business. This is one of my favourite ways of keeping in touch. As Chairman, it's your job to get everyone talking, then keep quiet. After an hour the real truth comes out, they will speak their mind about the business. If you want to discuss a specific problem, round up a group of specialists. When I met with experts on computer engraving, the most useful discovery had nothing to do with computers. They told me our engraving prices were too low.

Rehearse

We sometimes communicate through big road shows, 19 meetings covering the country. A road show can work for an area manager. A meeting which involves every member of the area once a year helps communicate your plans. But it's important to rehearse carefully, and make sure the meeting is worth everyone's time and effort. The more you involve the delegates, the more they think the meeting is worthwhile.

Meetings should not make decisions but they can change people's minds and change the business.

A good manager in every shop

LOOK AT THE SALES

Every area has its worst performing shops

+2% +6% +15% +22% +27% +33% +42% +50%

I don't have a problem at the moment

FAMOUS LAST WORDS

Keep examining your worst performers

Why so poor??

Good Reason   ROAD CLOSED
Poor Manager
Assistant Manager off the boil
Good Manager wrong shop
Good Manager weak team

PROBLEMS DON'T DISAPPEAR ON THEIR OWN

Do it NOW!

The secret behind continual improvements

GOOD MANAGER CHECK LIST

1 What is their track record?   **LOOK AT THE FIGURES**

2 Mr MEN + Make you money   Mr MEN − Make you tired

MR AMBITIOUS   MR HAPPY   MR FRIENDLY   MR CAN'T DO IT   MR CARELESS   MR DISHONESTY

MR KEEN   MR FAITHFUL   MR HONEST   MR DULL   MR FIB   MR GRUMPY

MR PERSONALITY   MR QUICK   MR SKILLFUL   MR LAZY   MR SLOW   MR SCRUFFY

FACT   **A GOOD A.M. PICKS PEOPLE WHO CREATE SUCCESS**

Stars everywhere

My Father used to tell me that if only we could sell one extra pair of shoes in each shop per day, we would make a fortune. Recently I told James that success would be assured if we had a good manager in every shop. These are dreams that will never come true but we shouldn't stop seeking perfection. The better the managers, the better the business.

Always a problem

With so many outlets, it's foolish to say we never have any problems. You only have to look at the figures, some shops are always doing better than others. You must wonder what is wrong with the worst performers. If the reason isn't obvious, you probably have a management problem.

Good managers in every branch

Everyone has problems, but good area managers never have a crisis, they deal with their difficulties before they get too big. Their motto is "Do it now." It's vital to know your managers very well. Our 'Mr Men' cartoons are a good aid to judging character, so is a person's track record. People seldom change, the good stay good and the poor find it difficult to improve. Never mind where technology takes the business, even if the High Street becomes dominated by the computer, people will still be important. In several generations, fathers will still be passing the same advice on to their sons, "the secret to success is having a good manager in every branch."

If you are ill

Doctor's orders

When I had influenza last February I was desperate to get back to work as soon as possible. "You love that office so much you would crawl back if you could." said Alex. Her sarcasm didn't stop me, I went back too early and got pneumonia. "Next time perhaps you will listen to me," said an irritated Alex.

Switch off your mobile

When it comes to illness 'Upside-down Management' should come to the rescue. It only takes two 'phone calls to release you from the business, one to your boss and the other to the person who will look after things while you are away. Once you have made those calls you can switch off your mobile. Go and see the doctor and do as you're told. You may receive a home visit from Personnel. The rest of your colleagues will look forward to seeing you when you are better.

Signs of a good manager

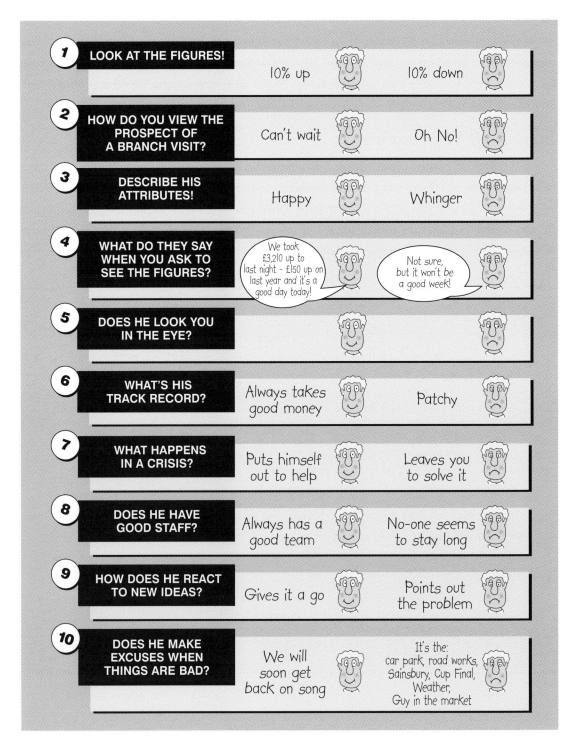

Signs of success

Some people recognise superstars and detect rogues by instinct, others spend their lives being misled by their fellow men. They resolutely ignore the signs that are there for all to see. The best guide to performance is figures. We once employed a man in Scotland who managed six different shops. The turnover dropped in all of them, but the area manager said he was a good bloke, indeed he was a good talker, but when we put a camera into his shop, we found he was pinching £250 a week and closed the shop at 4 0'clock in the afternoon.

We often lack confidence when judging other people, but our opinion is probably shared by everyone else.

Look at the figures

I ask for the turnover figures within two minutes of entering a branch. Keen managers don't need to look for the books, they know the exact takings. Weaklings are vague "It's a bit quiet this week." "I don't think it's very good." They give a shifty reply and never look you in the eye. A poor manager is good at making excuses for poor performance, he blames the weather, the Cup Final, the road works and his own staff. A good manager attracts good people to work for him.

Signs of weakness

Poor people get in a fix by not solving problems. You don't rely on your weaklings in a crisis, they moan rather than finding a solution. If someone suggests an answer, they find something wrong with it. Poor managers can't solve problems because they are the problem themselves.

The secret of success is to know your people. If you want a good manager in every shop, you need to know who the good managers are.

Don't hide the truth

Clear conscience

In our open style of management, honesty pays off handsomely. Even white lies can catch up with you. Don't tell anyone, but my wife Alex doesn't always tell the truth, but she lies with a clear conscience, white lies designed to hide hard truths. She can't turn down an invitation, without quoting a specific reason. We are away in Portugal, we are going to a wedding, John is ill. It is fairly easy to tell a white lie, but can be difficult to remember what you said, that's when lies catch up with you.

Honesty pays

Mistakes can play on your mind. It's better to admit you are wrong than bottle things up. It's not too painful to let people poke fun at you, so go through life sharing your frailty with everyone else.

If you see a problem, don't walk past it, blow the whistle. If you find an idea that works, don't keep it to yourself, let the rest of the company get the benefit.

You don't expect to go through life with other people lying to you, so don't lie to them, it's the best way - honestly.

Visiting another area

Away days

A change is as good as a rest and brings new ideas into the bargain. James visits other companies almost every month. Last year he saw Pret a Manger, Quickfit and Richer Sounds. At our last Area Managers' Conference, we had a talk from David Bryant, Managing Director of Johnsons the Cleaners. It's good to hear about other businesses, new experiences that can produce good ideas.

Talk to your colleagues

Most companies broaden their executives minds by sending them on training courses. A two-day seminar can cost over £1000 per person, a visit with another area manager costs nothing.

At our Area Managers' Conferences, most of the benefit is gained in the bar.

You can find lots of creative ideas in another area manager's car. Visiting another area doesn't need to be hard work, all you do is take a camera and a notebook. As long as you have an open mind, the ideas will come out and hit you. If you think your area is perfect, you won't see ways to improve.

Don't spend your time bragging about your area. You are there to learn, not to teach. At the end of a day on another area, you should have a long list of things to do. Keep the list carefully, when you get back, you could be too busy to remember all the ideas.

Press and publicity

WE **DON'T** ADVERTISE ON TELEVISION

BUT WE PLACE 250,000 ADS A WEEK

One every time we serve a customer

Therefore YOU DON'T HAVE AN ADVERTISING BUDGET

But YOU CAN SPEND AS MUCH AS YOU LIKE ON PUBLIC RELATIONS

Christine can help

Jools can help

BUT YOU CAN MAKE THE NEWS YOURSELF!

IF YOU GET A CALL FROM THE MEDIA

Can we come and interview you?

Can we film in your shop?

Will you talk to us about car keys

ALL NEWS IS GOOD PR → Say YES

IF YOU ARE INTERVIEWED

1 Be Honest

2 Stick to topics you know well

3

Don't flannel*

4 Smile when you are talking

Spreading the word

We advertise every day, but don't appear on T.V. commercials. We make 250,000 sales a week and every amazed customer can turn into a brilliant advert. Public Relations gets the company message across without paying for the privilege. Every time our name appears in the paper, it strengthens the business.

You shouldn't always believe what you read in the papers, but most people do. Employees are much more likely to trust an article in the Daily Mail than a memo from the Managing Director.

Everyone can be on TV

It's not just the Chairman who should appear on the radio, anyone can be called upon to do an interview. Mark Collier our manager at Wilmslow has become an expert at self publicity, so can anyone. Don't be shy, have a go. You can learn interview techniques, like everything else, you just need experience. The trick is to be yourself and talk about things you know well. Mark Collier got to know the reporters on his local paper, most shops could do the same. The papers need us as much as we need them, they want interesting stories to fill their paper, day after day, week after week.

Kelvin Redicliffe, in Newport is another who has created lots of news. Kelvin looks for ways to impress the press, like unusual jobs or a customer of the month. He has been featured winning customer care awards and plays in a band which released a compact disc to a barrage of publicity. Kelvin sends me a newspaper cutting every few weeks.

Make the news

Look through your local rag and see who makes the news. We are more interesting than most businesses, who else has provided pet tags for an elephant, engraved a chastity belt or repaired a clown's shoe.

Company awards give a good excuse to contact the paper, especially the skill diplomas, where else can you find craftsmen on the High Street? If the local paper wants to take a photograph, make sure you are in the picture. Your face in the local paper, can put 20% on sales. Whenever you make the news you bring in new customers to discover the secrets of your success.

Shoe shine promise to firefighters

BY SARAH FREEMAN

FIREFIGHTERS who tackled a blaze which ripped through a Northampton shoe repairers', were among the first customers when the town centre store re-opened for business today.

Timpson in The Drapery was gutted in the fire which started when a spark from a polishing machine ignited a bag of dust on October 12.

Neighbouring shops had to be evacuated as smoke from the fire billowed into the air but three weeks on from the blaze the shop officially opened for business this morning.

To mark the reopening the store managers have agreed to shine the boots of the members of red and white watches from Moulton and The Mounts stations who spent more than four hours making the premises safe.

Manager Richie Tugman said: "The courage and professionalism shown by firemen is something I think most of us take for granted. It is not until you are faced with a crisis like we were recently that we stark reality of the dangers they face are brought sharply into focus.

"I said all the senior executives of Timpson felt very strongly that we wanted to express our thanks in a positive way.

"From now on the red and white watch crews are welcome to bring their boots into the branch any time for a professional polish with our compliments."

The store will also be placing tin on the items-silent fund collection on the counter in the hope that customers will take the opportunity to show their own appreciation of the country's fire service."

■ RISE AND SHINE - Richie Tugman with Russell Kean and Gary Rose

Upper class

SHOE repairer Nobby Northover won a top award from his company for getting things off his chest.

Nobby, who manages Timpson, in North Street, Taunton, was voted the firm's top charity fund-raiser.

He received a trophy from chairman John Timpson at a recent awards ceremony for the firm. "I was stunned to get nominated and it was absolutely brilliant winning such a prestigious award," said Nobby.

"I raised just over £3,000 by having my chest waxed and we made a further £1,400 with a collection in the shop and by staff donating their tips."

Cobbling his way to top UK prize

A Huddersfield cobbler has been hailed the best in Britain.

Peter Smith (pictured) is head over heels with delight after being voted the UK's shoe repair craftsperson of the year.

It is the second time in three years the manager of Timpson in the Imperial Arcade has scooped the accolade.

Mr Smith, of Newsome Road, Newsome, demonstrated the highest levels of technical and artistic skill on the six pairs of repaired shoes he submitted. His entry included the pictured pair of men's shoes re-soled and heeled with brass rivet-patterned soles.

The awards were organised by the Society of Master Shoe Repairers and sponsored by products manufacturer Meltonian. He won £750 and John Timpson, the chairman and chief executive of the Timpson chain, was so impressed that he matched the prize money.

Mr Smith said: "I helped judge the contest last year so I couldn't enter. My competition success is all about hard work."

(4037/15/01)

Manager off to sunny Spain

A COMPETITION organised by Timpsons Ltd gave a holiday to Spain worth £650 to an Eastbourne manager.

Ben Hill, manager of the Eastbourne branch of Timpsons in the Arndale Centre, won the customer care service competition.

Ben is planning to go on the holiday in September with his wife Kim.

After winning the prize a surprised Ben said, 'I was absolutely stunned to find out that my chairman, John Timpson, had a load of letters about me and that I'd won this holiday as a result.

'I like to give my customers lots of time and attention. I've got a great rapport with a lot of lovely regulars and I'm really grateful for their kind words.'

(AP15/28)

Do these men hold the key to election result?

A SHREWSBURY shoe repairs and key engraving shop is running its own alternative charitable 'opinion poll' in a tongue-in-cheek poke at election pollsters.

Forget the complex sampling polls, the questions and the statistical analysis used by the psephologists at the staff at Timpson, in Claremont Street, think they have found a much better litmus test of public opinion.

The shop has been conducting its own unique method of measuring how people will cast their vote in the general election.

The Timpson team has not been asking its customers about their considered political views on the pressing questions of the day, European integration, taxation, education and asylum.

Instead, they are inviting people to select plastic key caps in the colours of the party they will support on June 7.

Blue, red and yellow key caps, representing each of the main political parties, are all up for grabs.

There is also a choice for 'the undecided' or those who do not intend to vote – a white coloured cap. And for each cap taken, the company will donate money to the children's charity Childline.

So far the Timpson's poll puts Labour on a 26 percent, the Conservatives on 32 percent, and the Liberal Democrats on 21 percent.

But the most interesting figure is the 21 percent figure for the number of undecided voters who say they are suffering from general election fatigue and would rather watch paint dry than watch a party political broadcast.

Although election buffs may scoff at the poll, in 1997, the Timpson poll put Labour just 5.8 percent adrift of its actual 44 percent share of the vote.

Not bad for a whoeze.

Timpson's Shrewsbury branch manager, Glen Plavell, said: "It's just a bit of fun which is raising money for a great cause.

"Most customers don't seem to mind our asking them how they'll vote although there are a lot of people saying they probably won't bother to vote at all.

PICTURE: Testing voters' opinions in their own election poll is the team from Timpson. From the left are Martin Bowen, Damian Goldson and Glen Plavell.

215

Area conference

Letter to an unwilling conference delegate

Dear Area Manager

Most of the year you can set your own timetable but you have to go to every Area Managers' Conference. We try and make them worthwhile, we know the keener you are to come, the more you will get from the Conference. They are designed to help you make more money and, as a result, earn a bigger bonus. So because it's money (your money) we are talking about, it's worth reading a few tips on how to make the most of your two days at a Conference.

Read the papers before you arrive, checking the venue and time, if you turn up late you will get a big cheer from all your colleagues but you will feel stupid. You should have delegated all the day-to-day jobs before you left home.

Arrive with a clear mind and leave your mobile and briefcase in the car. Enjoy yourself, we do our best to entertain. If you can relax and join in, you are likely to find some new ideas. Enjoy the free time, especially in the bar, but it's best to go to bed before 1 o'clock. The second day may be even better than the first.

John Timpson

John Timpson

Area review

RELAX

We are there to help you increase your bonus

1 KNOW YOUR FIGURES

2 KNOW YOUR PEOPLE

3 BE READY FOR THE LIKELY QUESTIONS...

Why has the profit fallen at.........?

Why are sales down at......?

Why are these costs so high?

...AND HAVE THE ANSWERS

YOU'RE RIGHT! MY PLAN IS........

4 BRING YOUR WISH LIST

REFITS

COMPUTERS

AREA DINNER

NEW SHOP

5 HAVE A MOAN

TOO MUCH PAPERWORK

LATE DELIVERIES

CAN'T GET DISPLAY MATERIALS

POOR MATERIALS

6 WRITE AN ACTION LIST

7 DO IT NOW!

ACTION LIST

On parade

For four hours every six months, area managers attend their review meeting. The purpose is to improve profit, not to appraise individual performance. But to some, it's like going to the dentist, the review is preceded by several sleepless nights. There is nothing to fear as long as you know the job, it's your best chance to be the area's representative.

Be prepared

Do your homework before you come, know the profit and turnover of every branch and know as much as you can about your people. List all the problems. You should tell us what is going wrong before we have a chance of telling you. If possible, suggest solutions, or even better tell us you have already fixed the problem.

Wish list

If you know something needs doing in your area, do it before you come to the meeting. To get the best out of the review, you must know what you are fighting for. Bring a wish list, the refits, new machinery, help with training and anything where you need help. Have a moan if you want, you will find we are getting better at listening.

Refits - *ALSO APPLIES TO NEW SHOPS*

1 COMMENT ON THE PLAN

OK
D.J.

Send it back to Rod.

2 SET YOUR TURNOVER TARGET

+20%

Does that justify the investment

3 PICK UP ACTION POINTS FROM ROD'S WARNING NOTICE!

TIMING		ACTION
Sat 23rd Sept	Branch to cease trading at 5.00 p.m. Clear all merchandise and displays from area concerned.	AB/420
	Shopfitting work to commence at 5.00 p.m.	RAU/AH
Sat 23rd Sept to Tues 26th Sept	Branch to remain closed. Shopfitting to continue and complete.	AB/420
Wed 27th Sept to Thurs 28th Sept	Branch to remain closed. Dressing out to be carried out.	AB/420

4 INVOLVE THE BRANCH STAFF...

...tell them everything

REPORT BULLETIN

WHY

WHEN

5 DECIDE WHO DOES WHAT

Branch Manager   ADM

Yourself
(You don't have to be there.)

TIP

USE THE PEOPLE WITH DISPLAY TALENT!

6 SHOUT! IF YOU HAVE A PROBLEM!

BUT

KEEP CALM
There is no need to irritate Rod

Closed for improvements

The company pays the bill for new shops and refits but we want everyone to be happy with the way we spend the money. Be persistent at the planning stage, everyone gets a chance to comment, don't sit back and let us make mistakes. There is no profit to be made out of the people who say "I told you so."

Keep calm

If you expect perfection you will be disappointed. We never get it dead right, and if we did, it would only be with help from the branch and area team. There will always be problems. Refits test whether you have a short temper. Keep calm. Before work commences, check the guidance notes that list your action points. They put you on the line but don't do everything yourself, delegate.

Don't waste the money

A good area manager can open a new shop without being there himself. But it won't be successful unless he picks good staff to take advantage of the investment. The vital part of any refit isn't the shopfitting, it's the staff and their training. We waste our money if we have the wrong people.

It's important to keep the business up-to-date, provide customers with a better service and it gives us the chance to make more money.

New starters

THEY ARE JOINING A VERY SPECIAL BUSINESS

PEOPLE MATTER

Your personal touch can do so much to bring the Apprentice Manual to Life!

School Leaver

Young Apprentice

Mature Recruit

Seasoned Cobbler

ENSURE ALL PAPERWORK IS SENT IN BEFORE THEY JOIN SO THEY ARE PAID AND UNIFORMED IN TIME AND RECEIVE THEIR APPRENTICE MANUAL ETC.

THINGS THAT REALLY WORK

1 MEET DURING THE FIRST WEEK

IT'S WORTH A SPECIAL VISIT

2 GO OUT FOR COFFEE

3 RING MUM AND DAD

*For school leavers!

HELLO MRS SYKES, HAVE YOU SEEN OUR COMPANY VIDEO?

WARNING

CUT YOUR LOSSES IF THEY ARE BELOW OUR STANDARDS TERMINATE THEIR CONTRACT - IT'S ONLY FAIR TO THEM AS WELL AS THE COMPANY

A warm welcome

Three years ago I met a Mr Minit manager who had been with their business for seven months and still hadn't met his area manager. You can't ignore new recruits, you must spend extra time with new team members, it's the only way to get to know them. Make sure you give a warm welcome. Demonstrate they haven't just got a job, but have joined an extraordinary business. They have become a member of an exceptional club.

Help on day one

They must find out how 'The Club' works. It won't be what they expect, we have turned conventional ideas on their head, we need to sell the concept of 'Upside-down Management.' As part of our culture, managers are there to help. You can show it to new recruits on their first day by buying them a coffee or giving a ring that evening to Mum and Dad to report how things have gone.

First hurdle

Once you know them, you must ask "Are they going to make it?" Don't waste time training people who don't care and can't get to work on time. If they pass the test, more training is available at Timpson than any similar business on the High Street. We spend more money on training than refits and new shops combined. The young people are the future of this business, it's important you get to know them as soon as possible.

Help is at hand

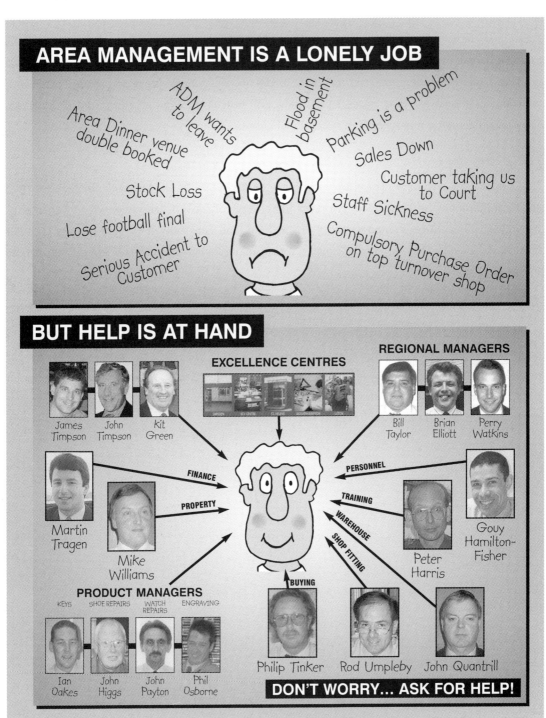

AREA MANAGEMENT IS A LONELY JOB

ADM wants to leave

Flood in basement

Parking is a problem

Area Dinner venue double booked

Sales Down

Customer taking us to Court

Stock Loss

Staff Sickness

Lose football final

Serious Accident to Customer

Compulsory Purchase Order on top turnover shop

BUT HELP IS AT HAND

EXCELLENCE CENTRES

REGIONAL MANAGERS

James Timpson

John Timpson

Kit Green

Bill Taylor

Brian Elliott

Perry Watkins

FINANCE

PERSONNEL

PROPERTY

TRAINING

Martin Tragen

WAREHOUSE

SHOP FITTING

Gouy Hamilton-Fisher

Mike Williams

BUYING

Peter Harris

PRODUCT MANAGERS

KEYS   SHOE REPAIRS   WATCH REPAIRS   ENGRAVING

Ian Oakes

John Higgs

John Payton

Phil Osborne

Philip Tinker

Rod Umpleby

John Quantrill

DON'T WORRY... ASK FOR HELP!

SOS

Area managers spend most of their time helping others, but sometimes they need help themselves. It's a lonely job spending your life in a car with a mobile 'phone that delivers a succession of problems. Before the shops have opened you have already heard of someone off sick and been asked for time off for a best friend's funeral. Experience provides the answer to most problems. Most solutions are delegated to ADM's but there will be times when you are stumped. In Timpson there are plenty of people to help. Everyone at Timpson House knows their main job is to help people in the field. All you have to do is ask. Ask for advice, and you will get an opinion not an instruction. We are there to help you make up your mind not to make the decision. So share your troubles, if you need advice, support or a word in the right ear, pick up the 'phone and ask Timpson House for help.

Chapter 5

Dealing with people problems

Dealing with people problems

Most weeks I challenge my friend Tom at tennis. Tom has been retired some years and thinks I am mad not to do the same. "The most wonderful thing about retirement," says Tom "is not having to employ people, all they bring is trouble and the longer time goes on the more trouble they seem to bring."

Tribunal phobia

Tom has a good point. Although we believe in looking after our people, too much management time is spent worrying about facing of an Industrial Tribunal. The Civil Service seems to assume that business is based on conflict, management against the workers making profits by exploiting the people we employ. We pay a big price for the poor personnel practices of the past. If you are not careful, employment legislation gets in the way of running a business. Too much time spent keeping to the regulations instead of looking after people. The objective is to avoid getting the blame. Never mind what you do as long as the paperwork is perfect.

Solving people problems

After I issued my manual on looking after people, one of the area managers wrote. "That's fine as far as it goes, but what we really need, John, is a detailed explanation of the disciplinary procedure." So here it is, a section devoted to dealing with problems. Most of it, I must admit, is pretty unconstructive. It talks of oral warnings and grievance procedures. All the things that are needed to make sure that if we ever appear in an Industrial Tribunal, we do so on the winning side. But I go beyond the legal requirements, into an area I consider more important. The manual gives guidance on how we can help our people with problems, whether they be illness, credit cards, drugs or divorce. Often the best help we can give is to listen to their problem or find experts who can give the help they need.

Politically correct?

I have tried to toe the line of political correctness, but someone pointed out there are very few women in the illustrations. No offence is intended, we don't have many women working in our shops, our trade doesn't attract them but that doesn't mean that we are guilty of sex discrimination.

Employment legislation has eliminated many bad practices and for that reason I am willing to put up with it, but at the same time I intend to make sure that the Law does not stop us looking after the people we employ.

People problems

Trouble at home

If someone goes off the boil, the reason for the lapse often lies at home. Something has gone wrong. Try to solve the problem, not deal with the symptoms. At first you see the poor turnover and look to change the displays or standard of salesmanship. Dig a bit deeper and you may discover stress and anxiety due to money or marriage problems, or a tired performer suffering from the effect of drink, drugs or ill health.

Managers are not experts in medicine or psychology, but they can be sympathetic listeners. If they themselves can't help, they can find someone else who can.

Avoid the pitfalls, Industrial Tribunals are full of firms that did too little, too late. Every time you fudge dealing with a problem, you create a bigger problem. Go out of the way to help. Deal with everyone equally and treat every problem seriously. But prepare for a shock, however hard you try to be fair, you may still finish up in an Industrial Tribunal, so make sure you keep careful notes. We don't want an undeserving employee to win in court, that would be unfair to the rest of the team.

Money problems

TYPICAL SCENARIOS

I can't pay that new demand

I need £1000 toward a new car

She's run up a £2000 credit card debt

TIMPSON

HELPFUL QUESTIONS

Are you still using your credit card?

Have you looked at your total financial alternatives?

Do you have a bank account?

Who have you spoken to?

Does your wife know about it?

Which bills do you have to pay now?

THINGS YOU COULD DO

APPLY FOR A COMPANY LOAN.

HELP FILL IN FINANCE CHECK FORM.

See next page ....

EXPERTS   BANK MANAGER   citizens advice bureau

WARNING   DO NOT TALK TO LOAN SHARKS

Finance check form

INCOME

WHAT IS YOUR NET PAY ....

OTHER INCOME

BENEFITS ....

INTEREST ....

OTHERS ....

TOTAL INCOME ....

EXPENDITURE

MORTGAGE/RENT ....

REPAYMENTS ....

CIGARETTES ....

WEEKLY EXPENSES ....

NIGHTS OUT ....

OTHER ....

TOTAL EXPENDITURE ....

☺ OR ☹ ....

DEBTS

CREDIT CARDS ....

PERSONAL LOANS ....

OVERDRAFT ....

TOTAL DEBT ....

ASSETS

CAR (resale value) ....

MONEY IN BANK ....

PREMIUM BONDS etc ....

INVESTMENTS ....

HOUSE ....

OTHER ....

TOTAL ASSETS ....

☺ OR ☹ ....

Bereavement

TYPICAL PROBLEM

How will I be able to cope?

My whole world has been turned upside down!

I can't think of anything else!

HELPFUL QUESTIONS

Who is organising the funeral?

Have you told all the friends and relations?

Is there a post mortem?

Are you worried about anything in particular?

THINGS YOU COULD DO

Send a letter.

Attend the Funeral.

Arrange time off.

Ask work colleague for support.

> Dear Bob
>
> I was very sorry to hear of Mary's death. I know it has come as a shock to you.
>
> I have met her several times at company dinners and remember her kindness to the young apprentice and partners at the table.
>
> Please do not hesitate to ask if there is any help I can give.
>
> All your Timpson colleagues express their sincere sympathy.
>
> Regards.

EXPERTS › **UNDERTAKER • LOCAL SOLICITOR • MINISTER**

Illness

TYPICAL PROBLEMS

I have to go in for an OP

I still don't feel myself

TIMPSON

HELPFUL QUESTIONS

What does the doctor say?

Who is looking after you at home ?

Have you any worries?

THINGS YOU COULD DO

HOSPITAL / HOME VISITS..........

WRITE A LETTER...

SEND A GIFT / FLOWERS.

CONTACT THE NEAREST RELATIVE.

EXPERT ADVICE   DOCTOR • HOSPITAL

Gambling

TYPICAL PROBLEM

Can I have a company loan?

He would be better off if he kept out of the bookies!

HELPFUL QUESTIONS

FIND WAYS TO TALK ABOUT THIS PROBLEM

What are your major items of expenditure?

Do you always have a bet?

How much do you win?

When did you last have a bet?

How much do you spend on betting?

THINGS YOU COULD DO

KEEP TALKING

EXPERTS

Romance and marriage

TYPICAL PROBLEMS

HELPFUL QUESTIONS

GET THEM TALKING!

How long have you felt like this?

I can't help thinking something is on your mind?

Who have you spoken to?

What does she say?

Have you told me everything?

THINGS YOU COULD DO

Give some time off.

Meet out of business hours.

EXPERTS ⟩ citizens advice bureau **RELATE**

Children

TYPICAL PROBLEMS

I'm not getting any sleep!

BABIES!

I just don't know what to do about Stacy?

TEENAGERS!

HELPFUL QUESTIONS

Who can you talk to?

Who can give you some help?

How long has it been going on?

Have you seen the doctor?

Have you spoken to school?

What does your daughter say?

THINGS YOU COULD DO

Allow time off.

Talk to the wife / husband / partner.

EXPERTS

FAMILY DOCTOR • YOUTH LEADERS
SCHOOLS

Drink

TYPICAL PROBLEMS

I keep fighting this bad infection

I've heard he has a drink problem

HELPFUL QUESTIONS

Do you have problems with your health?

Have you told your doctor everything?

Do you have a drink problem?

NOTE

MANY ALCOHOLICS DENY THEY HAVE A PROBLEM

THINGS YOU COULD DO

Keep looking for opportunities to raise the topic!

Insist on a doctors note if there is an regular pattern of illness!

EXPERTS

Alcoholics Anonymous
registered charity No 226745

Family illness

TYPICAL PROBLEMS

My dad can't do anything for himself - and my sister lives in Birmingham

My partner has cancer

QUESTIONS TO ASK

When did you find out ?

What does the doctor say now?

What treatment is she getting?

How does he feel?

Lots of questions to get people talking - (IT HELPS)

You need to listen a lot

THINGS YOU COULD DO

Time off.

Change hours.

Write a letter.

Visit the patient.

EXPERTS   DOCTOR • HOSPITALS • HELP GROUPS

Violence at home

TYPICAL PROBLEMS

I fell over in the garden

QUESTIONS TO ASK

TRY TO GET THEM TALKING

How exactly did it happen?

Have you seen a doctor?

Are you sure everything is all right?

Can I take you to "A&E".

TIP

LOOK OUT FOR EXAGGERATED OR INVENTED PROBLEMS!

HOW YOU CAN HELP

Look out for further problems.

Give them a copy of this manual.

EXPERTS ▷ citizens advice bureau **RELATE**

Banana skins

A boss must be on his best behaviour at all times, as one chief executive found to his cost, when at a Retail Awards Dinner he pinched a girl's bottom, and lost his job. But you don't have to be so blatant, much smaller things can cause trouble.

Life has changed, banter has become sexual innuendo, flattery is now thought to be foreplay, careless talk can create a lot of costs in court. You must not only be fair, but must be seen to be fair. Think carefully about the minority view, the gays, the blacks, the disabled. Although we only have a small percentage of women in our company, it's not the result of any sex discrimination, that's just the way that the business is. You can avoid people problems by being sensible and sensitive. A thoughtless slip of the tongue, can prove to be very expensive.

Your best approach

People problems

How to spot a thief

HOW TO SPOT A THIEF

SCAM 1 — THE UNDER-RING
Key in the till less money than the customer has tendered and later remove the excess money for your own use(Under-ring).

SCAM 2 — POCKET IT
Remove money from the till to your pocket for own use.

SCAM 3 — TILL BYPASS
When a customer gives the correct money fail to enter it into the till and place the money in your pocket for your own personal use.

SCAM 4 — CANCEL SALE
Complete a customer transaction and place the money in the till. When the customer has left the shop refund the transaction out and remove the money for your own use.

SCAM 5 — SPOOF REFUND
Complete a refund or customer compensation slip either yourself or use a friend, then remove the amount of the refund for your own use.

SCAM 6 — THE X READING
When a customer gives money for goods complete an "X" reading and place the money in the till. Later remove the money for your own use.

SCAM 7 — CHARITY BOX
Use the Charity box as a personal bank by removing money for your own use.

SCAM 8 — STOCK TAKING
Remove stock from your shop in order to sell or give to a friend or relative in the trade.

SCAM 9 — WORK IN PROGRESS
Remove customer's items entrusted to us and left in the shop in order to sell or keep for your own use.

SCAM 10 — CREDIT CARD TRICK
Complete a credit card transaction and hand the credit card slip to the customer as the receipt, without entering the transaction through the till. When the till is next opened swap the value of the credit card for the same amount of cash and keep it for your own use.

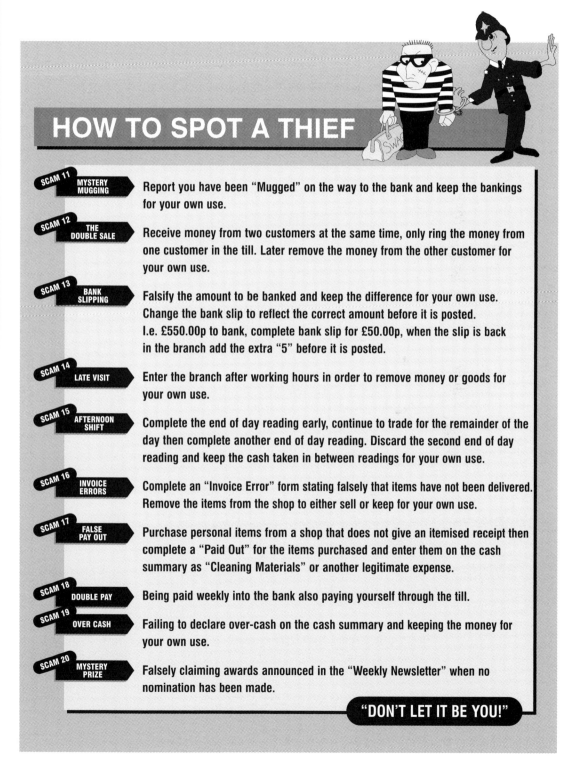

HOW TO SPOT A THIEF

SCAM 11 — MYSTERY MUGGING
Report you have been "Mugged" on the way to the bank and keep the bankings for your own use.

SCAM 12 — THE DOUBLE SALE
Receive money from two customers at the same time, only ring the money from one customer in the till. Later remove the money from the other customer for your own use.

SCAM 13 — BANK SLIPPING
Falsify the amount to be banked and keep the difference for your own use. Change the bank slip to reflect the correct amount before it is posted. I.e. £550.00p to bank, complete bank slip for £50.00p, when the slip is back in the branch add the extra "5" before it is posted.

SCAM 14 — LATE VISIT
Enter the branch after working hours in order to remove money or goods for your own use.

SCAM 15 — AFTERNOON SHIFT
Complete the end of day reading early, continue to trade for the remainder of the day then complete another end of day reading. Discard the second end of day reading and keep the cash taken in between readings for your own use.

SCAM 16 — INVOICE ERRORS
Complete an "Invoice Error" form stating falsely that items have not been delivered. Remove the items from the shop to either sell or keep for your own use.

SCAM 17 — FALSE PAY OUT
Purchase personal items from a shop that does not give an itemised receipt then complete a "Paid Out" for the items purchased and enter them on the cash summary as "Cleaning Materials" or another legitimate expense.

SCAM 18 — DOUBLE PAY
Being paid weekly into the bank also paying yourself through the till.

SCAM 19 — OVER CASH
Failing to declare over-cash on the cash summary and keeping the money for your own use.

SCAM 20 — MYSTERY PRIZE
Falsely claiming awards announced in the "Weekly Newsletter" when no nomination has been made.

"DON'T LET IT BE YOU!"

Disciplinary code

We receive more calls for help with disciplinary matters than any other aspect of our business. Warning letters and the threat of an Industrial Tribunal are now an every day part of business life. Even with our 'Upside-down Management' system, we can't escape the employment law. Everyone needs to know the rules, and know where they stand. To make it easy, what follows is an illustrated version of the current Employment Code.

Different types of problems

Different types of problems

Formal stages

THE FORMAL STAGES OF OUR DISCIPLINARY PROCEDURES

MAKE A NOTE

STAGE	WHO	WHEN
NOTE IMPORTANT EVENTS	MANAGER IN CHARGE OF SHOP	EVERYTIME AN EVENT OCCURS
INFORMAL COUNSELLING	AREA MANAGER	MINOR MISCONDUCT MINOR LAPSE IN STANDARDS

ISSUE A FORMAL WARNING

STAGE	WHO	WHEN
ORAL WARNING	AREA MANAGER	AFTER 1 COUNSELLING 2 FURTHER BREAKING OF RULES
WRITTEN WARNING	AREA MANAGER	AFTER 1 ORAL WARNING
FINAL WRITTEN WARNING	AREA MANAGER	AFTER 1 WRITTEN WARNING

DISMISSAL

STAGE	WHO	WHEN
DISMISSAL	AREA MANAGER	AFTER 1 FINAL WRITTEN WARNING 2 GROSS MISCONDUCT 3 NOTIFICATION FROM PERSONNEL

NOTE

EVERY DECISION IS CONFIRMED IN WRITING BY THE PERSONNEL DEPT

Who can do what?

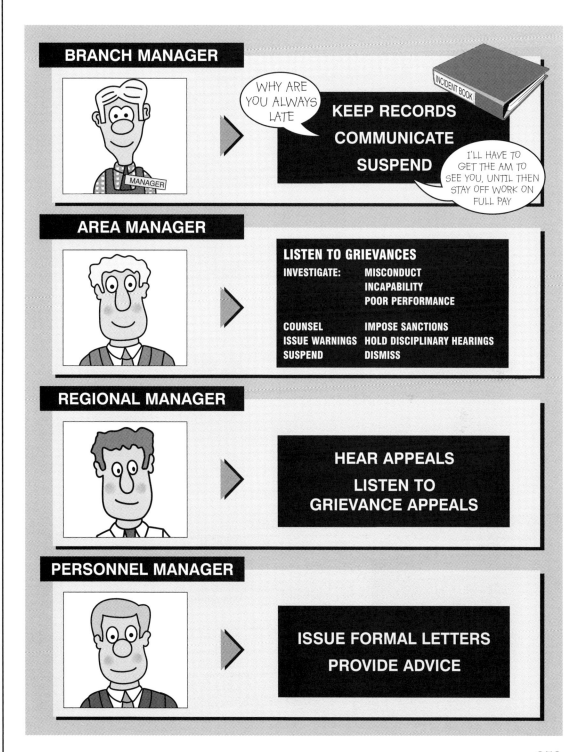

Manager record keeping

THE FOLLOWING SHOULD ALWAYS BE
ENTERED IN THE BRANCH INCIDENT BOOK

INCIDENT BOOK

LATENESS	UNSHAVEN	IMPROPER DRESS
SMOKING	SMELLING OF ALCOHOL	HEALTH AND SAFETY PROBLEM
POOR CUSTOMER CARE	MILD INSUBORDINATION	POOR HOUSEKEEPING

NOTE

YOU MUST ALWAYS TELL THE EMPLOYEE YOU ARE TAKING NOTE OF THE INCIDENT

IMPORTANT: DON'T IGNORE A PROBLEM

ALWAYS NOTE

NAME
DATE
INCIDENT
BACKGROUND
ACTION

GEORGE SMITH
WED 17 DEC
ARRIVAL 9.37AM
SAID THE BUS WAS LATE
AGREED TO GET EARLIER
BUS AND ARRIVE AT 8.45

JANE JONES
THURS 7 JAN
SMOKING IN SHOP
PROMISED NOT TO DO IT AGAIN
LEAVING CIGARETTES IN HER HANDBAG

TIP

DEAL WITH IT NOW - THIS IS THE BEST WAY TO KEEP UP STANDARDS

Investigating problems

BEFORE YOU ACT... GET ALL THE FACTS

WHO?

...was involved.
...were the witnesses.
...verified the incident.

WHEN?

...did the incident occur.

JANUARY

WHAT?

...evidence can you produce.
...statements have been made.
...video evidence do you have.
...is the previous history.

STATEMENT
On 20th January 2001 Bill
Franks took some cash
from the till.
David
Peterson

WHERE?

...did incident happen.
...were the other people involved.

WHY?

...did it happen.
...was it reported.

???

TIPS

WRITE IT ALL DOWN

**KEEP A COPY OF
ALL YOUR NOTES**

THEN THINK

WHAT DO
I DO NEXT

Check list

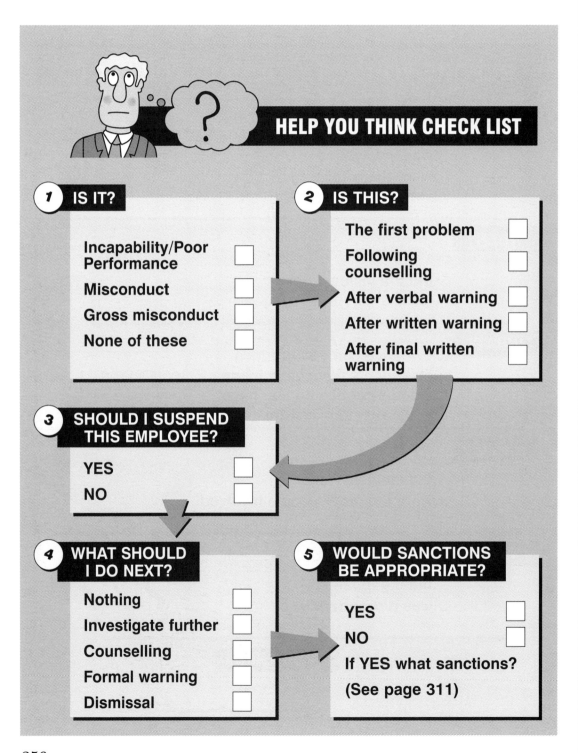

HELP YOU THINK CHECK LIST

1 IS IT?

Incapability/Poor Performance ☐

Misconduct ☐

Gross misconduct ☐

None of these ☐

2 IS THIS?

The first problem ☐

Following counselling ☐

After verbal warning ☐

After written warning ☐

After final written warning ☐

3 SHOULD I SUSPEND THIS EMPLOYEE?

YES ☐

NO ☐

4 WHAT SHOULD I DO NEXT?

Nothing ☐

Investigate further ☐

Counselling ☐

Formal warning ☐

Dismissal ☐

5 WOULD SANCTIONS BE APPROPRIATE?

YES ☐

NO ☐

If YES what sanctions?

(See page 311)

Poor performance counselling

YOUR AIM...
TO HELP AND IMPROVE

4 **SET TARGETS**

Level 1 Keys in 6 weeks

Give me a report from your doctor in a month

5 **POINT OUT CONSEQUENCES**

If you don't reach the target I will have to use the formal disciplinary procedure

REMEMBER

1 **KEEP A WRITTEN RECORD.**

2 **SEND A COPY TO PERSONNEL.**

NOTE

PERSONNEL WILL SEND A COPY OF NOTES TO THE EMPLOYEE.

Communication

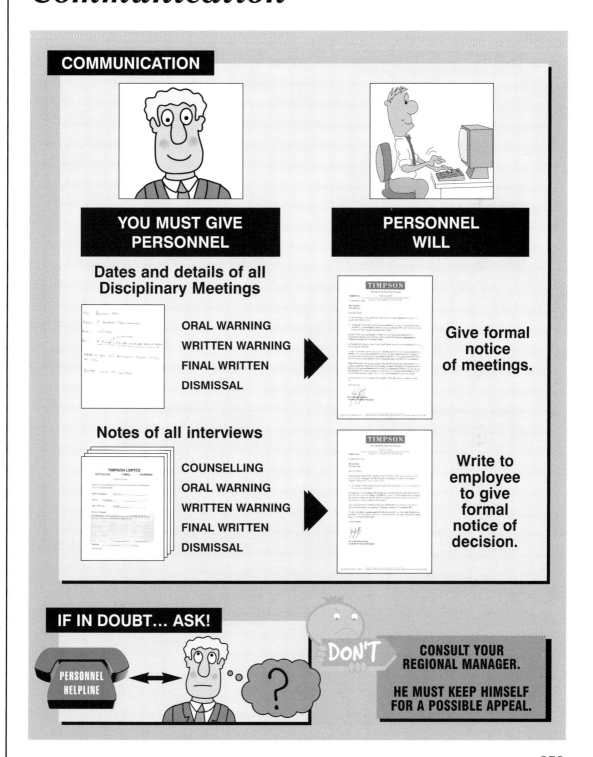

COMMUNICATION

YOU MUST GIVE PERSONNEL

PERSONNEL WILL

Dates and details of all Disciplinary Meetings

ORAL WARNING

WRITTEN WARNING

FINAL WRITTEN

DISMISSAL

Give formal notice of meetings.

Notes of all interviews

COUNSELLING

ORAL WARNING

WRITTEN WARNING

FINAL WRITTEN

DISMISSAL

Write to employee to give formal notice of decision.

IF IN DOUBT... ASK!

PERSONNEL HELPLINE

DON'T

CONSULT YOUR REGIONAL MANAGER.

HE MUST KEEP HIMSELF FOR A POSSIBLE APPEAL.

Counselling interview

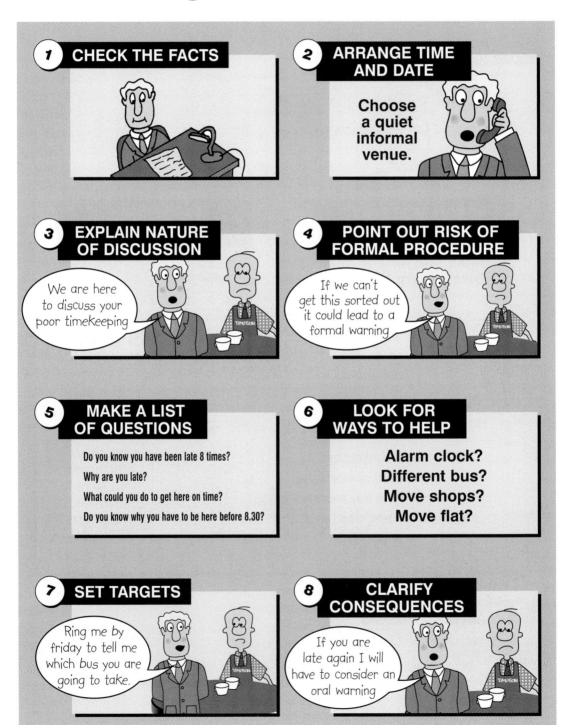

Counselling interview

Formal interviews

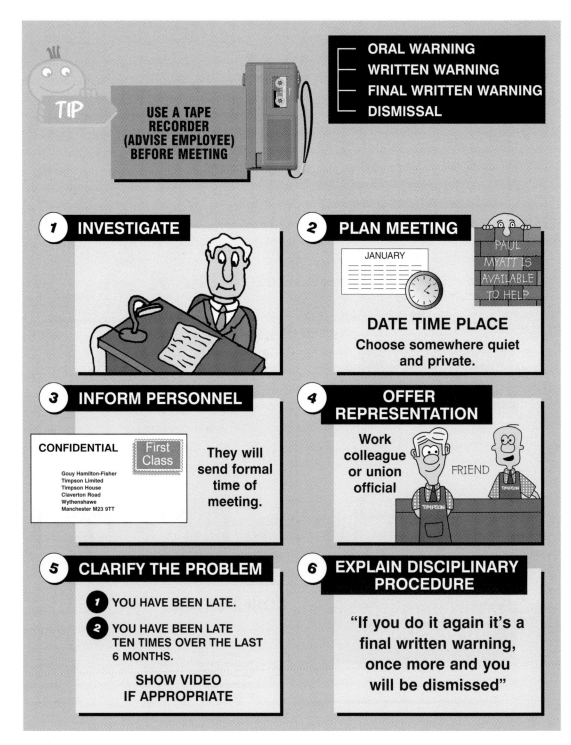

TIP

USE A TAPE RECORDER (ADVISE EMPLOYEE) BEFORE MEETING

- ORAL WARNING
- WRITTEN WARNING
- FINAL WRITTEN WARNING
- DISMISSAL

1 INVESTIGATE

2 PLAN MEETING

JANUARY

PAUL MYATT IS AVAILABLE TO HELP

DATE TIME PLACE
Choose somewhere quiet and private.

3 INFORM PERSONNEL

CONFIDENTIAL — First Class

Gouy Hamilton-Fisher
Timpson Limited
Timpson House
Claverton Road
Wythenshawe
Manchester M23 9TT

They will send formal time of meeting.

4 OFFER REPRESENTATION

Work colleague or union official

FRIEND

5 CLARIFY THE PROBLEM

1 YOU HAVE BEEN LATE.

2 YOU HAVE BEEN LATE TEN TIMES OVER THE LAST 6 MONTHS.

SHOW VIDEO IF APPROPRIATE

6 EXPLAIN DISCIPLINARY PROCEDURE

"If you do it again it's a final written warning, once more and you will be dismissed"

Formal interviews

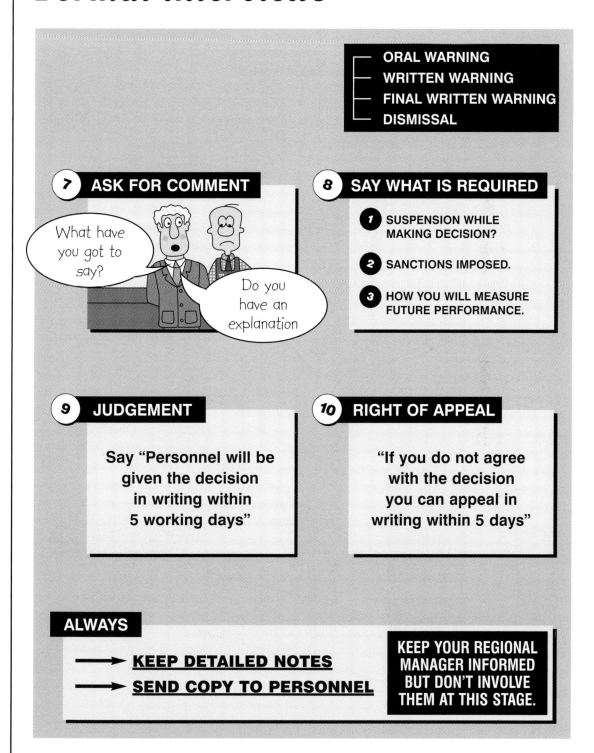

ORAL WARNING
WRITTEN WARNING
FINAL WRITTEN WARNING
DISMISSAL

7 ASK FOR COMMENT

What have you got to say?

Do you have an explanation

8 SAY WHAT IS REQUIRED

1 SUSPENSION WHILE MAKING DECISION?

2 SANCTIONS IMPOSED.

3 HOW YOU WILL MEASURE FUTURE PERFORMANCE.

9 JUDGEMENT

Say "Personnel will be given the decision in writing within 5 working days"

10 RIGHT OF APPEAL

"If you do not agree with the decision you can appeal in writing within 5 days"

ALWAYS

→ **KEEP DETAILED NOTES**

→ **SEND COPY TO PERSONNEL**

KEEP YOUR REGIONAL MANAGER INFORMED BUT DON'T INVOLVE THEM AT THIS STAGE.

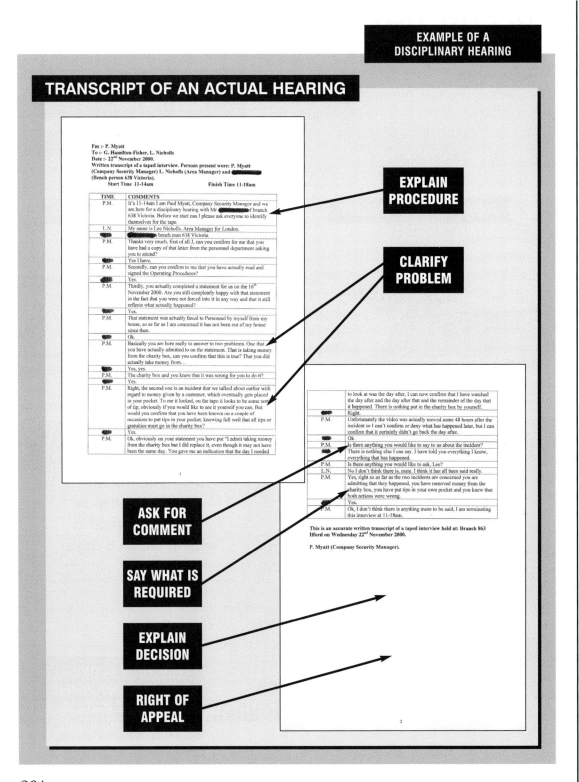

EXAMPLE OF A DISCIPLINARY HEARING

TRANSCRIPT OF AN ACTUAL HEARING

Fm :- P. Myatt
To :- G. Hamilton-Fisher, L. Nicholls
Date :- 22nd November 2000.
Written transcript of a taped interview. Persons present were: P. Myatt (Company Security Manager) L. Nicholls (Area Manager) and ████████ (Bench person 638 Victoria).
Start Time 11-14am   Finish Time 11-18am

TIME	COMMENTS
P.M.	It's 11-14am I am Paul Myatt, Company Security Manager and we are here for a disciplinary hearing with Mr ████████ of branch 638 Victoria. Before we start can I please ask everyone to identify themselves for the tape.
L.N.	My name is Lee Nicholls, Area Manager for London.
████	████████ bench man 638 Victoria.
P.M.	Thanks very much, first of all J, can you confirm for me that you have had a copy of that letter from the personnel department asking you to attend?
████	Yes I have.
P.M.	Secondly, can you confirm to me that you have actually read and signed the Operating Procedures?
████	Yes.
P.M.	Thirdly, you actually completed a statement for us on the 16th November 2000. Are you still completely happy with that statement in the fact that you were not forced into it in any way and that it still reflects what actually happened?
████	Yes.
P.M.	That statement was actually faxed to Personnel by myself from my house, so as far as I am concerned it has not been out of my house since then.
████	Ok.
P.M.	Basically you are here really to answer to two problems. One that you have actually admitted to on the statement. That is taking money from the charity box, can you confirm that this is true? That you did actually take money from…
████	Yes, yes.
P.M.	The charity box and you knew that it was wrong for you to do it?
████	Yes.
P.M.	Right, the second one is an incident that we talked about earlier with regard to money given by a customer, which eventually gets placed in your pocket. To me it looked, on the tape it looks to be some sort of tip, obviously if you would like to see it yourself you can. But would you confirm that you have been known on a couple of occasions to put tips in your pocket, knowing full well that all tips or gratuities must go in the charity box?
████	Yes.
P.M.	Ok, obviously on your statement you have put "I admit taking money from the charity box but I did replace it, even though it may not have been the same day. You gave me an indication that the day I needed

1

EXPLAIN PROCEDURE

CLARIFY PROBLEM

	to look at was the day after, I can now confirm that I have watched the day after and the day after that and the remainder of the day that it happened. There is nothing put in the charity box by yourself.
████	Right.
P.M.	Unfortunately the video was actually moved some 48 hours after the incident so I can't confirm or deny what has happened later, but I can confirm that it certainly didn't go back the day after.
████	Ok.
P.M.	Is there anything you would like to say to us about the incident?
████	There is nothing else I can say. I have told you everything I know, everything that has happened.
P.M.	Is there anything you would like to ask, Lee?
L.N.	No I don't think there is, mate. I think it has all been said really.
P.M.	Yes, right so as far as the two incidents are concerned you are admitting that they happened, you have removed money from the charity box, you have put tips in your own pocket and you knew that both actions were wrong.
████	Yes.
P.M.	Ok, I don't think there is anything more to be said, I am terminating this interview at 11-18am.

This is an accurate written transcript of a taped interview held at: Branch 863 Ilford on Wednesday 22nd November 2000.

P. Myatt (Company Security Manager).

2

ASK FOR COMMENT

SAY WHAT IS REQUIRED

EXPLAIN DECISION

RIGHT OF APPEAL

Formal interviews - useful words

THE FOLLOWING PHRASES MAY BE HELPFUL WHEN HEARING AN INTERVIEW

ADVISING EMPLOYEE OF MEETING

"We need to discuss certain aspects of the job. It will be on an official basis and you are entitled to have a witness present for our discussion."

INTRODUCTION (CLARIFYING PROBLEM)

"We are meeting today to discuss certain problems you seem to be encountering with regard to our rules and procedures. The items are........"

EXPLAINING PROCEDURE

"The procedure you should have used is ....
Do you understand the procedures I have just explained?"

ASK FOR COMMENT

"Having heard what I have to say are there any comments you would like to make?"

SAY WHAT IS REQUIRED

A. "We now need to move on and begin using the correct procedure."

B. "I now expect you to follow my example."

EXPLAIN DECISION

"Having listened to your answers today, my decision is................."

RIGHT OF APPEAL

"You are able to appeal against this decision.
It must be initiated in writing no later than 5 working days from today.
This appeal should be forwarded to the Personnel Department."

Letters from personnel

FORMAL NOTICE OF MEETINGS

To:- Personnel Dept

From:- D. Randall (Area Manager)

Date:- 15/11/00

Re:- A Fisher - failed customer service again
→ 123 Anytown.

Hearing at 123 Anytown, Friday 24/11/00 at 2pm.

Please write to confirm

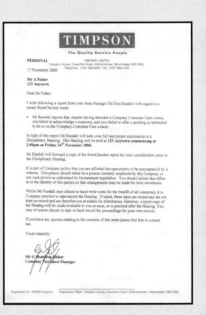

FORMAL NOTICE OR DECISION

Dealing with...

**SUSPENSION
DEMOTION
DISMISSAL**

SUSPENSION

Until this hearing takes place you will be suspended on full pay - you should not turn up for work here or anywhere else until the hearing

WHEN CAN YOU SUSPEND

1 WHILE WAITING FOR A DISCIPLINARY HEARING.

2 WHILE WAITING FOR A FORMAL DECISION FOLLOWING A HEARING.

3 TO PROVIDE 'BREATHING SPACE'.

WHAT CONDITIONS APPLY

How does he get his pay?

1 FULL PAY (NORMALLY UP TO FIVE DAYS ON FULL PAY).

2 STAY AWAY FROM PLACE OF WORK.

THINK?

3 SET TIME LIMIT (NORMALLY DATE OF HEARING OR DECISION).

DEMOTION

In view of your performance I propose to demote you to Benchman - I am arranging a hearing for us to discuss the situation

1 MUST HAVE A GOOD REASON.

2 ONLY AFTER DISCIPLINARY HEARING.

3 EMPLOYEE HAS RIGHT OF APPEAL.

4 SUSPENSION MAY BE APPROPRIATE DURING DISCUSSION PERIOD.

DISMISSAL

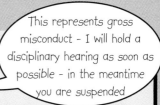

This represents gross misconduct - I will hold a disciplinary hearing as soon as possible - in the meantime you are suspended

1 SUSPENSION SHOULD START AS SOON AS DISCIPLINARY HEARING ARRANGED.

2 FULL PAY UNTIL FORMAL DECISION.

3 RIGHT OF APPEAL.

Sanctions

WHAT YOU COULD DO		POSSIBLE REASON
DEMOTION	MISS MANAGEMENT	SHOWN TO BE INCAPABLE OF PRESENT JOB
CHANGE TO BONUS POINTS	MR CARELESS	EVIDENCE OF POOR QUALITY WORK
TELEPHONE AREA MANAGER AT 8.30 EVERY DAY	MR LATE	POOR TIMEKEEPING
CHANGE SHOP	MR ANGRY	INSUBORDINATION TO BRANCH MANAGER
CHANGE JOB	MISS FIT	POOR PERFORMANCE
APPLY RESTRICTIONS e.g Can't enter a branch	MR RUDE	ROW BETWEEN BRANCH STAFF

SANCTIONS CAN TAKE EFFECT

1. AFTER DISCIPLINARY HEARING.
2. AFTER ANY APPEAL.
3. IF EMPLOYEE FAILS A TRIAL PERIOD.

NOTE

SANCTIONS MAY BE REVERSED.

Record keeping

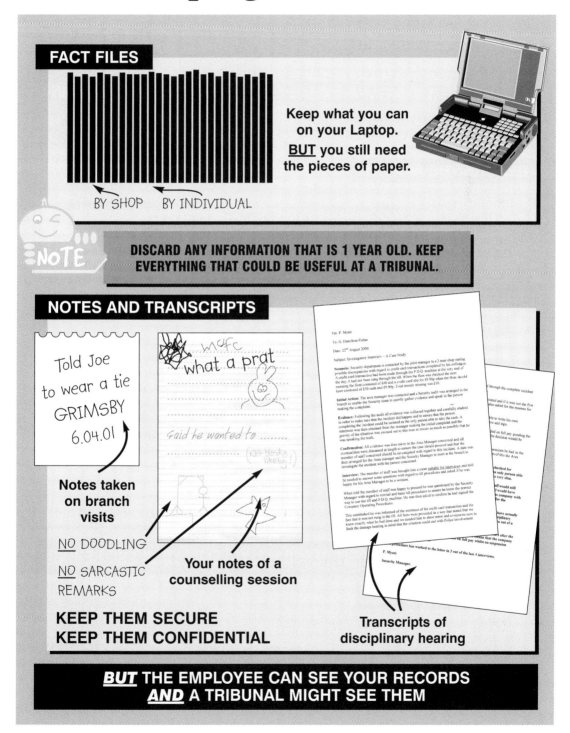

FACT FILES

Keep what you can on your Laptop.

BUT you still need the pieces of paper.

← BY SHOP   ← BY INDIVIDUAL

NOTE

DISCARD ANY INFORMATION THAT IS 1 YEAR OLD. KEEP EVERYTHING THAT COULD BE USEFUL AT A TRIBUNAL.

NOTES AND TRANSCRIPTS

Told Joe to wear a tie GRIMSBY 6.04.01

what a prat

Said he wanted to ....

Notes taken on branch visits

NO DOODLING

NO SARCASTIC REMARKS

Your notes of a counselling session

Transcripts of disciplinary hearing

KEEP THEM SECURE
KEEP THEM CONFIDENTIAL

BUT THE EMPLOYEE CAN SEE YOUR RECORDS
AND A TRIBUNAL MIGHT SEE THEM

Appeals

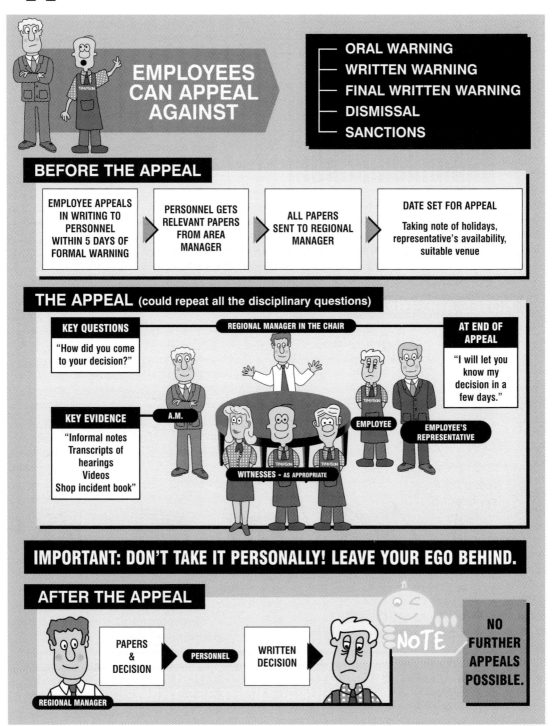

EMPLOYEES CAN APPEAL AGAINST

- ORAL WARNING
- WRITTEN WARNING
- FINAL WRITTEN WARNING
- DISMISSAL
- SANCTIONS

BEFORE THE APPEAL

EMPLOYEE APPEALS IN WRITING TO PERSONNEL WITHIN 5 DAYS OF FORMAL WARNING → PERSONNEL GETS RELEVANT PAPERS FROM AREA MANAGER → ALL PAPERS SENT TO REGIONAL MANAGER → DATE SET FOR APPEAL — Taking note of holidays, representative's availability, suitable venue

THE APPEAL (could repeat all the disciplinary questions)

KEY QUESTIONS
"How did you come to your decision?"

KEY EVIDENCE
"Informal notes
Transcripts of hearings
Videos
Shop incident book"

REGIONAL MANAGER IN THE CHAIR

A.M.

WITNESSES - AS APPROPRIATE

EMPLOYEE

EMPLOYEE'S REPRESENTATIVE

AT END OF APPEAL
"I will let you know my decision in a few days."

IMPORTANT: DON'T TAKE IT PERSONALLY! LEAVE YOUR EGO BEHIND.

AFTER THE APPEAL

REGIONAL MANAGER → PAPERS & DECISION → PERSONNEL → WRITTEN DECISION →

NOTE

NO FURTHER APPEALS POSSIBLE.

Representation

WHEN CAN AN EMPLOYEE BRING A REPRESENTATIVE

COUNSELLING	✗
ORAL WARNING	✓
WRITTEN WARNING	✓
FINAL WRITTEN WARNING	✓
DISMISSAL	✓

WHO CAN AN EMPLOYEE CHOOSE AS A REPRESENTATIVE

PARTNER	MUM	UNION REP	WORK COLLEAGUE	BEST MATE
✗	✗	✓	✓	✗

Grievance procedure

Grievance procedure

WHAT HAPPENS NEXT?

1 **BUILD BACK THE BRIDGES!**

MEET AGAIN AS SOON AS POSSIBLE

DON'T AVOID THE SUBJECT!

Can't change what happened but hope things now go well

OFFER YOUR HELP!

2 **STAND BY OUR PRINCIPLES**

TIMPSON ON TRIBUNALS

If we have a solid case with all the supporting paperwork we will fight our case at a Tribunal – even if it may be cheaper to settle out of court.

John Timpson

Chapter 6

Start as we mean to go on

Start as we mean to go on

We bring employees into our culture as soon as they join as apprentices or new starters.

I still remember my first day as a shop assistant. Like a new boy at school, I knew nothing and felt the world was watching waiting for my first mistake. I dreaded the first customer, a humourless man who thankfully bought a pair of Tuf boots for 42/9d. I still sense the feeling of elation when he finally paid and I went to open the door as he left the shop.

I also remember what happened on my third day when one of the Directors called. He spent twenty minutes in the shop and never spoke to me. He saw me but looked right through me. He knew me but he didn't use my name. He was only interested in talking to the manager.

Thank goodness my branch manager had plenty of time to talk to me. He was great. You can learn more in your first month with a business than you will ever learn in another year and thanks to Bill Branston that's what I did. He was my apprentice trainer who not only taught me how to serve customers but gave me the enthusiasm to enjoy it. I was able to thank Bill personally for the start he in my business career when I met him during our visit to the Sydney Olympics. Then aged 95, Bill had left to live in Australia as soon as he retired and has been there for over 30 years. He could still remember a lot of our customers, the styles of the shoes, the way we dressed the windows and our conversations at tea time when he taught me the rudiments of the trade. It's amazing what people like Bill were able to achieve without the help of a computer.

Timpson Apprentice Scheme

In 1996 we introduced our apprentice scheme, a sixteen week course leading to basic skills in shoe repairing, key cutting and engraving (later we introduced watch repairs.) When I wrote the introduction to the manual I aimed to give new starters a sense of purpose within the first few days. It was written before I had been converted to 'Upside-down Management'. If it was written today, I would speak less of rules and more about guidelines. But in my defence, when you join a new club you need to know the rules as soon as possible. That's why we make it clear from the outset what our employees should look like and what they shouldn't do.

I also wanted to make them feel welcome, so I gave a short guide to what the business does and where they fit in. It's uncomfortable when customers know more than you do. In our shops new starters have a real problem. Until they have some training, they can't repair shoes or watches and they can't cut a key, so our first two days training concentrates on jobs they can do - housekeeping and talking to customers. People are surprised we allow apprentices to handle cash on their first day. But I believe we should trust them from the very beginning – it helps our customers.

Warm welcome

The nearest our apprentice manual came to 'Upside-down Management' was the two pages headed "People Matter at Timpson". They were written by my daughter Victoria. She is a teacher only involved in our business as a customer. I was writing the manual at home so I asked her opinion. "Have you put yourself in the position of the person reading this?" she asked. "Do you really think you would feel welcome if all you get on your first day is a set of rules and instructions? Shouldn't you say why people are important to the business? You keep telling me your success depends on the people who serve customers, tell them how valuable they are." She was right.

The apprentice

Sowing the seed

Outsiders wonder where we find staff with all the skills required in our shops. We train most of them ourselves. When I started work in 1960, an apprentice was expected to spend years doing nothing very useful. Today the world can't wait for a four year apprenticeship. Within months we need to make sure everyone has the skills to be worth the money they think they deserve.

There are many different ways to create a training scheme. For years our competitor Mr Minit had a shoe repair school in Sheffield, their recruits went on a residential course, some businesses rely on NVQ'S. We believe in 'on the job' training and our apprentice scheme makes sure it works.

We teach values as well as skills. The first test is time keeping. People who can't turn up for work are no good to us. There is a special problem on Saturdays and Mondays, all night raves and key cutting do not go together. Despite the care we take with recruitment, a lot of people leave within the first few weeks.

Our biggest investment

Each year we invest over £2m improving the look of our shops but we spend even more on training. We start investing the day a person joins us. Most of the work is done by their apprentice trainer, usually a shop manager who has passed a diploma in training skills, and earns a special bonus for successfully training a new recruit.

You no longer have to wait for middle age before being acknowledged as an expert. Pretesh Pravda managed one of our biggest turnover shops in London, when 19 years old.

Our history

The business is owned by our Chairman and Chief Executive John Timpson, whose Great Grandfather William Timpson started working in the shoe business in 1865.

At the age of 16 William Timpson opened a shoe shop in a North Manchester suburb in partnership with his uncle. Three years later in 1868, William Timpson broke away from his uncle and started his own business opening a shoe shop in Manchester's busy Oldham Street.

The business prospered, gaining a reputation for good value and good service. William Timpson ploughed his profits back into the business opening shops throughout the Manchester area.

By 1903 he had 23 shops and started a shoe repair service from a central factory near Manchester's city centre.

William Timpson had a large family - six girls and five boys, and many of his children worked in the business. Two of his sons, William and Noel were the prime movers who turned the Company into a national business.

In 1960, when the present chairman, John Timpson, started work as a shop assistant, the business had 260 shoe shops, 165 small shoe repair factories and a large shoe factory in Kettering, Northamptonshire, manufacturing 25,000 pairs of shoes each week.

During the 1960's cheap imports made life difficult for shoe makers and Timpson stopped making their own shoes in 1971.

Family history

The introduction to our apprentice manual shows a new recruit is working for a family business with a history. I think history is important. In 1999 when the DotCom gold rush took place, the new entrepreneurs were seeking instant success. The business world was becoming a casino. In the end very few became millionaires, most made the same mistakes many had made before them. All businesses find pitfalls, businesses with a history can show how they learned from past problems.

Life does not stand still, every business has to manage change to survive. History shows how well they achieved it and business history is always dominated by people. Everyone in a business plays a part in its development. Senior managers are the vital factor.

Merchant Banks

Shortly after the merchant bank UBS took over our main competitor, Mr Minit, I went to see the director in charge, Ian Siddall, who tried to put me firmly in my place. "We're specialists at picking up family businesses," he said "and turning them into professionally run enterprises." The implication was clear, all family businesses would do better with a professional manager including Timpson. We had a short and frosty meeting.

Independent family businesses don't earn fees for merchant banks unless they take the plunge and go public or sell out, it is not, therefore, surprising that the City takes a jaundiced view of a business like ours. They assume professionally run PLC's are bound to produce a better performance. I don't think that is necessarily true.

Another incorrect assumption is that a family business is handed to each generation on a plate. I admit my biggest break was that my Great Grandfather started a shoe shop. When I wanted to join the family business, I was hardly likely to fail the interview. But it's not that easy to survive, as our history has shown. Very few family companies reach the fifth generation unscathed.

Our history

When John Timpson was appointed Managing Director in 1975, he soon saw the importance of customer care - he became the customers' champion in the shoe industry. But twelve years later, in 1987, John correctly forecast difficult times ahead for shoe shops - as a result he sold the shop part of the business and has concentrated ever since on shoe repairs.

Between 1987 and 1997 the shoe repair business has grown from 150 shops to 325 branches throughout England, Scotland and Wales. At the same time the company has added expert key cutting and engraving to the range of services on offer.

The company now repairs more shoes, cuts more keys and does more engraving than any other retailer in the UK.

Despite its size, John Timpson still visits almost all of his shops every year, knows most of his staff personally and insists that individual branch staff are given the authority to give customers the best possible service.

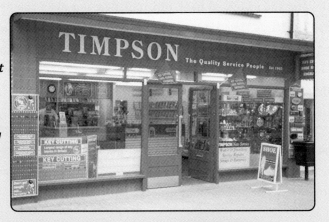

John Timpson and his wife Alex live in Cheshire - they have five children, two of whom are adopted and are long established foster parents having fostered nearly 60 children during the past 18 years. Two of his children now work in the business, determined to continue the Timpson reputation for quality, value and service into a fifth generation.

Keep it in the family

I don't think there is much point in retaining family control unless the family are visible in the business. People like to know the boss and it helps to know he will still be there in a few years time. Such consistency reduces management politics. We are not hampered by Stock Exchange regulations, fund managers or market analysts. We don't have to improve profits every six months, we can build for the long-term, that's why history is so important. When making decisions, it's helps to look at how the business developed. Family businesses have worked well, because they look after their employees who in turn look after their customers. Our history shows that there is a lot going for independence, we have benefited from being private, I intend to keep it that way !

Where do I fit in?

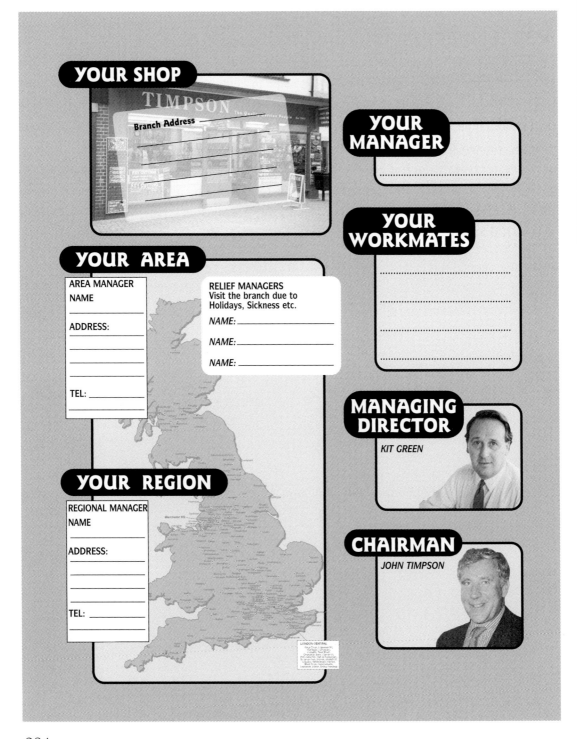

YOUR SHOP

Branch Address

YOUR MANAGER

YOUR WORKMATES

YOUR AREA

AREA MANAGER
NAME

ADDRESS:

TEL:

RELIEF MANAGERS
Visit the branch due to
Holidays, Sickness etc.

NAME:

NAME:

NAME:

MANAGING DIRECTOR

KIT GREEN

YOUR REGION

REGIONAL MANAGER
NAME

ADDRESS:

TEL:

CHAIRMAN

JOHN TIMPSON

Raw recruit

The first day at work can be pretty difficult. I was overawed by my first experience of school and my first day as a shop assistant. Apprentices used to spend the first month sweeping up and it was six months before they met a customer. But I am talking of a different world. When I started the pay was £5.7s.6d per week with up to 20 people working in a shop. Plenty of hands to do the housekeeping and lots of time for training.

Look after the new boy

Starting a new job should not be an ordeal. We at Timpson believe it's our job to look after our people including the newest recruit. Having been in the business for 40 years, it's easy for me to assume everyone knows what it is all about. But it's wrong to think new recruits know what goes on behind the name on the High Street. We tell them who we are, what we do and something about the people they are likely to meet. Everyone who joins the business contributes to its culture. We think it's important they know the sort of organisation they have joined from the very first day. That includes getting to know the people who run the business. Employees in a large company seldom meet the Chief Executive and many don't know who he or she is. We want to be different, we want to take an interest in our people and for them to take an interest in the company. Communication is important, it should start on the first day.

Working hours? Pay day?

WORKING HOURS

MOST TIMPSON BRANCHES WORK 8.30AM - 5.30PM, BUT CHECK WITH YOUR AREA MANAGER

LUNCH

MOST TSR PEOPLE HAVE A WORKING LUNCH TO MAXIMISE THEIR BONUS

DAYS OFF

ALL STAFF WORK A FIVE OR SIX DAY BASIC WEEK - THE DAY OFF IS ARRANGED BY AGREEMENT WITH YOUR MANAGER

NAME	MON	TUE	WED	THUR	FRI	SAT
JOE BLOGGS	✓	✓	✗	✓	✓	✓
FRED BLOGGS	✓	✗	✓	✓	✓	✓
JOHN BLOGGS	✓	✓	✓	✗	✓	✓
MARK BLOGGS	✗	✓	✓	✗	✓	✓

BONUS

TIMPSON ENCOURAGE ALL BRANCHES TO EARN BONUS, WHICH IS BASED ON THE TOTAL WAGE BILL IN THE BRANCH AND THE TURNOVER ACHIEVED. YOU WILL QUALIFY FOR BONUS AS SOON AS YOU ARE AWARDED YOUR BASIC SKILLS DIPLOMA

OVERTIME

THERE WILL SOMETIMES BE OPPORTUNITIES TO WORK -

- REST DAYS
- SUNDAYS
- EXTRA HOURS

PAY DAY

15TH OF EACH MONTH

WEEKLY PAID STAFF THURSDAY

TIMPSON PAY ON THE 15TH OF EACH MONTH -

2 WEEKS IN ADVANCE
2 WEEKS IN ARREARS

PENSION SCHEME

ANY TIMPSON EMPLOYEE AGED 22 - 57 WHO HAS COMPLETED 2 YEARS SERVICE WITH THE COMPANY CAN JOIN THE TIMPSON PENSION SCHEME. APPLY TO THE PENSION ADMINISTRATOR. TIMPSON HOUSE

STAFF DISCOUNTS

STAFF DISCOUNT IS AVAILABLE TO ALL MEMBERS OF STAFF AND THEIR CHILDREN & WIVES. OTHER FAMILY MEMBERS ARE NOT INCLUDED

KEYS	60%
REPAIRS	60%
ENGRAVING	40%
MERCHANDISE	25%

SAVINGS SCHEME

FACILITIES ARE AVAILABLE FOR EMPLOYEES TO SAVE WITH THE HALIFAX BUILDING SOCIETY BY REGULAR DEDUCTIONS FROM PAY. FURTHER INFORMATION MAY BE OBTAINED FROM THE PERSONNEL DEPARTMENT.

HOLIDAYS

21 DAYS AFTER ONE YEAR'S SERVICE

QUERIES

Personnel Dept
0161 946 6200

The basics

We have less regulations than most businesses but every club has to have some rules. Most of the new starters who fail to stay with the company for more than a month fall down on the fundamentals.

Timekeeping is a good thermometer. 50% of the young recruits who fail to make the grade can't get out of bed. Our success depends on having good people, it is essential for our 'Upside-down Management' style to work.

Pay is most important

As well as good timekeeping, we require loyalty and honesty, but we don't expect everyone's priority to be the business. My wife Alex accuses me of thinking about nothing but shoe repairs and engraving. She may be right, but I don't expect everyone else to be obsessed with, key cutting and watch repairs. It is important to remember people come to work to earn money, that's why we clarify the pay package on the first day, it's an early demonstration of our open management style and I hope gains us the trust of employees as soon as they join the company.

The small print

A GUIDE TO THE
IMPORTANT PART
OF OUR CONTRACT
OF EMPLOYMENT

YOUR BRANCH NOTICE BOARD WILL HAVE A FULL SET OF THE
TIMPSON DOCUMENTS WHICH YOU WILL NEED TO READ.

Legal language

We believe rules are there to be broken. While chairing a discussion group in Bristol in 2001, I asked what they thought about working for Timpson. "What I like" said one, "Is that when I really need a day off, I can have one." Our willingness to look outside the regulations helps us look after the good employees. The 'Upside-down Management' style lets middle management help their staff even if it means breaking the rules. But that doesn't mean we are a soft touch. No manager can walk past a problem. At times we must be tough but to make sure no one is victimised, we have a grievance procedure that really works. Someone with a problem can complain to anyone they wish. 'Upside-down Management' doesn't allow a boss to stop people going over his head.

Equal opportunities

Timpson is sociologically imbalanced. We don't have enough women and employ a high proportion of white workers. We are keen to change, but not just to reach an equal opportunities target. Some of our highest quality shoe repairers are women and some of our best managers are Asian. We will seek to strengthen minority groups, it's good for business.

Employment legislation has placed a heavy burden on business. Some feel it is one-sided. Companies can go to a lot of trouble to toe the line and find employees still go to an industrial tribunal. Employing people costs more each year and the law seems to protect employees who abuse their sickness benefit and sue for harassment at the slightest whim. We believe it is right to protect our employees' interest. The Timpson code goes much further than any legislation. We set out to amaze our employees but we will still stand up to anyone who tries to take the company for a ride.

Staff dress

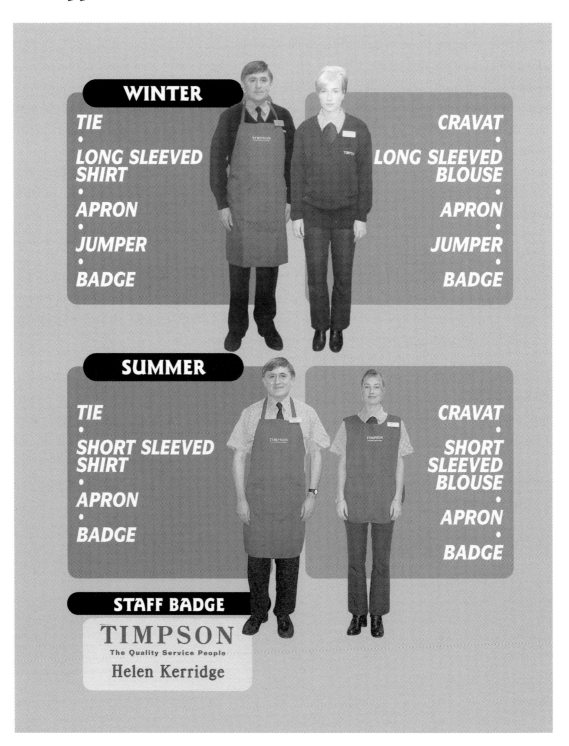

WINTER

TIE
•
LONG SLEEVED SHIRT
•
APRON
•
JUMPER
•
BADGE

CRAVAT
•
LONG SLEEVED BLOUSE
•
APRON
•
JUMPER
•
BADGE

SUMMER

TIE
•
SHORT SLEEVED SHIRT
•
APRON
•
BADGE

CRAVAT
•
SHORT SLEEVED BLOUSE
•
APRON
•
BADGE

STAFF BADGE

TIMPSON
The Quality Service People
Helen Kerridge

Look the part

In Timpson, uniform is a big issue. When I wanted to improve our standards in 1979, I asked everyone to wear a tie. Just like Eddie Stobart the haulier, ties mark the difference between us and our competitors. I consider it such a symbol of excellence that I reprimand more people about inappropriate dress than anything else. As a result, I am used to the list of excuses. "My tie is at home". "I overslept." "I ordered the aprons but they haven't arrived." or my favourite from someone who hadn't shaved for three days, "My girlfriend likes me like this."

Our annual attitude survey usually reveals criticism about our uniform but guess what, it was chosen by our employees. Although some say they look like traffic wardens, or prison officers, many wear the uniform on their day off. If during a shop visit, I want to take a picture of the staff, they look in the mirror to make sure their tie is straight.

Best turned out

If employees leave to set up their own shop, they usually get rid of the uniform, dress down into jeans and a dirty shirt and in the process downgrade the quality of their shop. There is one exception, Stacey Weeks who runs an excellent shoe repair shop in the centre of Oxford. Stacey always goes to work in a bow tie, he looks immaculate until you look at his shoes, he always has a brown shoe on one foot and a black shoe on the other.

I am convinced it's important to be smart. In April 2001, I was talking to a group of department stores at their Annual Conference when one of the delegates came up to me. "The greatest thing about your company," he said "Is that you make everyone wear a tie."

Staff dress

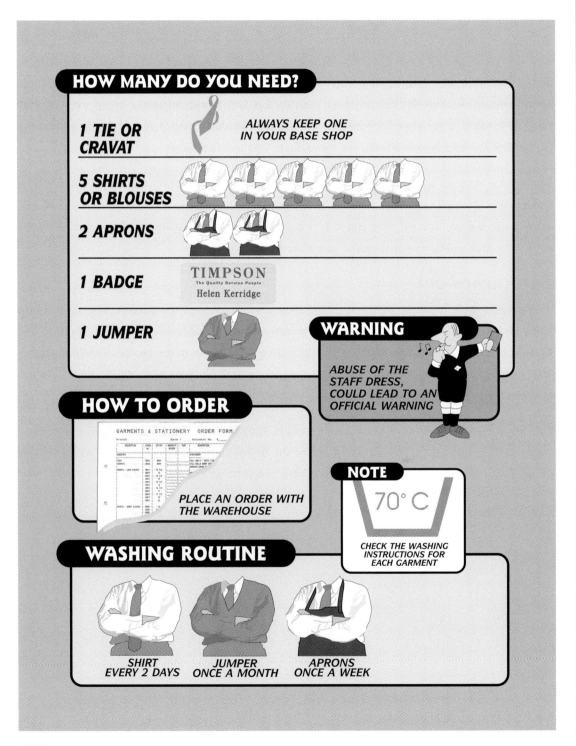

HOW MANY DO YOU NEED?

1 TIE OR CRAVAT — ALWAYS KEEP ONE IN YOUR BASE SHOP

5 SHIRTS OR BLOUSES

2 APRONS

1 BADGE — TIMPSON — The Quality Service People — Helen Kerridge

1 JUMPER

WARNING

ABUSE OF THE STAFF DRESS, COULD LEAD TO AN OFFICIAL WARNING

HOW TO ORDER

GARMENTS & STATIONERY ORDER FORM

PLACE AN ORDER WITH THE WAREHOUSE

NOTE

70° C

CHECK THE WASHING INSTRUCTIONS FOR EACH GARMENT

WASHING ROUTINE

SHIRT EVERY 2 DAYS

JUMPER ONCE A MONTH

APRONS ONCE A WEEK

Retail is detail

We hardly have any rules but produce lots of guidelines, because with 'Upside-down Management' you must give as much detailed help as possible. The illustration on the opposite page about staff dress shows how 'Upside-down Management' works in practice. This is not an instruction, it's a guideline. No one has to wash their shirt every two days and they won't get a warning letter if they don't have a spare apron, but they must be smart and if they follow our guidelines they will look the part.

These are not rules, if anyone thinks they have got a better way of doing things, they should give it a go. If it works, they should let us know (they might get some money from the suggestion scheme,) but if it fails, they should forget all about it and use our guidelines.

The golden rules

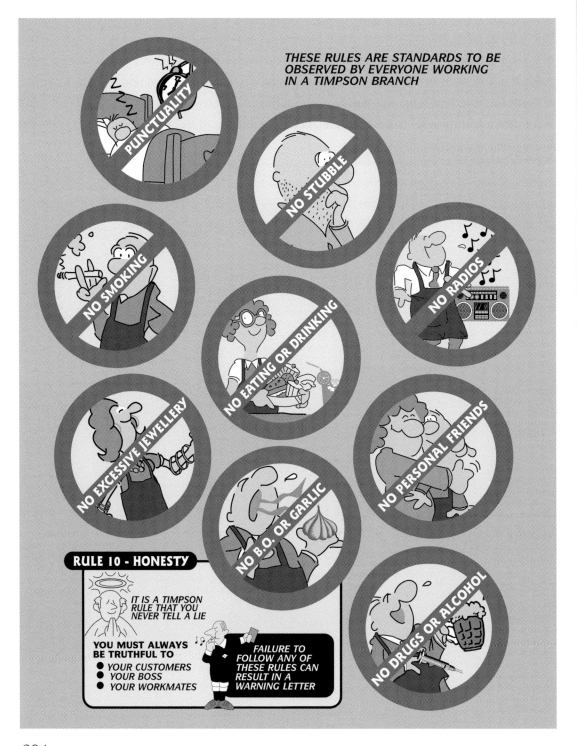

Must do

Our rules are restricted to things which are beyond question. You can't improve business by opening the shop late and looking scruffy. It can't be right to listen to the radio or talk to a friend when a customer is waiting to be served. Our business is based on trust. Dishonesty has no place in Timpson. Our honesty rule covers theft and states you must never lie. Trust relies on truthfulness to customers and between business colleagues.

A disciplined bunch

10 years ago one of the senior managers from Mr Minit came to see me. He asked, "How do you get your guys to look so smart?" The answer is simple, we have a clear rule and make sure everyone sticks to it. Anyone seen breaking our rules can expect to be apprehended. We have proved a company full of cobblers can be a disciplined bunch.

Sometimes we allow rules to be broken. During the World Cup radios were permitted, I thought it was reasonable for staff to listen while most of the population were at home watching on television. This lenience was justified when I saw a notice in a competitor's shop, "this branch will close at 1pm due to family illness." At least we were around to serve customers.

Occasionally during my shop visits I discover a problem. Like the manager I found on the 'phone to his bookie. Sometimes I see someone reading a newspaper. Once I observed a competitor where the two members of staff were sat either side of the counter playing chess. I hope we get too many customers to play that game.

Setting the standards

Some rules lead to problems, we have to keep up with new jewellery fashions and it needs a sensitive touch to deal with B.O. and garlic. Our insistence on punctuality, no stubble, no smoking and honesty have made a difference to the look of our shops and to the service we give our customers, the golden rules have made us a better business.

People matter at Timpson

My job is to help the people in our shops give customers the best possible service. This help extends to personal problems and business Worries.

John Timpson

In Timpson there are many ways an individual member of staff can air their views.

DIRECT ACCESS TO JOHN TIMPSON

I receive 50 - 100 notes each week from members of branch staff.

SUGGESTION SCHEME

Employees suggestions are always a source of new ideas, in the last year we have received 570 suggestions. Last year we paid out over £7000 in awards.

INTRODUCE A FRIEND

Many of our best employees have a relation or a friend who could also do a good job for us. Introduce us to a friend and if he / she is successful, you will get £150 after they complete 16 wks + a further £250 when they complete 12 months service.

H.Q. COMMENT

We encourage comment from all branches on the level of service they receive from our Wythenshawe Head Office.

HOW TO COMPLAIN

We do not like to think that any of our employees are unhappy. We have a simple way to make it easy for anyone to get a big grumble out into the open- you are free to talk to anyone in the company you feel able to.

ATTITUDE SURVEY

Each year we check your views which play an important part in our future strategy.

People make a business

At first it was difficult to persuade people to take on authority. We encouraged initiative, but soon realised people seldom do something for nothing.

Contributors to our suggestion scheme all get an award. The best suggestions attract the biggest cash sums but everyone can expect something. Our most regular contributors Tony Doreboize from Ashford and Gillian Briggs from Leeds, have submitted 42 suggestions between them in the past year providing them with considerable extra pocket money.

Journalists

An average of 100 people contribute to our newsletter every week, most items of good news get a prize. The payment encourages people to speak up, but the company must listen to what they say. Too many managers have a 'not invented here' attitude that can get in the way. Businesses are full of people with the reasons why new ideas won't work. But if management doesn't listen, the ideas stop coming in.

Channels of communication

Many companies have strict lines of communication, everything is channelled through your boss, James discovered this problem when he worked for Apparalmaster, part of Johnson's the Cleaners. James has always been full of ideas and this period of his life was no exception. He went to see the Managing Director with his suggestions. When he returned to his workplace he was in trouble with his boss. I learned a lesson from his experience, so now in Timpson, you can talk to anyone without fear of recrimination. We don't put barriers in the way of people who want to contribute to our success.

Employees have played a big part in our development through our 'Introduce a Friend' scheme. It provides £400 to anyone who introduces a successful recruit. Our success has been created by our people, experience shows the best place to look for new talent is amongst their friends.

Housekeeping standards

Looking good

When I started in the business, it was assumed shoe repairers were shoddy and housekeeping was women's work. Every branch employed a counter girl, it was her job to clean the shop. No one was told why cleanliness was important or that tidy shops make more money. Shoe repairers don't seem to see a scruffy shop could be a sign of poor quality shoe repairing. Shoe repairers might not see it but customers certainly do.

My wife Alex believes tidiness is next to godliness and judges our shops by their standard of housekeeping. We were in our ASDA concession in Reading on a Saturday morning before we went to a wedding, Alex was so appalled she started to clean the shop herself. The manager was late. When he turned the corner to see Alex hoovering, he was so aghast he couldn't face us and went away to have a coffee. He was almost in tears when he finally arrived and pleaded with Alex to stop and let him do the job himself.

Morning and night

Our housekeeping will never be perfect, some people do it naturally, others don't. The secret is to clean the shop morning and night. Tidiness is so important it is the first job we teach a new recruit. Don't assume they know how to use a hoover, give a demonstration. These days housekeeping is not just the junior's job, everyone is involved. The manager should set an example by mucking in. Good housekeeping has become a health and safety issue, the new legislation will help us to keep our shops clean. But still expect problems. Most competitors are so scruffy a tidy shoe repair shop will always stand out from the crowd.

Health & safety

EACH BRANCH HAS A HEALTH & SAFETY MANUAL, MAKE SURE YOU READ IT, SO THAT YOU KNOW THE COMPANY'S HEALTH & SAFETY POLICY

Timpson Shoe Repairs
HEALTH & SAFETY AT WORK Regulations

KNOW ALL ABOUT FIRE EXTINGUISHERS

| CO² | WATER | FOAM | POWDER | VAPOURISING LIQUID |
| INSTRUCTIONS | INSTRUCTIONS | INSTRUCTIONS | INSTRUCTIONS | INSTRUCTIONS |

| CARBON DIOXIDE (CO²) | WATER | FOAM | POWDER | VAPOURISING LIQUID |
| For burning liquid and electrical fires NOT TO BE USED ON FLAMMABLE METAL FIRES | For wood, paper, textile, fabric and similar material NOT TO BE USED ON BURNING LIQUID, ELECTRICAL OR FLAMMABLE METAL FIRES | For use on burning liquid fires | For burning liquid and electrical fires | For use on electrical fires |

KEEP ALL PASSAGEWAYS CLEAR

FIRE

KNOW WHERE YOUR FIRE EXITS ARE

↑ FIRE EXIT

DO NOT SWITCH ON OR USE ANY MACHINERY WITHOUT SUPERVISION

STORE ALL SOLVENT INKS AND SOLUTIONS ETC. IN THE GALVANISED BIN- ONLY KEEP A MINIMUM IN THE MINI BOYS - KEEP LIDS ON WHEN NOT IN USE

DANGER PETROL SPIRIT NO SMOKING NO NAKED LIGHTS

KEEP LOCKED

Keep this book where people can easily get to it.
Consecutive number of this book.
Form BI 510

ACCIDENT BOOK
FOR USE AT

This book satisfies the regulations about keeping records of Accidents to people at work
▶ Social Security Administration Act 1960
▶ Reporting of Injuries, Diseases and Dangerous Occurrences ─── Regulations 1980
The instructions on how to use this book are overleaf

HMSO

ALL ACCIDENTS MUST BE RECORDED IN THE ACCIDENT BOOK.

- SERIOUS ACCIDENTS MUST BE REPORTED BY TELEPHONE AT ONCE TO THE PERSONNEL OFFICE, FORM RF17 MUST BE COMPLETED AND MAILED TO HEAD OFFICE THAT SAME DAY.

Safety first

We take health and safety very seriously. Bill Platt, our Health and Safety Officer, makes sure we do. A lot of the legislation requires defensive action, putting up notices, keeping an accident book and publishing health and safety manuals. We want to go further than the letter of the law. We have a duty to make our workplaces safe for everyone.

The company can carry out risk assessments and make sure all machinery is safe, but individuals still have responsibility for their own health and safety. The company can't put on the goggles that protect their eyes when they cut a key. In a one man shop the manager must look after himself. There are health and safety sections in all our technical manuals and we have health and safety courses leading to a diploma. Holders of this health and safety qualification are paid a better bonus.

Who's to blame

No one can challenge the common sense of health and safety legislation but I don't like the current culture with everyone encouraged to look for someone else to blame. Finding a scapegoat has become an industry in itself. I am often stopped in the street by someone with a clip board asking "Have you had an accident at work?" People make mistakes, nothing is totally safe, life is about taking risks. The current climate can lead to innocent people getting the blame. A friend of mine has a company that runs its own fleet of vans. Tragically, one of his drivers was manoeuvring his vehicle and ran over a child who ultimately died. Although his health and safety precautions were better than most, he still lived for two years under the threat of a corporate manslaughter charge.

There is a danger that Government will put so much of the responsibility, so much of the blame and so much of the ultimate cost on individual companies, that the businesses, won't be able to afford health and safety. I believe in making our workplace safe but individual employees must play their part and look after their own safety. That's 'Upside-down Management.'

Key cutting - can we cut it?

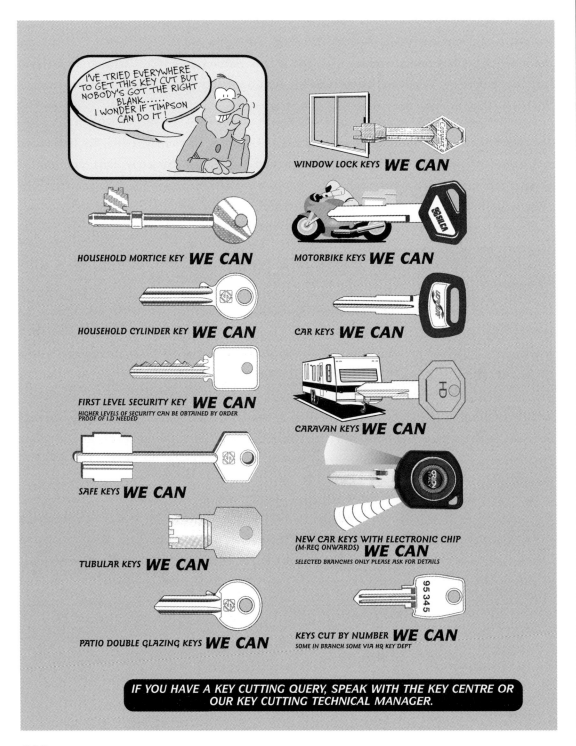

IF YOU HAVE A KEY CUTTING QUERY, SPEAK WITH THE KEY CENTRE OR OUR KEY CUTTING TECHNICAL MANAGER.

"I'll have to ask the manager"

It's embarrassing working in a shop during your first week. When a queue forms what do you do? You can't stare at the ground and ignore customers. We don't like to keep people waiting, so one of your first jobs at Timpson is to serve a customer.

The trainee badge gets sympathy. Our Apprentice manual lists the major services we offer, but it takes 16 weeks to learn the basic skills to give a proper service.

When James worked during his school holidays in Northwich, he was keen to take as much money as possible from each customer. He was very disappointed when he lost a sale for shoe care. "You could have offered a leather dye" said his manager. Without hesitation, James grabbed two packets of leather dye and raced off down the street accosting the customer outside Boots. He made his sale.

The way to learn

New recruits can only learn through experience. Don't flannel customers, always tell the truth. If you don't know ask. We aim to help customers and solve their problems. If we don't have the answer, we find someone else who does. Help is available from Timpson House at the end of a 'phone. If we can't give a reply immediately, we take the customer's telephone number and ring them later.

We believe our special attitude towards customers isn't found in many places on the High Street. The best way for new recruits to discover our secret is to serve customers.

Induction training

TUTOR AND MENTOR

Your day to day tutor will be .... Your Mentor will be ....
(Manager)   *(AM/RDM/ADM)*

TUTORS JOB
To help you with the day to day elements of the Apprenticeship.

MENTORS JOB
To monitor your progress having welcomed you to Timpson and give you any support you need.

WELCOME TO TIMPSON
Your first day is spent with your Mentor introducing you to your company before you meet a customer.
Your Mentor will go through the basic Health & Safety procedures:
- *Fire Exit / Assembly Point*
- *Fire Extinguishers*
- *No unsupervised use of machinery*

WEEK 1
During your first week you will learn the branch housekeeping routine and the Till Operation.
Your Tutor will go through the Health and Safety manual with you.

BY WEEK 16 YOU SHOULD BE ABLE TO

KEY CUTTING
- FIND & CUT POPULAR CYLINDER, MORTICE & CAR KEYS
- DECODE & CUT TIBBE
- USE OF- KEY GAUGES, FILES & KEYSAW
- USE OF THE CATALOGUES
- KNOWLEDGE OF : PARTS OF A KEY
  OPERATION OF KEY MACHINES
  USE OF TEST LOCKS
  KEYBOARD LAYOUT
  PRICING
  CUSTOMER SERVICE
  HEALTH & SAFETY

ENGRAVING
- PET TAGS
- TROPHY PLATE (SINGLE LINE)
- CALCULATIONS
- BACK STOP / MOTOR TENSION / ARM TENSION
- CENTRE PANTOGRAPH
- WORKING HEIGHT
- CHECK VICE IS PARALLEL TO COPY TABLE
- USE OF SPINDLE / CHANGE AND SET CUTTERS
- KNOWLEDGE OF ROTARY DIAMOND / DRAG DIAMOND AND CUTTERS
- FONTS & JIGS
- TILT
- ARM SETTINGS
- MOTOR (BASIC KNOWLEDGE)
- LOCK AND COLLAR
- VICE CONTROLS & VICE SETTINGS
- CUSTOMER SERVICE & BRANCH TICKET
- HEALTH AND SAFETY

SHOE REPAIRS
- TOP PIECE REMOVAL
- SOLUTIONING & PRESOLUTIONING
- USE OF: HAMMER & PINCERS
- PATCHING & STITCHING LEVEL 'A'
- INKING & POLISHING & WAIST PAINTING
- KNOWLEDGE OF: SHOE CONSTRUCTION (INTRO)
  MATERIALS (INTRO)
  TYPE OF REPAIRS OFFERED
  PRICING
  TICKET BOOK
  CUSTOMER SERVICE
  HEALTH & SAFETY

CUSTOMER CARE

YOU MAY BE ASKED TO ATTEND A ONE DAY COURSE AWAY FROM YOUR BRANCH, GIVING A GUIDE TO THE EASY WAY TO ADVISE CUSTOMERS

INDUCTION DIPLOMA COVERS....
1 KEY CUTTING   **3** ENGRAVING
2 SHOE REPAIRS   **4** CUSTOMER CARE

This Induction Diploma to be assessed by your area manager

Nursery class

Not everyone is good at training, just because you produce a first class job, doesn't mean you can help someone else do the same. We value people who have the talent to teach.

Stan Knagg had the patience to look after raw recruits. One of his toughest assignments was to teach James Timpson how to repair shoes. He succeeded and still found time to practice Yoga at lunchtime and become an accomplished oil painter in the evening.

Despite the input of their tutor and mentor, every Timpson individual is still responsible for their own training. The induction programme is designed to take each recruit step by step towards competence within 16 weeks.

Ideally, they will be trained in a different shop to the one where they finally work. We find it is better that way. But they won't spend all of their time in the base branch, everyone has an 'away day' on our Customer Care Course.

Most succeed

We can't guarantee success, some people are ham fisted, and not made for a practical job. Others have the wrong personality, they find it difficult to get on with customers. Some sadly are overpowered by problems at home and aren't able to concentrate on the job. But, I am pleased to say, most succeed. The Timpson induction is not as tough as joining the SAS.

There is a lot to learn but within 16 weeks most people can expect to be sufficiently qualified to earn a bonus.

Health & safety induction

FIRST MORNING

On your first morning your mentor will go through the basic Health & Safety procedures as listed below:-

TOUR OF PREMISES

New starter signature	Date
Tutor signature	

FIRE EXITS

New starter signature	Date
Tutor signature	

FIRE EXTINGUISHERS

New starter signature	Date
Tutor signature	

GOGGLES

New starter signature	Date
Tutor signature	

LONG HAIR / LOOSE CLOTHING

New starter signature	Date
Tutor signature	

FIRST AID KIT

New starter signature	Date
Tutor signature	

USE OF MACHINERY UNSUPERVISED

New starter signature	Date
Tutor signature	

KEEP PASSAGEWAYS CLEAR

New starter signature	Date
Tutor signature	

PROCEDURE IN CASE OF ACCIDENT

New starter signature	Date
Tutor signature	

Keep it safe

I make no apology for returning to the subject of health and safety. It is high on our agenda, especially for new recruits.

My Father sent me to Oundle school in Northamptonshire because it had workshops. One week every term was spent in a foundry, doing woodwork or in the metal shop. My Father would have loved it, that's why he sent me to that school, I hated it. I find practical tasks almost impossible. If a mistake could be made, I made it. In the foundry I produced a faulty mould and hot metal poured onto the floor. In the metal workshop I left a chuck key in the lathe and it flew dangerously round the room, I was given detention, banned from the workshop and was delighted.

Risk management

In a business that tackles 250,000 jobs a week, it's inevitable that accidents happen. But we can head off trouble by good risk management. The best way to start is to train everybody in health and safety. We specify our safety rules in minute detail. Note they are rules not guidelines. Even 'Upside-down Management' does not allow leeway when it comes to safety. But, however good our risk management, we won't eliminate every problem.

Everyone is responsible

Most legislation is the result of stable door government, regulations written to prevent a repeat of something that has already gone wrong. Our company approach goes further than the regulations. We want to shut our stable door before problems occur. But safety measures won't work unless they have everyone's support. We all have the right to a safe and healthy working environment. To make this happen, everyone is responsible for their own safety and the safety of people around them. Health and safety rules will not prevent every accident, risk assessments however thorough, will miss the unexpected. It's not just rules that ensure safety but a culture that aims to improve the environment for everyone's benefit.

How to use the cash register

FOR THE COMPLETE OPERATING INSTRUCTIONS FOR YOUR TILL SEE THE DETAILED INSTRUCTIONS ISSUED WHEN THE TILL WAS INSTALLED

VALIDATING A CHEQUE

IMMEDIATELY AFTER COMPLETING A CHEQUE TRANSACTION, PLACE THE CHEQUE FACE-UP INTO THE TILL'S VALIDATION PRINTER

AND PRESS THE VALIDATION PRINT KEY

ALL OTHER CASH REGISTER TRANSACTIONS MUST ONLY TAKE PLACE WITH THE MANAGERS AUTHORITY

ENTERING THE SALE

TIP ALWAYS SMILE ALWAYS SAY THANK YOU

1 ENTER THE PRICE

2 PRESS THE DEPARTMENT

TIP IF THE CORRECT CASH IS OFFERED, STEPS 3 & 4 CAN BE OMITTED

3 PRESS SUB TOTAL

REPEAT STEPS 1, 2 & 3 FOR ANY ADDITIONAL ITEMS THEN...

(IF) KEY CUTTING, ENGRAVING AND MERCHANDISE

4 ENTER THE AMOUNT TENDERED

5 PRESS FOR THE METHOD OF PAYMENT - CHEQUE, CREDIT CARDS OR CASH

THE TILL WILL AUTOMATICALLY DISPLAY ANY CHANGE DUE

6 ALWAYS GIVE A RECEIPT

ALWAYS OFFER A RECEIPT

WHEN YOU HAVE MADE A SALE

THAT WILL BE £3.50 PLEASE!

HOW WOULD YOU LIKE TO PAY?

CASH

CHEQUE

CREDIT CARD OR SWITCH

MAKING A REFUND

1 ENTER THE AMOUNT

2 PRESS REFUND

3 PRESS THE DEPARTMENT

4 PRESS TL

ASK THE CUSTOMER TO FILL IN DETAIL. IE. NAME, ADDRESS & SIGN THE BOTTOM. STAPLE THE REFUND RECEIPT TO THE REFUND FORM. REFUND SLIPS MUST BE VALIDATED THROUGH THE TILL.

Handling the cash

When I started as a shop assistant, I wasn't allowed to touch the till for four months, it didn't make any difference that my Father was the Managing Director. Today our recruits can handle cash on the first day.

When I consulted my son Oliver he said "Apprentices should be taught how to use the till before they learn to cut a key." "At least" he said "They will be able to serve some customers." He was right. If a new recruit is let loose on key cutting or shoe repairs, the customer could suffer through a job poorly done and the machine may be broken in the process. With the cash register, the only harm they can do is to charge the wrong price or pinch our money.

Our attitude to cash handling is an early indication of 'Upside-down Management'. We trust our people and that trust starts on their first day. The ability to handle cash encourages new staff to serve customers and gets them used to our kind of customer care. Initially they are surprised they can accept £50 notes without question, there is no minimum amount for credit sales and we are willing to give change for the telephone or car park. Hopefully, they soon get the message that their job is to amaze our customers.

Cash security

- ● All Managers/staff are responsible for banking and security of cash in their branch.
- ● Improper use of cash register will be considered a serious misconduct and can lead to instant dismissal.

- ● Failure to follow banking procedures will be considered a serious misconduct and can lead to instant dismissal.
- ● Suspected theft will involve the Police.

SALES

1 All Sales must be rung through the cash register.
2 A receipt must be offered to every customer.
3 Cash must be checked and balanced each and every night. All Over/Short Cash must be declared daily on the Cash Summary (lines 30/31).
4 Each night all money must be removed from the cash register and held overnight in a secure place agreed by Area Manager within the branch.
5 The empty Cash Register drawer must be left open at night.

WARNING Mystery shoppers check regularly

BANKING

1 All money except the float must be banked with local Post Office on the Monday and Friday of each week (extra bankings/other arrangements must be authorised by Area Manager/Personnel Dept. HQ)
2 The amount banked must agree with amount shown on Line 37 of the cash summary.
3 A copy of each Paying In Slip, stamped by the Bank, must be attached to the Weekly Cash Summary to be sent to Finance Dept. (2nd copy attached to branch copy of Cash Summary).
4 Wages are paid Thursday of each week. No prior payments of Wages (subs) unless authorised by Personnel Dept.
5 Area Managers are required to check the cash and bankings on each visit.
6 All employees should be aware that Lodge Services are authorised to do 'test shopping checks' in any TSR branch.
7 The Company reserves the right to install security cameras as deemed necessary and to search all members of staff/vehicles/bags.

We use hidden cameras

SECURITY

1 Branch keys must only be held by the Manager unless otherwise arranged by Area Manager (Spare keys kept at home - NOT AT BRANCH).
2 We do not authorise the use of Cash Register drawer keys except in an emergency. These must be kept in a sealed envelope in the Safe or Cash Box or a place agreed with the Area Manager. After use (emergency only) they should immediately be re-sealed in an envelope and put back.
3 No staff to enter premises after closing, unless authorised by Area Manager or Police.

We carry out random audits into branch security

EXPENSES

1 V.A.T. receipts must be obtained for all expenses claimed.

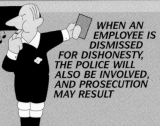

PROSECUTION

WHEN AN EMPLOYEE IS DISMISSED FOR DISHONESTY, THE POLICE WILL ALSO BE INVOLVED, AND PROSECUTION MAY RESULT

Broken trust

Here is the saddest statistic about our business. Last year we fired 40 people for theft. For years, shoe repairing has had a big security problem. We faced theft at its worst when we acquired Automagic in 1995 and found a protection racket operating in London with the ring leaders threatening anyone who was honest.

We have cut out major crime in our business but still regularly detect petty theft. Despite sophisticated security systems, it will always be easy to pinch money from our shops. We usually know where crimes are being committed, but can't take any action without concrete proof. We spend much time and money on mystery shoppers and hidden cameras.

The reduction of theft brought a substantial improvement to our profits. We estimate staff were pinching £1.5m a year, it's now probably half that figure, but still big enough to treat the problem very seriously.

Betrayed

Early in 1999, things suddenly got worse, we caught 25 people in 6 weeks. As a result, I wrote an article for our weekly newsletter under the headline "Betrayed." Thieves not only harm the company and myself they also cheat colleagues out of their bonus, they betray everyone in the business. When criminals are caught and see the evidence on video, they are quick to apologise. They are really sorry when they find they have lost their job.

What looking after customers really means at Timpson

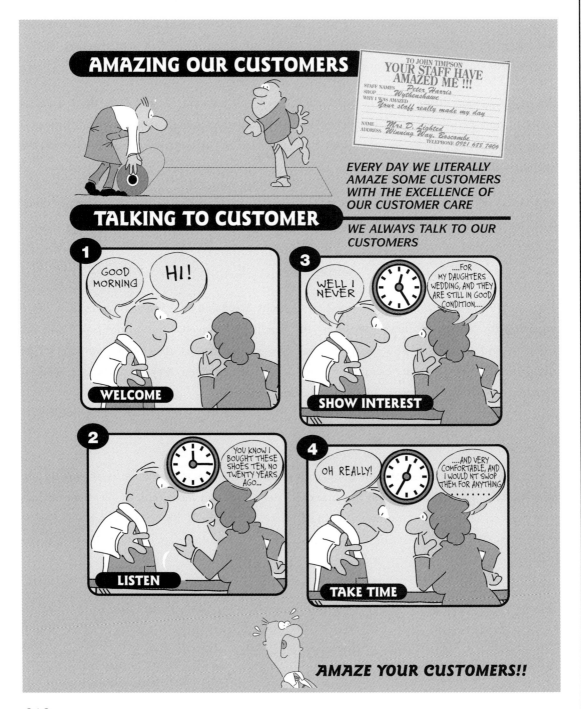

Amazing service

Nearly every time I go shopping, I encounter some of my High Street hates. "If it's not on display we haven't got it." "Haven't you anything smaller than a £10 note?" "I can't sell you that, the computer won't take it."

Mystery shopper

I am not the only one in Timpson who spots sloppy service. Since we started customer care courses and asked our staff to amaze their customers, Timpson people have been doing their own shopping surveys. Whenever I discuss customer service with a group of managers there is always somebody with a tale to tell about terrible treatment from a High Street trader.

Kerry Burke has my favourite story. He was in his local supermarket wanting to buy swedes. The only swedes available were offered free with 5 lbs of potatoes. He had plenty of potatoes at home so just took the swedes to the checkout. "I can't sell you those." said the girl. "They are free with the potatoes." "I don't want potatoes." said Kerry "But am happy to pay for the swedes." "You can't pay for the swedes." said the girl "because they are free, you've got to buy potatoes." So it went on until Kerry finally got help from the customer service manager who had the authority to allow Kerry to purchase his swedes for the price of 5lbs of potatoes.

Winning formula

We want new recruits to start serving customers straight away and to do it properly. That's why we teach them to talk (you can do a days shopping in total silence). We teach them to solve problems and most of all, we encourage them to amaze our customers.

The combination of expertise and good conversation is a winning formula as shown by Jim Malcolm who for many years ran our branch in Selfridges and more recently has been on the road helping to improve turnover in a whole range of locations. Jim can do everything in our business but he wouldn't describe himself as a quality competition winner, where he wins is the way he talks to customers.

What looking after customers really means at Timpson

New recruits soon discover the job is not just about shoe repairing and key cutting, they need to look after customers. Customers who have been amazed provide the best form of advertising. When they tell their friends "You will never believe what happened when I got my shoes repaired..." their positive impression brings us more business.

My biggest buzz comes when a friend says "I visited your shop and the people could not have been more helpful."

Total authority

New recruits find it difficult to come to terms with delegation. They can't believe they get so much authority. "Can we really do that?" they ask. If they have any doubts, the way we let anyone spend £500 to settle a complaint, makes it clear we really mean to delegate. We have never given a warning letter for being too generous to a customer.

To make our policy crystal clear, we display a notice in every branch. "The staff in this shop have my total authority to do what they think will best give their customers an amazing service." These words are over the door facing into the shop so our staff can see them.

Let you get on with it

It has taken us four years to establish the delegation that 'Upside-down Management' brings but it is well worth it. During a recent shop visit, a newly recruited manager told me. "It's different working here, you let us get on with it but we can always get help." That showed 'Upside-down Management' is starting to work.

Conclusion

Our 'Upside-down Management' approach has already made a big difference. We now have a business where people take a pride in their work and the main objective is to look after customers rather than sticking to rules.

When I visit our shops each week and when I re-read the extracts from our manuals which are reprinted here, I realise there is still long way to go. When you first look at my management structure, with the shop staff at the top trusted with control, and me at the bottom, purely there to help, you will think that I have an easy job, but it doesn't work like that.

It's hard persuading people to accept authority, but it's worth the trouble when 1000 people help you to run the business.

Index

Index

Index

Ridgways

The
Complete
TEA BOOK

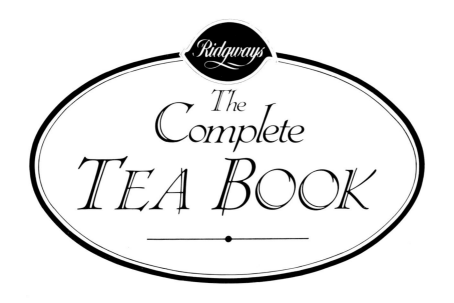

Ridgways

The
Complete
TEA BOOK

EBURY PRESS
LONDON

Published by Ebury Press
Division of The National Magazine Company Ltd
Colquhoun House
27–37 Broadwick Street
London W1V 1FR

First impression 1988
Copyright © 1988 The National Magazine Company Ltd

ISBN 0 85223 761 8

Editors:	*Heather Rocklin and Bridget Jones*
Art Director:	*Frank Phillips*
Designer:	*Tony Paine*
Photographer:	*Tim Imrie*
Home Economist:	*Janet Smith*
Stylist:	*Cathy Sinker*

Filmset by Advanced Filmsetters (Glasgow) Ltd
Printed and bound in Italy by New Interlitho S.p.a., Milan

Cookery Note
*Follow either metric or imperial measures for the
recipes in this book as they are not interchangeable.*

CONTENTS

INTRODUCTION

The British characteristic of consuming several cups of tea a day is one that is recognised all over the world, and the custom of taking afternoon tea is probably one of this country's best-known culinary traditions. Even though the daily tea break may not be a celebration, there are times when everyone indulges in the true pleasure of tea with all the trimmings.

THE HISTORY OF TEA-TIME

Tea was first introduced into Britain in the 1650s, but it wasn't until the 1680s that tea drinking really caught on. An expensive luxury, its popularity can be partly attributed to Charles II's Portuguese wife, Catherine of Braganza, who brought a large chest of tea with her as part of her dowry. At this time, tea was drunk only at breakfast and after dinner. Not until two centuries later did the habit of taking afternoon tea catch on.

By the eighteenth century, tea was being consumed throughout Britain, although it was still regarded as a luxury. So much so, that even the very rich used the same leaves two or three times over. Multi-coloured caddies complete with blending bowls were necessary for storing the tea. They were frequently locked and the keys would be kept by the mistress of the house. The vessels for brewing and serving the beverage were often elaborate, made of the finest porcelain and rich silver and they became an essential part of the tea blending and preparation of the brew that made up the household's tea-taking ritual.

AFTERNOON TEA

The custom of taking afternoon tea between the main meals of the day came later, in the nineteenth century. The custom is believed to have been introduced by Anna, 7th Duchess of Bedford, in 1840, for herself and her friends, but as more tea was imported and special ships ('tea clippers') were employed for this purpose, so the precious leaf became more popular for all levels of society. From the simple refreshment consisting of a cup of tea served with plain bread and butter grew the social occasion with elaborate spreads of fine sandwiches, rich pastries and splendid cakes.

As the habit of afternoon tea drinking spread, so too did the demand for a good quality tea service both to impress friends and improve the pleasures of taking tea. Manufacturers such as Josiah Wedgwood and Josiah Spode (who invented bone china) fed this demand and soon few households were without an elegant tea service.

HIGH TEA

The tradition for high tea was born in rural homes where the family worked on the land. One of the brightest gatherings of the day, high tea is still a popular family meal in the northern counties of England and also in Scotland. For this custom, the delicacies of the genteel social gatherings were replaced by a combination of both savoury and sweet dishes that made up the last meal of the day—hot savouries with salad accompaniments, fruit cakes, fresh scones and light pancakes were served to satisfy raging appetites.

THE FINEST TEAS FROM RIDGWAYS

Ridgways has played a significant role in the history of tea—the company was founded in 1836, when Thomas Ridgway opened his first tea shop in London. His business philosophy was one offering 'the best quality at a fair price'.

RIDGWAYS AND THE ART OF BLENDING

Over 150 years of experience and expertise in buying and blending teas has led the company to produce a varied selection of finest quality tea blends.

The job of the blender is to overcome any naturally occurring inconsistencies that arise from changing weather conditions and seasonal variations. Individual blends are developed from a selection of as few as two or three teas to as many as twenty-five teas. When the result meets the stringent requirements of the blender who works on a small scale, it can then be copied in bulk from a blend sheet which outlines the entire production process. The skill of the blender is partly based on long experience but more importantly, on a natural gift enabling him to detect minute differences between the hundreds of tea samples which he tastes. It is this natural ability which lends to the art of tea blending an air of mystique for which it is famous.

TEA VARIETIES

Teas are selected from the major tea-producing areas of the world: India, Sri Lanka (Ceylon), China and Africa. They are shipped to England where they are blended to create beverages to suit every taste and occasion. If you are unfamiliar with the many blends that are available, then you may find the following guide to teas both helpful and fascinating.

Assam: grown in the Brahmaputra Valley in the far North East of India. Each tea in this blend has been carefully selected to enhance the natural flavour, strength and bouquet for which Assam tea is so richly famous.

Ceylon: the Broken Orange Pekoe Teas in this blend are grown in tea gardens on the mountain slopes in the centre of Sri Lanka (Ceylon). Sri Lanka is known as the 'pearl of the East,' and it is due to the perfect climate of the island that Ceylon Tea has the unique fragrance and flavour that makes it such a delightful and refreshing drink.

China Caravan: in the past, the finest teas from China were carried overland by caravan in order to preserve and protect their delicate flavour. Today the method of transport has changed but the name 'Caravan' is a reminder that this is a blend of Keemun and other China teas of the highest quality.

Darjeeling: Darjeeling is in the North of India, 5,000 feet up on the slopes of the Himalayan foot-hills. Because of the fullness and richness of Darjeeling teas, combined with their particular flavour, frequently described as 'muscatel,' they are sought throughout the world by connoisseurs of fine tea.

Earl Grey: this world-renowned blend has been a favourite for generations because of its rare flavour. It is composed of teas gathered from the world's finest Tea Gardens and is delicately scented by a special process which enhances the natural qualities of the tea and produces its unique flavour.

Her Majesty's Blend (H.M.B.): a blend of carefully selected teas from the finest Tea Gardens of the world, as originally created for the personal use of Queen Victoria. This is a tea in which the art of blending has excelled to preserve the original appeal of a traditional tea.

Kenyan: the teas used to create this blend are specially selected for their rich, bright colour and their full and rounded flavour.

Lapsang Souchong: this is a unique blend of tea which is much admired by discerning tea drinkers the world over. The distinctive 'smoky' or 'tarry' flavour of this tea results from a special process during the tea's production in the Fukien Province of China.

Lemon: high-grown teas from Sri Lanka (Ceylon) subtly blended with pure Oil of Lemon to create a delicately flavoured drink. Equally refreshing whether taken with or without milk.

THE VERSATILE BREW

To make the perfect cup of tea, boil fresh water and warm the pot. Add a heaped teaspoon of tea or one tea bag for each person, plus one extra for the pot. Take the teapot to the kettle and pour in the water as soon as it boils, then allow the tea to brew for 3–6 minutes. Stir the tea before pouring it on to cold, fresh milk, if used.

You may like to try some simple variations on traditional afternoon tea. The following examples of ways in which tea can be spiced or flavoured are intended to inspire you to experiment with your favourite ingredients and different blends.

Iced Tea: add cold water to Ridgways China Caravan tea and allow to infuse for at least one hour before straining. This will ensure that the tea remains clear; tea made with hot water may cloud on cooling. Chill the strained tea in the refrigerator. Just before serving, pour the tea into glasses half-filled with ice. Add a slice of lemon and a few mint sprigs if you like.

Spiced Indian Tea: take 4 cardamom pods and 2 cloves, then bring them to the boil in 600 ml (1 pint) water. Reduce the heat and add 2–3 teaspoons Ridgways Darjeeling tea. Leave for 5 minutes before straining into cups. Pour milk in first if you like, then sweeten to taste.

Hot Cinnamon Tea: bring 3 cloves, 5 cm (2 inch) cinnamon stick and 1.1 litres (2 pints) water to the boil in a saucepan. Put 3 teaspoons Ridgways Assam tea into a bowl and pour on the spiced water. Infuse for 5 minutes before straining. Add about 50 g (2 oz) sugar. When the sugar has dissolved, stir in 65 ml (2½ fl oz) orange juice and the juice of 1 lemon. The tea is ready to serve, with each cup decorated with a cinnamon stick. If you wish to reheat the tea before serving, make sure you do not boil it.

CHAPTER ONE

TRADITIONAL CAKES

CRUMPETS

Makes about 24
350 g (12 oz) strong white flour
15 g (½ oz) fresh yeast or 7.5 ml
    (1½ level tsp) dried yeast and a
    pinch of sugar
300 ml (½ pint) tepid water

2.5 ml (½ level tsp) salt
2.5 ml (½ level tsp) bicarbonate of
    soda
225 ml (8 fl oz) milk
vegetable oil

1. Sieve 175 g (6 oz) flour into a mixing bowl and crumble in the fresh yeast. Make a well in the centre of the flour and pour in the water. Gradually mix together until smooth, beating well as the flour is worked into the liquid. Cover and leave to stand in a warm place for about 15 minutes, or until frothy.
2. If using dried yeast, sprinkle it into the water with the pinch of sugar and leave in a warm place for 15 minutes until frothy.
3. Meanwhile, sieve the remaining flour, salt and bicarbonate of soda into a large bowl (if dried yeast is being used, all the flour will be added at this stage). Make a well in the centre, then pour in the yeast mixture and the milk. Mix to give a thick batter consistency.
4. Using a wooden spoon, vigorously beat the batter for about 5 minutes to incorporate air. Cover and leave in a warm place for about 1 hour, until sponge-like in texture. Beat the batter for a further 2 minutes to incorporate more air.
5. Place a large, preferably non-stick frying pan on to a high heat and, using absorbent kitchen paper, rub a little oil over the surface. Grease the insides of three crumpet rings or three 8 cm (3¼ inch) plain metal pastry cutters. Place the rings blunt edge down on to the hot surface and leave for about 2 minutes, or until very hot.
6. Pour the batter into a large measuring jug. Pour a little batter into each ring to a depth of 1 cm (½ inch). Cook the crumpets for 5–7 minutes until the surface of each appears dry and is honeycombed with holes.
7. When the batter has set, carefully remove each metal ring. Flip the crumpet over and cook the second side for 1 minute only. Cool on a wire rack.
8. Continue cooking the crumpets until all the batter is used. It is important that the frying pan and metal rings are well oiled each time, and heated before the batter is poured in. When required, toast the crumpets on both sides and serve hot, spread with butter.

clockwise from back:
Crumpets (page 11),
Lardy Cake (page
22), Orange Madeira
Cake (page 46)

MUFFINS

Makes about 14
5 ml (1 level tsp) caster sugar
300 ml (½ pint) warm milk
10 ml (2 level tsp) dried yeast
450 g (1 lb) strong white flour
5 ml (1 level tsp) salt
5 ml (1 level tsp) plain flour, for
*   dusting*
5 ml (1 level tsp) fine semolina, for
*   dusting*

1. Dissolve the sugar in the milk, sprinkle the yeast over the surface and leave in a warm place for about 20 minutes until frothy.
2. Sift the flour and salt together, then form a well in the centre. Pour the yeast liquid into the well, draw in the flour and mix to a smooth dough.
3. Knead the dough on a lightly floured surface for about 10 minutes until smooth and elastic. Place in a clean bowl, cover with a tea towel and leave in a warm place until doubled in size.
4. Roll out the dough on a lightly floured surface using a lightly floured rolling pin to about 0.5–1 cm (¼–½ inch) thick. Leave to rest, covered, for 5 minutes, then cut into rounds with a 7.5 cm (3 inch) plain cutter.
5. Place the muffins on a well floured baking sheet. Mix together the 1 teaspoon flour and semolina, and use to dust the tops. Cover with a tea towel and leave in a warm place until doubled in size.
6. Grease a griddle, electric griddle plate or heavy frying pan and heat over a moderate heat, until a cube of bread turns brown in 20 seconds.
7. Cook the muffins on the griddle or frying pan for about 7 minutes each side. Serve warm or leave to cool, then split and toast the muffins before serving.

GRIDDLE SCONES

Makes 8–10
225 g (8 oz) self raising flour
pinch of salt
2.5 ml (½ level tsp) freshly grated
    nutmeg

50 g (2 oz) butter or block
    margarine
50 g (2 oz) caster sugar
1 egg, beaten
45–60 ml (3–4 tbsp) milk

1. Preheat and grease a griddle, or heavy-based frying pan.
2. Sift the flour, salt and nutmeg together and rub in the fat until the mixture resembles fine breadcrumbs. Stir in the sugar. Mix with the egg and milk to a firm dough.
3. On a lightly floured surface roll out to 1 cm (½ inch) thick and cut into rounds or triangles. Cook on a moderately hot griddle until brown on both sides—about 10 minutes in all.

Variation
Add 50 g (2 oz) dried fruit with the sugar.

FRUIT SCONES

Makes 10
225 g (8 oz) self raising flour
5 ml (1 level tsp) baking powder
pinch of salt
50 g (2 oz) butter or margarine

15 ml (1 level tbsp) caster sugar
75 g (3 oz) sultanas
1 large egg, lightly beaten
75 ml (5 tbsp) plus 5 ml (1 tsp)
    milk

1. Sift the flour, baking powder and salt together. Rub in the butter until the mixture resembles breadcrumbs, then stir in the sugar and sultanas. Add the egg and 75 ml (5 tbsp) of the milk. Mix lightly to a soft dough.
2. Roll out the dough on a lightly floured surface to 2 cm (¾ inch) thick. Using a 5 cm (2 inch) plain or fluted biscuit cutter, cut out 10 rounds, re-rolling the dough as necessary.
3. Place the scones on a greased baking sheet and brush the tops with the remaining milk. Bake at 220°C (425°F) mark 7 for 12–15 minutes or until golden brown and well risen.
4. Cool on a wire rack. Serve warm or cold, split and buttered.

Fruit Scones (page 15), Irish Apple Cake (page 42)

Scotch Pancakes or Drop Scones (below)

SCOTCH PANCAKES OR DROP SCONES

Makes about 15–18 pancakes
100 g (4 oz) self raising flour
30 ml (2 level tbsp) caster sugar

1 egg, beaten
150 ml ($\frac{1}{4}$ pint) milk

1. Lightly grease a griddle or heavy-based frying pan.
2. Mix the flour and sugar. Make a well in the centre and stir in the egg, with enough of the milk to make a batter of the consistency of thick cream. The mixing should be done as quickly and lightly as possible. Do not beat.
3. Drop the mixture in spoonfuls on to a hot surface. For round pancakes, drop it from the point of the spoon, for oval ones, drop from the side.
4. Keep the griddle at a steady heat and when bubbles rise to the surface of the pancakes and burst—after 2–3 minutes— turn the pancake over, using a palette knife. Cook for a further 2–3 minutes, until golden brown on the other side.
5. Place the cooked pancakes on a clean tea towel, cover with another towel and place on a rack to cool. (This keeps in the steam and the pancakes do not become dry.) Serve with butter or with whipped cream and jam.

Variation
For richer drop scones, add about 25 g (1 oz) fat, rubbing it into the flour. If you prefer, use 100 g (4 oz) plain flour, 2.5 ml ($\frac{1}{2}$ level tsp) bicarbonate of soda and 5 ml (1 level tsp) cream of tartar instead of the self raising flour.

DEVONSHIRE SPLITS

Makes 14–16

15 g (½ oz) fresh yeast or 7.5 ml
(1½ level tsp) dried yeast and a
pinch of sugar
about 300 ml (½ pint) tepid milk
50 g (2 oz) butter or block
margarine

30 ml (2 level tbsp) sugar
450 g (1 lb) strong white flour
5 ml (1 level tsp) salt
Devonshire or whipped cream and
jam for serving
icing sugar for dusting

1. Grease two baking sheets.
2. Blend the fresh yeast with half the milk. If using dried yeast, sprinkle it into 150 ml (¼ pint) of the milk with the pinch of sugar and leave in a warm place for 15 minutes, until frothy.
3. Dissolve butter and sugar in remaining milk.
4. Mix together the flour and salt in a large bowl, make a well in the centre, add the butter mixture and yeast liquid.
5. Beat to an elastic dough, turn out on to a lightly floured surface and knead until smooth. Cover with a clean tea towel and leave in a warm place until doubled in size.
6. Turn on to a lightly floured surface and divide into 14–16 pieces. Knead lightly and shape into round buns.
7. Place on the baking sheets and flatten lightly with the hand. Cover with a clean tea towel and leave to prove in a warm place until doubled in size.
8. Bake in the oven at 220°C (425°F) mark 7 for 15–20 minutes. Cool on a wire rack. Split and spread with jam and cream. Dust with icing sugar.

MINIATURE BUTTER MUFFINS

Makes 12–14

115 g (4½ oz) self raising flour
5 ml (1 level tsp) baking powder
2.5 ml (½ level tsp) salt

100 g (4 oz) butter
1 egg
100 ml (4 fl oz) milk

1. Sift together the flour, baking powder and salt. Rub in the butter.
2. Beat together the egg and milk, then lightly stir this into the flour mixture, leaving the mixture quite lumpy.
3. Three-quarters fill 12–14 well-greased miniature brioche tins and bake at 220°C (425°F) mark 7 for 12–15 minutes or until golden.
4. Turn out and cool slightly on a wire rack. Serve while still warm.

SULTANA TEACAKES

Makes 12
225 g (8 oz) strong white flour
225 g (8 oz) plain wholemeal flour
5 ml (1 level tsp) salt
about 30–45 ml (2–3 level tbsp)
    caster sugar

50 g (2 oz) polyunsaturated
    margarine
100 g (4 oz) sultanas
about 300 ml (½ pint) milk
15 g (½ oz) fresh yeast
1 egg white

1. Mix together the flours and salt with 15 ml (1 level tbsp) of the caster sugar. Using a fork, cut in the margarine until evenly blended. Stir in the sultanas.
2. Warm the milk until just tepid then remove from the heat and crumble in the yeast. Stir until smooth. Beat into the flour mixture until a soft dough is formed, adding a little more milk if necessary.
3. Turn out the dough on to a lightly floured surface and knead until smooth and elastic—about 10 minutes. Place in a large oiled bowl. Cover with oiled cling film and leave in a warm place until doubled in size—about 1 hour.
4. Divide the dough into 12 even-sized

pieces. Knead each one into a flat round and place on greased baking sheets. Cover with oiled cling film and leave to double in size.
5. Place a roasting tin of boiling water in the bottom of the oven. Uncover the rolls, flatten slightly, then bake at 200°C (400°F) mark 6 for 12 minutes. Brush with lightly beaten egg white and sprinkle with caster sugar. Return to the oven and bake for a further 5–10 minutes, or until well browned and hollow-sounding when tapped. Cool on a wire rack or serve immediately. Alternatively, cool then refrigerate in a polythene bag for the next day.

CHELSEA BUNS

Makes 12
225 g (8 oz) strong white flour
15 g (½ oz) fresh yeast or 7.5 ml
(1½ level tsp) dried yeast
2.5 ml (½ level tsp) caster sugar
50 ml (2 fl oz) milk, lukewarm
50 ml (2 fl oz) water, lukewarm
2.5 ml (½ level tsp) salt

15 g (½ oz) lard
1 egg, lightly beaten
100 g (4 oz) mixed dried fruit
25 g (1 oz) chopped mixed peel
50 g (2 oz) light soft brown sugar
25 g (1 oz) butter, melted
clear honey, to glaze

1. Sift 50 g (2 oz) of the flour into a warmed bowl. Blend the fresh yeast with the caster sugar then pour in the milk and water stirring until smooth. Then pour this yeast mixture over the flour in the warmed bowl. If using dried yeast, then sprinkle it over the flour, sugar, milk and water. Leave in a warm place for 20 minutes or until puffed up and frothy.
2. Sift the remaining flour with the salt and rub in the lard. Make a well in the centre and pour in the yeast mixture and the egg. Mix to a dough and knead for 10 minutes. Place the dough in a bowl, cover with cling film and leave in a warm place for 1½ hours or until doubled in size.
3. Turn the dough out on to a lightly

floured surface and knead lightly. Roll the dough out into a 30 × 23 cm (12 × 9 inch) rectangle.
4. Mix the fruit, mixed peel and brown sugar together. Brush the dough with melted butter and sprinkle with the fruit mixture to within 2.5 cm (1 inch) of the edge. Roll the dough tightly, starting from one long edge. Press the edges to seal. Slice the roll into 12 pieces and pack into a greased baking tray with sides.
5. Cover with cling film and leave in a warm place for 30 minutes or until risen slightly, then bake at 190°C (375°F) mark 5 for 30 minutes.
6. Remove from the oven and brush with honey. Leave to cool in the tin.

WELSH CAKES

Makes about 16
225 g (8 oz) plain flour
5 ml (1 level tsp) baking powder
pinch of salt
50 g (2 oz) butter

50 g (2 oz) lard
75 g (3 oz) sugar
50 g (2 oz) currants
1 egg, beaten
about 30 ml (2 tbsp) milk

1. Grease a griddle or large frying pan.
2. Sift together the flour, baking powder and salt. Rub in the fats and add the sugar and currants. Bind with egg and milk to give a stiff paste similar to shortcrust pastry.
3. Roll out to about 0.5 cm ($\frac{1}{4}$ inch) thickness and cut out circles with a 7.5 cm (3 inch) cutter.
4. Cook the cakes slowly on the griddle for about 3 minutes on each side, until golden-brown. Cool on a wire rack.
5. Eat while fresh; if you like, toss them in caster sugar before leaving them to cool.

*Chelsea Buns
(opposite)*

LARDY CAKE

Makes 8 pieces
5 ml (1 level tsp) caster sugar
300 ml (½ pint) warm water
10 ml (2 level tsp) dried yeast
450 g (1 lb) strong white flour
10 ml (2 level tsp) salt

175 g (6 oz) lard, chilled
175 g (6 oz) mixed sultanas and
    currants
50 g (2 oz) chopped mixed peel
175 g (6 oz) sugar

1. Grease a 20.5 × 25 cm (8 × 10 inch) tin. Dissolve the sugar in the water, sprinkle the yeast over the surface then leave in a warm place for about 20 minutes until frothy.
2. Sift the flour and salt together into a bowl. Dice 15 g (½ oz) of the lard, toss in the flour, then rub it in. Form a well in the centre, pour in the yeast liquid, then draw in the dry ingredients and mix to a dough that leaves the sides of the bowl clean.
3. Turn on to a lightly floured work surface and knead well for 10 minutes until smooth and elastic. Place in a clean bowl.
4. Cover with a damp cloth, put the bowl inside a large polythene bag and leave until doubled in size. This will take about 1 hour in a warm room, about 2 hours at normal room temperature.
5. Turn the dough on to a floured surface and roll out to a rectangle about 0.5 cm (¼ inch) thick. Cut the remaining lard into small pieces and dot one third of it over the surface of the dough and sprinkle over one third of the fruit, peel and sugar. Fold the dough in three, folding the bottom third up and the top third down. Give a half turn and roll out as before, repeating the process twice more.
6. Roll the dough out to fit the prepared tin. Cover with oiled polythene and a cloth and leave to rise in a warm place for 20–30 minutes until puffy.
7. Score the top into 8 rectangles, then bake at 220°C (425°F) mark 7 for about 45 minutes.

CHAPTER TWO

SMALL
CAKES

clockwise from back:
Fluted Caraway Buns
(page 30), Banana
and Honey Teabread
(page 63), Welsh
Cakes (page 21),
Orange-glazed Ginger
Cake (page 43)

BANANA ROCK CAKES

Makes about 10
200 g (7 oz) plain wheatmeal flour
7.5 ml (1½ level tsp) baking powder
75 g (3 oz) polyunsaturated
    margarine
15 ml (1 level tbsp) soft light brown
    sugar

50 g (2 oz) sultanas
225 g (8 oz) bananas
5 ml (1 tsp) lemon juice
1 egg, lightly beaten

1. Place the flour and baking powder in a bowl. Then, using a fork, cut in the margarine until the mixture resembles breadcrumbs. Stir in the sugar and sultanas; make a well in the centre.
2. Mash the bananas with the lemon juice; stir in the egg. Pour this mixture into the dry ingredients and beat until well mixed.

3. Spoon the mixture into about 10 'lumps' on a greased baking sheet, allowing room for spreading.
4. Bake at 200°C (400°F) mark 6 for about 15 minutes or until the cakes are well risen and golden brown. Allow to cool on a wire rack.

BOSTON BROWNIES

Makes about 16
50 g (2 oz) plain chocolate
65 g (2½ oz) butter or block
    margarine
175 g (6 oz) caster sugar

65 g (2½ oz) self raising flour
1.25 ml (¼ level tsp) salt
2 eggs, beaten
2.5 ml (½ tsp) vanilla flavouring
50 g (2 oz) walnuts, roughly chopped

1. Grease and line a shallow 20.5 cm (8 inch) square cake tin. Break up the chocolate and put it in a bowl with the butter, cut into pieces. Stand the bowl over a pan of hot water and heat gently, stirring occasionally, until melted. Add the caster sugar.
2. Sift together the flour and salt into a bowl. Add the chocolate mixture, eggs, vanilla flavouring and walnuts. Mix

thoroughly.
3. Pour the mixture into the prepared tin and bake in the oven at 180°C (350°F) mark 4 for 35–40 minutes until the mixture is risen and just beginning to leave the sides of the cake tin.
4. Leave in the tin to cool, then cut the Boston brownies into squares with a sharp knife.

WALNUT AND SULTANA ROCKIES

Makes about 12
225 g (8 oz) plain flour
pinch of salt
2.5 ml ($\frac{1}{2}$ level tsp) mixed spice
50 g (2 oz) butter
50 g (2 oz) lard

100 g (4 oz) demerara sugar
50 g (2 oz) walnut halves, chopped
50 g (2 oz) sultanas
25 g (1 oz) chopped mixed peel
1 egg, beaten
a little milk

1. Sift the flour, salt and spice into a bowl. Rub in the fats until the mixture resembles fine breadcrumbs.

2. Add the sugar, walnuts, sultanas and peel. Using a fork, bind them together with egg, adding a little milk, if necessary, to give a stiff dough that just knits together.

3. Continue using a fork to make small rough heaps on greased baking sheets. Bake at 200°C (400°F) mark 6 for 15–20 minutes. Leave to cool for a short time before transferring to a wire rack to cool completely.

ST CATHERINE'S CAKES

Makes about 30
125 g (4 oz) butter
125 g (4 oz) caster sugar
1 large egg, beaten

225 g (8 oz) self raising flour
2.5 ml ($\frac{1}{2}$ level tsp) mixed spice
60 ml (4 level tbsp) ground almonds
50 g (2 oz) currants

1. Cream the butter and sugar together until light and fluffy; gradually beat in the egg. Sift in flour and spice; add almonds and currants.

2. Mix, handling lightly, until the dough begins to bind together, then knead again lightly. Roll the dough out on a floured surface to 5 mm ($\frac{1}{4}$ inch) thick and 20.5 cm (8 inches) wide. (This is easier if only half the dough is handled at once.)

3. Cut into 1 cm ($\frac{1}{2}$ inch) strips and wind round to form a Catherine wheel. Arrange on greased baking sheets and bake at 190°C (375°F) mark 5 for 10–15 minutes, or until pale golden. Cool on a wire rack.

DOUGHNUT TIES

Makes 8–10
15 g (½ oz) fresh yeast
5 ml (1 level tsp) sugar
60 ml (4 tbsp) milk
225 g (8 oz) strong white flour

2.5 ml (½ level tsp) salt
knob of butter or margarine
1 egg, beaten
caster sugar and poppy seeds to coat

1. Crumble the yeast into a basin. Dissolve the 5 ml (1 level tsp) sugar in the milk and stir into the yeast until smooth. Leave until frothy.
2. Sift together the flour and salt and rub in the fat. Add the yeast mixture and egg and mix to a soft but manageable dough, adding more milk if necessary.

3. Beat well until smooth and divide into 8–10 pieces. Shape each into a roll 18 cm (7 inches) long. Tie each in a knot.
4. Deep fry in oil heated to 190°C (375°F) until golden. Drain on kitchen paper. Toss in a mixture of caster sugar and poppy seeds to coat. Serve freshly cooked.

ENGLISH MADELEINES

Makes 10
100 g (4 oz) butter or block
 margarine
100 g (4 oz) caster sugar
2 eggs, beaten
100 g (4 oz) self raising flour

50 g (2 oz) desiccated coconut
30 ml (2 tbsp) red jam, sieved and
 melted
5 glacé cherries, halved, and angelica
 pieces, to decorate

1. Grease 10 dariole moulds. Put the butter and sugar into a bowl and beat together until pale and fluffy. Add the eggs a little at a time, beating well after each addition. Fold in half the flour, using a metal spoon. Fold in the remaining flour.
2. Turn the mixture into the moulds, filling them three-quarters full. Bake in the oven at 180°C (350°F) mark 4 for about 20 minutes until well risen and firm to the touch. Turn out on to a wire rack to cool

for 20 minutes.
3. When the cakes are almost cold, trim the bases so they stand firmly and are about the same height.
4. Spread the coconut out on a large plate. Spear each cake on a skewer, brush with melted jam, then roll in the coconut to coat.
5. Top each madeleine with half a glacé cherry and small pieces of angelica.

ALMOND FINGERS

Makes 8–12
100 g (4 oz) plain flour
pinch of salt
50 g (2 oz) butter or block
*   margarine*
5 ml (1 level tsp) caster sugar
1 egg yolk

Filling
45 ml (3 level tbsp) raspberry jam
1 egg white
45 ml (3 level tbsp) ground almonds
50 g (2 oz) caster sugar
few drops almond flavouring
45 ml (3 level tbsp) flaked almonds

1. Lightly grease a shallow 18 cm (7 inch) square tin. Sift the flour and salt and rub in the butter until the mixture resembles fine breadcrumbs. Stir in the 5 ml (1 tsp) sugar and add the egg yolk and enough water to mix to a firm dough.

2. Knead lightly on a floured surface and roll out to an 18 cm (7 inch) square; use to line the base of the tin. Spread the pastry with the jam, almost to the edges.

3. Whisk the egg white until stiff. Fold in the ground almonds, sugar and flavouring. Spread the mixture over the jam.

4. Sprinkle with flaked almonds and bake in the oven at 180°C (350°F) mark 4 for about 35 minutes until crisp and golden. Cool in the tin, then cut into fingers and remove with a palette knife.

Maids of Honour (page 80), Almond Fingers (above)

FLUTED CARAWAY BUNS

Makes about 9
75 g (3 oz) butter or margarine
50 g (2 oz) caster sugar
2 eggs, beaten
30 ml (2 level tbsp) lemon cheese or
curd

100 g (4 oz) self raising flour
pinch of salt
2 5 ml (½ level tsp) caraway seeds
100 g (4 oz) icing sugar
15 ml (1 tbsp) water
glacé cherries, halved

1. Using lard, thoroughly grease 9 fluted patty tins measuring about 7 cm (2¾ inches) wide and 3 cm (1¼ inches) deep.
2. Cream the fat and sugar together until pale and fluffy. Add the egg, a little at a time, beating well after each addition. Fold in the lemon cheese.
3. Sift in the flour and salt and fold it in followed by the caraway seeds. Divide the mixture between the prepared tins and bake in the oven at 170°C (325°F) mark 3

for about 25 minutes.
4. Turn out and leave to cool bottom sides up on a wire rack.
5. Sift the icing sugar into a basin and beat in the water to make a smooth, stiff glacé icing.
6. Decorate each bun with a little blob of stiff glacé icing and half a glacé cherry. Or serve the other way up, simply dusted with sifted icing sugar.

GINGER WHIRLS

Makes 12
225 g (8 oz) butter or margarine
75 g (3 oz) icing sugar
200 g (7 oz) plain flour

25 g (1 oz) cornflour
10 ml (2 level tsp) ground ginger
30 ml (2 tbsp) ginger marmalade
stem ginger (optional)

1. Arrange 12 paper cases in patty tins. Cream the fat until soft, then sift in the icing sugar and cream together until pale and fluffy.
2. Sift together the flour, cornflour and ground ginger and fold into the creamed mixture.
3. Spoon the mixture into a piping bag fitted with a large star nozzle and pipe a whirl into each paper case.
4. Bake in the oven at 190°C (375°F) mark 5 for 15–20 minutes until golden brown. Leave to cool on a wire rack.
5. Fill the centre of each whirl with a little ginger marmalade and top with a sliver of stem ginger (if used).

FAIRY CAKES

Makes 12–16
100 g (4 oz) butter or block margarine
100 g (4 oz) caster sugar

2 eggs, beaten
100 g (4 oz) self raising flour
350 g (12 oz) icing sugar
about 45 ml (3 tbsp) warm water

1. Spread 12 to 16 paper cases out on baking sheets, or if wished put them into patty tins.
2. Cream the fat and sugar until pale and fluffy. Add the eggs, a little at a time, beating well after each addition. Fold in the flour using a metal spoon. Two-thirds fill the cases with the mixture.
3. Bake in the oven at 190°C (375°F) mark 5 for 15–20 minutes, until golden.
4. Sift the icing sugar into a bowl and beat in the water, adding enough to make a fairly thick smooth glacé icing.
5. Cool the cakes on a wire rack, then top each one with a little icing.

Variations
Add one of the following before folding in the flour:
- 50 g (2 oz) sultanas (known as Queen cakes)
- 50 g (2 oz) chopped dates
- 50 g (2 oz) chopped glacé cherries
- 50 g (2 oz) chocolate chips

LAMINGTONS

Makes 12
50 g (2 oz) butter
65 g (2½ oz) plain flour
15 ml (1 level tbsp) cornflour
3 large eggs

75 g (3 oz) caster sugar
450 g (1 lb) icing sugar
75 g (3 oz) cocoa
100 ml (4 fl oz) milk
75 g (3 oz) desiccated coconut

1. Grease a 28 × 18 cm (11 × 7 inch) cake tin. Line the tin with greaseproof paper and grease the paper.

2. Melt 40 g (1½ oz) butter and let it stand for a few minutes for the salt and any sediment to settle. Sift the flour and cornflour.

3. Put the eggs and sugar into a large bowl and whisk until light and creamy—the mixture should be thick enough to leave a trail on the surface for a few seconds when the whisk is lifted. If whisking by hand, place the bowl over simmering water, then remove from the heat and whisk for 5–10 minutes until cool.

4. Re-sift the flours and fold half into the egg mixture with a metal spoon.

5. Pour the cooled but still flowing butter round the edge of the mixture, taking care not to let the salt and sediment run in.

6. Fold the butter very lightly into the mixture, alternating with the rest of the flour.

7. Turn the mixture into the tin. Bake in the oven at 190°C (375°F) mark 5 until firm to the touch, 20–25 minutes. Turn out on to a wire rack and leave to cool.

8. Meanwhile, for the icing: sift the icing sugar and cocoa into the top part of a double boiler or into a heatproof bowl placed over simmering water.

9. Add the remaining butter and the milk and stir over a gentle heat to a coating consistency.

10. Cut the cake into twelve even-sized pieces. Place on a wire cooling rack. Spoon the icing over each cake to cover. Sprinkle the tops of each with coconut. Leave for 30 minutes until set.

CHAPTER THREE

LARGE
CAKES

FRUIT BRAZIL BUTTER CAKE

Makes one 20.5 cm (8 inch)
round cake
175 g (6 oz) butter or block
  margarine
175 g (6 oz) caster sugar
3 large eggs, beaten
125 g (4 oz) Brazil nuts
50 g (2 oz) candied lemon peel
125 g (4 oz) dried apricots

125 g (4 oz) sultanas
125 g (4 oz) plain flour
125 g (4 oz) self raising flour
30 ml (2 tbsp) sieved apricot jam
15 ml (1 tbsp) boiling water
225 g (8 oz) marzipan
a few whole Brazil nuts, soaked, then
  drained, dried and sliced

1. Line the bottom and sides of a 20.5 cm (8 inch) round cake tin or 1.7 litre (3 pint) loaf tin with greased greaseproof paper.
2. Cream the fat and sugar together until pale and fluffy. Add the beaten eggs gradually, beating all the time.
3. Roughly chop or coarsely grate the nuts and finely chop the candied peel. Snip the apricots into small pieces. Mix all the fruit and nuts together.
4. Fold the sifted flours into the creamed mixture followed by the fruit mixture. Spoon into the prepared tin.

5. Bake at 180°C (350°F) mark 4 for about $1\frac{1}{4}$ hours, covering the top of the cake towards the end of the cooking time, if necessary, to prevent it becoming too brown. Cool a little then turn out on to a wire rack.
6. To make an apricot glaze, stir the sieved jam and boiling water together.
7. To finish, brush the top of the cake with apricot glaze. Cover with rolled out marzipan. Score in a diamond pattern. Place a slice of Brazil nut in each diamond. Grill cake top until evenly browned.

CHOCOLATE AND HAZELNUT CAKE

Serves 10
275 g (10 oz) unsalted butter,
softened
225 g (8 oz) light soft brown sugar
4 eggs, separated
100 g (4 oz) self raising flour
pinch of salt
100 g (4 oz) ground hazelnuts

100 g (4 oz) plain chocolate, finely
grated
225 g (8 oz) icing sugar
50 g (2 oz) cocoa
30 ml (2 tbsp) milk
25 g (1 oz) hazelnuts, chopped to
decorate

1. Grease and line a 23 cm (9 inch) round cake tin. Put 225 g (8 oz) of the butter and the sugar into a bowl and beat together until pale and fluffy. Beat in the egg yolks one at a time, then fold in the flour and salt. Stir in the hazelnuts and chocolate.

2. Whisk the egg whites until stiff, then fold into the cake mixture. Pour into the prepared tin and bake in the oven at 170°C (325°F) mark 3 for 1 hour 15 minutes or until a fine warmed skewer inserted in the centre comes out clean. Leave to cool in the tin for 45 minutes.

3. Make the fudge icing. Sift the icing sugar and cocoa together, then put into a heavy-based pan with the remaining butter and the milk. Heat gently until the butter has melted; beat until smooth. Remove from heat.

4. Cut the cake in half horizontally. Spread a little icing over one half, then top with the other. Swirl remaining icing over and sprinkle with nuts.

clockwise from back:
Almond Custard
Tarts (page 81),
Jalousie (page 71),
Chocolate and
Hazelnut Cake
(page 35)

GRANDMOTHER'S BOILED FRUIT CAKE

Makes one 18 cm (7 inch) round cake
275 g (10 oz) plain flour
10 ml (2 level tsp) bicarbonate of soda
300 ml (½ pint) freshly made, strained Ridgways Ceylon tea

100 g (4 oz) margarine
150 g (5 oz) light soft brown sugar
175 g (6 oz) currants
175 g (6 oz) sultanas
15 ml (1 level tbsp) mixed spice
1 large egg, beaten

1. Grease and line an 18 cm (7 inch) round cake tin. Sift together the flour and bicarbonate of soda into a large bowl. Make a well in the centre.
2. Put the tea, margarine, sugar, currants, sultanas and spice in a pan and bring to the boil. Reduce the heat and simmer for 20 minutes. Remove from the heat and leave to cool. When cold, pour into the dry ingredients, add the egg and mix thoroughly.
3. Turn the mixture into the prepared tin and bake in the oven at 180°C (350°F) mark 4 for about 1 hour. When the cake is beginning to brown, cover with a piece of greaseproof paper. Turn out and leave to cool on a wire rack.

CIDER CAKE

Makes about 9 pieces
150 ml (¼ pint) dry cider
225 g (8 oz) sultanas
100 g (4 oz) butter

100 g (4 oz) light soft brown sugar
2 eggs, beaten
225 g (8 oz) plain flour
5 ml (1 level tsp) bicarbonate of soda

1. Grease an 18 cm (7 inch) square cake tin.
2. Put the cider and fruit in a bowl and leave to soak for 12 hours or overnight.
3. Cream the butter and the sugar together until pale and fluffy. Gradually beat in the eggs, a little at a time, beating well after each addition. Add half of the flour and the bicarbonate of soda and beat thoroughly together.
4. Pour over the sultanas and the cider and mix well together. Fold in the remaining flour, then pour quickly into the prepared tin.
5. Bake at 180°C (350°F) mark 4 for about 1 hour, until well risen and firm to the touch. Leave to cool in the tin for 30 minutes, then turn out on to a wire rack and leave to cool completely. Serve cut into squares.

MARZIPAN PINEAPPLE CAKE

Makes 8 pieces
175 g (6 oz) butter
150 g (5 oz) light soft brown sugar
finely grated rind of 1 orange plus
*   15 ml (1 tbsp) juice*
finely grated rind of 1 lemon plus
*   15 ml (1 tbsp) juice*
2 large eggs
2 egg yolks
100 g (4 oz) self raising flour

50 g (2 oz) cornflour
pinch of salt
75 g (3 oz) glacé pineapple, thinly
*   sliced*
75 g (3 oz) firm bought marzipan,
*   cut into small cubes*

Glacé icing
75 g (3 oz) icing sugar
15–30 ml (1–2 tbsp) lemon juice

1. Grease a 24 × 18 cm (9½ × 7 inch) cake or roasting tin. Line with greased greaseproof paper.

2. Put the butter and sugar into a bowl and beat together until pale and fluffy. Stir in the lemon and orange rind.

3. Lightly beat in the whole eggs and the yolks. Lightly beat in the self raising flour, cornflour and salt with the orange and lemon juice. Fold in the pineapple.

4. Turn the mixture into the prepared tin, level the surface and scatter with marzipan cubes.

5. Bake in the oven at 180°C (350°F) mark 4 for about 45 minutes or until a fine warmed skewer inserted in the centre comes out clean.

6. Meanwhile, make the glacé icing by sifting the icing sugar into a basin and beating in enough lemon juice to make a smooth fairly thick icing. When the cake is baked, turn it out on to a wire rack and immediately brush the top with the glacé icing. Leave to cool completely for about 1 hour.

ALMOND AND CHERRY CAKE

Makes one 23 cm (9 inch) round cake

275 g (10 oz) glacé cherries
65 g (2½ oz) self raising flour
225 g (8 oz) unsalted butter, softened
225 g (8 oz) caster sugar
6 eggs, beaten
pinch of salt
175 g (6 oz) ground almonds
2.5 ml (½ tsp) almond flavouring
icing sugar, to decorate

1. Grease a deep 23 cm (9 inch) round cake tin. Line with greaseproof paper and grease the paper.
2. Dust the cherries lightly with a little of the flour. Arrange in the bottom of the tin.
3. Put the butter and sugar into a bowl and beat together until pale and fluffy. Beat in the eggs a little at a time, adding a little of the flour if the mixture shows signs of curdling.
4. Sift in remaining flour with salt and add the almonds and almond flavouring.
5. Turn the mixture into the prepared tin. Bake in the oven at 180°C (350°F) mark 4 for 1 hour. Cover with greaseproof paper if browning too quickly. Leave in the tin for 1–2 hours to cool. Sift icing sugar on top to decorate.

Almond and Cherry Cake (above)

Victorian Seed Cake (below)

VICTORIAN SEED CAKE

Makes one 18 cm (7 inch) round cake
175 g (6 oz) butter
175 g (6 oz) caster sugar
5 ml (1 tsp) vanilla flavouring
3 eggs, beaten

100 g (4 oz) plain flour
100 g (4 oz) self raising flour
10 ml (2 level tsp) caraway seeds
15–30 ml (1–2 tbsp) milk (optional)

1. Grease an 18 cm (7 inch) round cake tin. Line with greased greaseproof paper.
2. Put the butter, sugar and flavouring into a bowl and beat until pale and fluffy. Beat in the eggs a little at a time.
3. Fold in the flours with the caraway seeds, adding a little milk if necessary to give a dropping consistency.
4. Turn the mixture into the prepared tin. Bake in the oven at 180°C (350°F) mark 4 for about 1 hour until firm to the touch. Turn out on to a wire rack to cool for 1–2 hours.

IRISH APPLE CAKE

Makes one 23 cm (9 inch) round cake

150 g (5 oz) butter
150 g (5 oz) caster sugar
15 ml (1 level tbsp) vanilla sugar
3 eggs, lightly beaten
finely grated rind of 1 lemon
150 g (5 oz) plain flour
150 g (5 oz) cornflour
10 ml (2 level tsp) baking powder
45 ml (3 tbsp) milk
400 g (14 oz) eating apples, peeled
   weight, cored and quartered
30 ml (2 tbsp) apricot jam
5 ml (1 tsp) water

1. Cream the butter with the caster and vanilla sugar until pale, light and fluffy. Add the egg, a little at a time, beating well after each addition. Stir in the lemon rind.
2. Sift the plain flour, cornflour and baking powder together twice. Gradually fold it into the cake mixture, then stir in the milk.
3. Spoon the mixture into a greased and floured 23 cm (9 inch) round spring form cake tin with a removable base. Arrange the apple quarters, rounded sides up, on top.
4. Bake the cake on the middle shelf of the oven at 190°C (375°F) mark 5 for 1 hour. The cake is cooked when a small skewer inserted into the centre comes out clean. Cool in the tin for 10 minutes, then remove the ring.
5. Heat the apricot jam with the water then rub it through a sieve. Brush the top of the cake with the glaze while it is still hot.

ORANGE-GLAZED GINGER CAKE

Makes one 23 cm (9 inch) round cake

125 g (4 oz) lard
125 g (4 oz) caster sugar
1 egg, beaten
275 g (10 oz) plain flour
7.5 ml (1½ level tsp) bicarbonate of soda

2.5 ml (½ level tsp) salt
5 ml (1 level tsp) ground cinnamon
5 ml (1 level tsp) ground ginger
100 g (4 oz) golden syrup
100 g (4 oz) black treacle
225 ml (8 fl oz) water
pared rind and juice of 1 orange
100 g (4 oz) icing sugar

1. Grease a 23 cm (9 inch) round cake tin. Line with greased greaseproof paper.
2. Put the lard and sugar into a bowl and beat together until pale and fluffy. Beat in the egg, then the flour, bicarbonate of soda, salt and spices.
3. Warm together the golden syrup and black treacle in a pan with the water and bring to the boil. Stir into the lard mixture, beating all the time until completely incorporated.
4. Turn the mixture into the prepared tin. Bake in the oven at 180°C (350°F) mark 4 for about 50 minutes or until a fine warmed skewer inserted in the centre comes out clean. Cool in the tin for about 10 minutes before turning out on to a wire rack to cool completely for 2 hours.
5. Cut the orange rind into strips; put into a pan and cover with water. Boil until tender, about 10 minutes and drain well.
6. Make an orange glacé icing by sifting the icing sugar into a basin, then beating in enough orange juice to make a smooth, fairly thick icing.
7. Evenly coat the top of the cake with the orange icing and leave to set for 1 hour. Sprinkle the orange strips around the top.

MARBLED CHOCOLATE RING CAKE

Makes 8 pieces
250 g (9 oz) plain chocolate
5 ml (1 tsp) vanilla flavouring
45 ml (3 tbsp) water
350 g (12 oz) butter
225 g (8 oz) caster sugar

4 large eggs, beaten
225 g (8 oz) plain flour
10 ml (2 level tsp) baking powder
2.5 ml (½ level tsp) salt
50 g (2 oz) ground almonds
30 ml (2 tbsp) milk

1. Grease a 1.7 litre (3 pint) ring mould. Break 50 g (2 oz) chocolate into a heatproof bowl. Add the vanilla flavouring and 15 ml (1 tbsp) water and place over simmering water. Stir until the chocolate is melted, then remove from heat and leave to cool for 10 minutes.

2. Put 225 g (8 oz) butter and the caster sugar into a bowl and beat together until pale and fluffy. Beat in the eggs one at a time.

3. Fold the flour, baking powder and salt into the creamed mixture with the ground almonds. Stir in the milk. Spoon half the mixture into base of ring mould.

4. Stir the cooled but still soft chocolate into the remaining mixture. Spoon into the tin.

5. Draw a knife through the cake mixture in a spiral. Level the surface of the mixture again.

6. Bake in the oven at 180°C (350°F) mark 4 for about 55 minutes or until a fine warmed skewer inserted in the centre comes out clean. Turn out on to a wire rack to cool for 1 hour.

7. Make the chocolate frosting. Break 150 g (5 oz) chocolate into a heatproof bowl with 30 ml (2 tbsp) water and the remaining butter. Place over simmering water and stir until the chocolate is melted, then pour over the cooled cake, working quickly to coat top and sides. Leave to set for 1 hour.

8. Melt the remaining chocolate over simmering water as before. Spoon into a greaseproof paper piping bag, snip off the tip and drizzle chocolate over the cake.

Marbled Chocolate Ring Cake (opposite)

HALF-POUND CAKE

Makes one 20.5 cm (8 inch) round cake

225 g (8 oz) butter or block margarine, softened
225 g (8 oz) caster sugar
4 eggs, beaten
225 g (8 oz) seedless raisins
225 g (8 oz) mixed currants and sultanas

100 g (4 oz) glacé cherries, halved
225 g (8 oz) plain flour
2.5 ml ($\frac{1}{2}$ level tsp) salt
2.5 ml ($\frac{1}{2}$ level tsp) mixed spice
60 ml (4 tbsp) brandy
few walnut halves

1. Line a 20.5 cm (8 inch) round cake tin with greased greaseproof paper.
2. Cream the fat and sugar until pale and fluffy. Add the eggs, a little at a time, beating well after each addition.
3. Mix the fruit, flour, salt and spice and fold into the creamed mixture, using a metal spoon. Add the brandy and mix to a soft dropping consistency.
4. Turn the mixture into the tin, level the top and arrange the nuts on top. Bake in the oven at 150°C (300°F) mark 2 for about 2$\frac{1}{2}$ hours, until a fine warmed skewer inserted in the centre comes out clean. Turn out and cool on a wire rack.

CARROT CAKE

Makes one 20.5 cm (8 inch) round cake

225 g (8 oz) butter or margarine, diced
225 g (8 oz) light soft brown sugar
4 eggs, separated
10 ml (2 level tsp) grated orange rind
15 ml (1 tbsp) lemon juice
175 g (6 oz) self raising flour

5 ml (1 level tsp) baking powder
50 g (2 oz) ground almonds
100 g (4 oz) walnuts, chopped
350 g (12 oz) young carrots, grated

Topping (optional)

200 g (7 oz) soft cheese
10 ml (2 tsp) runny honey
5 ml (1 tsp) lemon juice
25 g (1 oz) walnuts, chopped

1. Grease and line a 20.5 cm (8 inch) round cake tin. Beat the butter or margarine and sugar together in a bowl until light and fluffy. Beat in the egg yolks, then stir in the orange rind and lemon juice.
2. Sift the flour and baking powder, then stir into the mixture with the ground almonds and the walnuts.
3. Whisk the egg whites until stiff and fold into the cake mixture with the carrots. Pour into the prepared tin and hollow the centre slightly.
4. Bake at 180°C (350°F) mark 4 for about 1½ hours, covering the top with foil after an hour if it starts to overbrown.
5. Leave to cool slightly, then turn out on to a wire rack and remove the lining paper. Leave to cool.
6. For the topping (if used): beat the cheese, honey and lemon juice and spread over the cake. Sprinkle with walnuts.

ORANGE MADEIRA CAKE

Makes one loaf cake, about 900 g (2 lb) size

175 g (6 oz) butter or margarine
175 g (6 oz) caster sugar

3 eggs, beaten
150 g (5 oz) self raising flour
100 g (4 oz) plain flour
1 orange

1. Grease and base-line a 28 cm (11 inch) 1.4 litre (2½ pint) ovenproof loaf dish or tin.
2. Cream together the butter and caster sugar until pale and fluffy.
3. Gradually beat in the eggs. Fold in the self raising and plain flours, sifted together.
4. Grate in the orange rind and fold in with 30 ml (2 tbsp) orange juice. Spoon into the prepared tin. Smooth the surface with a palette knife.
5. Bake in the oven at 170°C (325°F) mark 3 for about 1 hour 15 minutes or until firm to the touch. Turn out on to a wire rack to cool.

LEMON SWISS ROLL

Makes 6–8 slices
3 large eggs
100 g (4 oz) caster sugar
100 g (4 oz) plain flour
150 ml ($\frac{1}{4}$ pint) double cream
about 275 g (10 oz) lemon curd

Glacé icing
100 g (4 oz) icing sugar
20 ml (4 tsp) warm water

1. Grease a 33 × 23 × 1 cm (13 × 9 × $\frac{1}{2}$ inch) Swiss roll tin. Line the base with greaseproof paper and grease the paper. Dust with caster sugar and flour.
2. Whisk the eggs and sugar in a bowl until thick enough to leave a trail on the surface when the whisk is lifted. Sift in flour and fold gently through the mixture.
3. Turn the mixture into the prepared tin and level the surface. Bake in the oven at 200°C (400°F) mark 6 for 10–12 minutes or until the cake springs back when pressed lightly with a finger and has shrunk away a little from the tin.
4. Sugar a sheet of greaseproof paper and turn the cake out on to it. Roll up with the paper inside. Transfer to a wire rack and leave to cool for 30 minutes.
5. Whip the cream until it just holds its shape. Unroll the Swiss roll and spread with three-quarters of the lemon curd. Top with cream then roll up again and place on a serving plate.
6. Make a thin glacé icing by sifting the icing sugar into a basin and beating in the water.
7. Coat the Swiss roll with the icing. Immediately, using the point of a teaspoon, draw rough lines of lemon curd across the icing and pull a skewer through to form a feather pattern. Leave to set, about 1 hour.

CHAPTER FOUR

GÂTEAUX
AND MERINGUES

*clockwise from back:
Strawberry
Shortbread Gâteau
(below), Iced Tea
(page 9), Palmiers
(page 77), Fig and
Almond Tart (page
83)*

STRAWBERRY SHORTBREAD GÂTEAU

Serves 8
*200 g (7 oz) plain flour
25 g (1 oz) cornflour
100 g (4 oz) caster sugar
100 g (4 oz) butter, softened*

*2 eggs
225 g (8 oz) fresh strawberries
300 ml (½ pint) double cream
45 ml (3 tbsp) milk
icing sugar*

1. Sift together 150 g (5 oz) of the flour, the cornflour and 50 g (2 oz) of the sugar. Knead in the butter, using finger tips, to give a soft dough. Roll out on a lightly floured board and trim, using a pan lid as a guide to give a 21.5 cm (8½ inch) round. Bake at 170°C (325°F) mark 3 for about 25 minutes until pale golden brown. Cut into 8 sections while still warm. Leave to cool on a wire rack.

2. Make a whisked egg sponge in the usual way with the eggs, remaining flour and sugar. Cook in a 21.5 cm (8½ inch) sandwich tin at 190°C (375°F) mark 5 for about 15 minutes until golden. Turn out and cool on a wire rack.

3. Wipe strawberries, hull and slice all but three.

4. Whip cream with milk until it holds its shape. Sweeten to taste with a little icing sugar if desired. Using a large star vegetable nozzle, pipe whirls of cream around the outside edge of the sponge. Fold sliced strawberries through the remaining cream and pile into the centre of the sponge.

5. Dust the shortbread with icing sugar and arrange at an angle on top of the cream. Top with the whole berries.

BLACK FOREST GÂTEAU

Serves 10
100 g (4 oz) butter
6 eggs
225 g (8 oz) caster sugar
75 g (3 oz) plain flour
50 g (2 oz) cocoa
2.5 ml (½ tsp) vanilla flavouring

two 425 g (15 oz) cans stoned black
  cherries, drained and syrup reserved
60 ml (4 tbsp) kirsch
600 ml (1 pint) whipping cream
100 g (4 oz) chocolate caraque (see
  note) to decorate
5 ml (1 level tsp) arrowroot

1. Grease and base-line a 23 cm (9 inch) round cake tin. Put the butter into a bowl, place over a pan of warm water and beat it until really soft but not melted.

2. Put the eggs and sugar into a large bowl, place over a pan of hot water and whisk until pale and creamy, and thick enough to leave a trail on the surface when the whisk is lifted.

3. Sift the flour and cocoa together, then lightly fold into the mixture with a metal spoon. Fold in the vanilla flavouring and softened butter.

4. Turn the mixture into the tin and tilt the tin to spread the mixture evenly. Bake in the oven at 180°C (350°F) mark 4 for about 40 minutes, until well risen, firm to the touch and beginning to shrink away from the sides of the tin.

5. Turn out of the tin on to a wire rack, covered with greaseproof paper, to cool for 30 minutes.

6. Cut the cake into three horizontally. Place a layer on a flat plate. Mix together 75 ml (5 tbsp) cherry syrup and the kirsch. Spoon 45 ml (3 tbsp) over the cake.

7. Whip the cream until it just holds its shape, then spread a little thinly over the soaked sponge. Reserve a quarter of the cherries for decoration and scatter half the remainder over the cream.

8. Repeat the layers of sponge, syrup, cream and cherries. Top with the third cake round and spoon over the remaining kirsch-flavoured syrup.

9. Spread a thin layer of cream around the sides of the cake, reserving a third to decorate. Press on the chocolate caraque, reserving a few to decorate the top.

10. Spoon the remaining cream into a piping bag, fitted with a large star nozzle and pipe whirls of cream around the edge of the cake. Top each whirl with a chocolate curl.

11. Fill the centre with the reserved cherries. Blend the arrowroot with 45 ml (3 tbsp) cherry syrup, place in a small saucepan, bring to the boil and boil, stirring, for a few minutes until the mixture is clear. Brush the glaze over the cherries.

Note

To make chocolate caraque, melt 100 g (4 oz) chocolate over a pan of hot water. Pour it in a thin layer on to a marble slab or cold baking tray and leave to set until it no longer sticks to your hand when you touch it. Holding a large knife with both hands, push the blade across the surface of the chocolate to roll pieces off in long curls. Adjust the angle of the blade to get the best curls.

COFFEE PRALINE GÂTEAU

Serves 6
2 large eggs
100 g (4 oz) caster sugar
50 g (2 oz) plain flour
15 ml (1 tbsp) coffee essence

25 g (1 oz) blanched almonds
150 ml ($\frac{1}{4}$ pint) double cream
30 ml (2 tbsp) coffee-flavoured
   liqueur
icing sugar, for dusting

1. Grease a 20 cm (8 inch) round cake tin. Base-line with greased greaseproof paper. Dust with caster sugar and flour.

2. Put eggs into a deep bowl with 75 g (3 oz) caster sugar and whisk vigorously until the mixture is very thick and light and leaves a trail. If hand mixing, whisk the mixture over a saucepan of simmering water.

3. Sift the flour evenly over the surface of the egg mixture and fold in lightly until no traces of flour remain. Lightly fold in the coffee essence.

4. Turn into the prepared tin and bake at once in the oven at 180°C (350°F) mark 4 for about 30 minutes or until the sponge springs back when pressed lightly with a finger and has shrunk away a little from the tin. Turn out on to a wire rack and leave for 1–2 hours.

5. Meanwhile, make the praline. Oil a baking sheet. Put the remaining caster sugar into a small frying pan with the blanched almonds and heat gently until the sugar dissolves and caramelises.

6. Pour the praline on to the prepared baking sheet and leave for 10–15 minutes to cool and harden.

7. When cold, grind or crush with end of a rolling pin in a strong bowl. Whip the cream until it holds its shape then whisk in the liqueur and fold in three-quarters of praline (ground nut mixture).

8. Split the sponge in half and sandwich with the cream. Dust the top with icing sugar and decorate with praline. Refrigerate for 1–2 hours before serving.

clockwise from back:
Iced Tea (page 9),
Coffee Praline Gâteau
(page 51), Mille
Feuilles (page 76),
Meringue Medley
(page 58)

MERINGUE NESTS

Makes 12
5 egg whites
275 g (10 oz) caster sugar

Cranberry filling
20 g (¾ oz) custard powder
15 ml (1 level tbsp) caster sugar
300 ml (½ pint) milk
225 g (8 oz) cranberries or
  blueberries
100 g (4 oz) granulated sugar

60 ml (4 tbsp) water
10 ml (2 level tsp) arrowroot
175 g (6 oz) curd cheese
150 ml (¼ pint) double cream

Chestnut filling
450 ml (¾ pint) double cream
5 ml (1 tsp) vanilla flavouring
500 g (1 lb) can sweetened chestnut
  purée
grated chocolate curls, to decorate

1. Line two baking sheets with non-stick baking paper. Draw twelve 10 cm (4 inch) circles on the paper.

2. Whisk the egg whites until they are very stiff, but not dry, then gradually whisk in the caster sugar a little at a time, whisking well between each addition, until the meringue is very stiff and shiny.

3. Put the meringue into a large piping bag fitted with a medium-sized star nozzle. Fill in each drawn circle on the baking paper, with a continuous spiral of meringue. Pipe stars around the edge of each base to form a little wall. Bake at 100°C (200°F) mark Low for 4–5 hours. Turn the oven off and leave the meringues until cool.

4. For cranberry filled nests, blend the custard powder with the caster sugar and a little of the milk to form a smooth paste. Bring the remaining milk to the boil, then stir it into the custard mixture. Return the custard to the saucepan and cook over a low heat, stirring, until the custard thickens. Pour the custard into a clean bowl, then cover the surface closely with greaseproof paper to prevent a skin forming. Allow to cool, then refrigerate.

5. Put the cranberries into a saucepan with the granulated sugar and water, cover and cook gently for about 15 minutes until the cranberries are softened. Blend the arrowroot with a little cold water to form a smooth paste, then stir into the cranberries. Bring to the boil, stirring until the mixture thickens and clears. Pour into a small bowl, cover the surface closely with greaseproof paper to prevent a skin forming, allow to cool, then refrigerate until well chilled.

6. Beat the curd cheese until it is soft and smooth. Whip the cream until it will hold soft peaks. Whisk the cold custard until it is very smooth, mix with the curd cheese, then fold in the cream. Divide the custard mixture between the meringue nests, then spoon the cranberries on top. Serve immediately, or chill until ready to serve.

7. For chestnut filled nests, whip the cream with the vanilla flavouring until just thick enough to pipe, then put it into a piping bag fitted with a medium-sized star nozzle.

8. Spoon the chestnut purée into the nests. Pipe or spoon the cream on top and sprinkle over the chocolate curls. Serve immediately, or chill until ready to serve.

LEMON MERINGUE PIE

Serves 6–8
Pâte sucrée
150 g (5 oz) plain flour
pinch of salt
25 g (1 oz) icing sugar
75 g (3 oz) butter, cubed
2 egg yolks
lightly whipped cream, to serve

Filling
pared rind and juice of 4 large lemons

600 ml (1 pint) water
65 g (2½ oz) cornflour
50–75 g (2–3 oz) caster sugar
3 egg yolks

Meringue
3 egg whites
175 g (6 oz) caster sugar

1. Sift the flour, salt and icing sugar into a bowl. Rub in the butter until the mixture resembles fine breadcrumbs. Add the egg yolks and mix with a round-bladed knife to form a dough. Turn on to a lightly floured surface and knead for a few seconds until smooth. Chill for 30 minutes.

2. Roll out the pâte sucrée on a lightly floured surface to a round 2.5 cm (1 inch) larger than a 23 cm (9 inch) fluted flan tin. Line the dish with the pastry, pressing it well into the flutes.

3. Trim the edge, then prick the pastry well, all over, with a fork. Chill for 30 minutes, then bake blind at 220°C (425°F) mark 7 for 25–30 minutes, until cooked and lightly browned. Allow to cool. Leave the oven on.

4. Meanwhile, prepare the filling, put the lemon rind in a saucepan with the water, bring to the boil, then remove from the heat, cover, and leave to stand for at least 30 minutes.

5. Remove all of the lemon rind from the pan, then stir in the lemon juice. Blend the cornflour with a little of the lemon liquid to form a smooth paste, pour it into the pan and stir well. Bring the lemon mixture to the boil, stirring continuously. Reduce the heat and continue cooking until every trace of raw cornflour disappears, and the mixture has thickened.

6. Stir in the sugar to taste, adding a little more if liked, then beat in the egg yolks. Pour the lemon filling into the pastry case.

7. To make the meringue, whisk the egg whites until stiff, but not dry, then gradually whisk in the sugar, adding a little at a time and whisking well between each addition, until the meringue is very stiff and shiny. Put the meringue into a large piping bag fitted with a large star nozzle, then pipe it attractively on top of the lemon filling. Alternatively, spoon the meringue on to the filling and shape it into swirls with a palette knife.

8. Bake for 5–10 minutes until the meringue is very lightly browned. Remove the pie from the oven and allow to cool, then refrigerate until quite cold. Serve with lightly whipped cream.

Lemon Meringue Pie
(page 55)

PINEAPPLE GRIESTORTE

Serves 6–8
3 eggs, separated
100 g (4 oz) caster sugar
376 g (13¼ oz) can pineapple pieces,
drained and juice reserved

75 g (3 oz) semolina
300 ml (½ pint) whipping cream
100 g (4 oz) chopped mixed nuts,
toasted

1. Grease a 20 cm (8 inch) round cake tin.
Base-line with greased greaseproof paper.
2. Whisk the egg yolks and sugar in a bowl
until pale and really thick. Stir in 30 ml
(2 tbsp) of the reserved pineapple juice
together with the semolina.
3. Whisk the egg whites until stiff, then
gently fold into the yolks and sugar
mixture.
4. Turn into the prepared tin. Bake in the
oven at 180°C (350°F) mark 4 for about
40 minutes or until the sponge springs back

when pressed lightly with a finger and has
shrunk away a little from the tin. Turn out
on to a wire rack and leave 30 minutes to
cool.
5. Roughly chop the pineapple pieces.
Lightly whip the cream. Split the cake in
half and fill with half the cream and half the
pineapple. Spread a little of the cream
around the sides and top of the cake and
press the nuts on the side. Pipe the
remaining cream in whirls and decorate
with pineapple.

HAZELNUT AND PASSION FRUIT ROULADE

Serves 6
5 eggs, separated
175 g (6 oz) caster sugar
30 ml (2 tbsp) runny honey
75 g (3 oz) ground hazelnuts

2 passion fruit
300 ml (½ pint) double cream
icing sugar, whipped cream and
    hazelnuts, to decorate

1. Grease and line a 33 × 23 cm (13 × 9 inch) Swiss roll tin. Whisk the egg yolks and sugar in a bowl over hot water for 10 minutes or until pale and thick. Remove from the heat and whisk for a further 2 minutes.
2. Whisk the egg whites until stiff, then gradually whisk in the honey. Fold the egg whites into the egg yolk and sugar mixture, then fold in the ground hazelnuts.
3. Pour the mixture into the tin. Shake the tin to level the mixture. Bake at 180°C (350°F) mark 4 for 12–15 minutes, until

firm to the touch. Leave to cool in the tin.
4. Cut the passion fruit in half and scoop out the seeds. Whip the cream until stiff then fold in the passion fruit seeds.
5. Dust a sheet of greaseproof paper with icing sugar. Turn the cooled cake out on to the paper and carefully remove the lining paper. Spread with the cream and roll up from one short edge, using the greaseproof paper to lift the cake. Carefully transfer to a serving plate and decorate with icing sugar, whipped cream and hazelnuts.

Hazelnut and Passion
Fruit Roulade
(above)

MERINGUE MEDLEY

Makes 44 small meringues
6 egg whites
350 g (12 oz) caster sugar
15 ml (1 level tbsp) finely chopped
   pistachio nuts
300 ml ($\frac{1}{2}$ pint) double cream

15 ml (1 tbsp) Grand Marnier
25 g (1 oz) pecans, walnuts, or
   hazelnuts, finely chopped
15 ml (1 tbsp) raspberry purée
75 g (3 oz) plain chocolate, melted

1. Line several baking sheets with non-stick baking paper cut to fit the sheets.
2. Put the egg whites and caster sugar together in a large bowl over a large saucepan of hot water and whisk until very stiff and shiny. Remove from the heat and continue whisking until the meringue will hold unwavering peaks—on no account let the meringue become too hot.
3. Fill a large piping bag, fitted with a large star nozzle, with meringue and pipe out as follows:—

To make whirls: pipe 24 whirls of meringue on the lined baking sheets, about 4 cm (1$\frac{1}{2}$ inch) in diameter.

To make oblong spirals: pipe the meringue in a spiral fashion to make 24 spirals about 7.5 cm (3 inch) long. Or, if you find it easier, pipe a joined line of shells to the same length.

To make pistachio fingers: simply pipe 20 straight lines of meringue about 7.5 cm (3 inches) long on the baking sheets, then sprinkle with chopped pistachio nuts.

4. Bake the meringues at 140°C (275°F) mark 1 for 2–2$\frac{1}{2}$ hours, or until completely dried out. Change the trays around in the oven during cooking, to ensure that they all dry evenly. Allow the meringues to cool, then remove from the paper and complete as follows, or store in an airtight tin until required.
5. To finish the whirls, whisk 150 ml ($\frac{1}{4}$ pint) of the double cream with the Grand Marnier until it will hold soft peaks, then fold in the chopped nuts. Sandwich the meringues together, in pairs, with the nut cream, then place in small paper cases for serving.
6. To finish the spirals, whisk the remaining cream until thick, then fold in the raspberry purée. Put the cream into a piping bag fitted with a large star nozzle. Sandwich the meringues together, in pairs, with piped cream. Put the meringues into small paper cases for serving.
7. To finish the pistachio fingers, dip the base of each meringue in the melted chocolate to coat it evenly, removing excess chocolate by gently pulling the meringue across the back of a knife. Place on greaseproof paper until set.

MOCHA MERINGUE

Serves 6–8
3 egg whites
175 g (6 oz) caster sugar
15 ml (1 level tbsp) instant coffee
   powder

Filling
300 ml (½ pint) double cream

2 egg whites
5 ml (1 level tsp) instant coffee
   powder
25 g (1 oz) chocolate, grated
25 g (1 oz) almonds, finely chopped
chopped almonds and grated
   chocolate, to decorate

1. Draw two 20.5 cm (8 inch) circles on non-stick paper and place on two baking sheets.
2. Whisk the egg whites until very stiff. Whisk in half the sugar, add the instant coffee and whisk until the mixture is really stiff and no longer speckled with coffee. Carefully fold in the remaining sugar with a metal spoon.
3. Divide the mixture between the baking sheets and spread evenly to fill the circles. Bake in the oven at 150°C (300°F) mark 2

for about 2 hours until dry. Leave to cool on the baking sheets before carefully lifting them off.
4. To make up the filling, whip the cream until thick. Whisk the egg whites until stiff, then carefully fold into the cream. Fold in the coffee, chocolate and nuts.
5. Sandwich the meringue layers together with half the cream mixture. Spread remainder on top; decorate with nuts and chocolate 30 minutes before serving.

Hazelnut Meringue Gâteau (below)

HAZELNUT MERINGUE GÂTEAU

Serves 6–8
3 egg whites
175 g (6 oz) caster sugar
50 g (2 oz) hazelnuts, skinned,
    toasted and finely chopped

300 ml ($\frac{1}{2}$ pint) double cream
350 g (12 oz) fresh raspberries
icing sugar for sifting
finely chopped pistachio nuts for
    sprinkling

1. Line two baking sheets with non-stick baking paper, then draw a 20.5 cm (8 inch) circle on each one.
2. Whisk the egg whites until they are very stiff, but not dry. Adding just a little sugar at a time, gradually whisk the caster sugar into the egg whites, whisking well between each addition until the meringue is stiff and very shiny. Carefully fold in the chopped hazelnuts.
3. Divide the meringue equally between the two baking sheets, then spread neatly into rounds. With a palette knife, mark the top of one of the rounds into swirls—this will be the top meringue. Bake at 140°C

(275°F) mark 1 for about 1½ hours until dry. Turn the oven off, and allow the meringues to cool in the oven.
4. Whip the cream until it will hold soft peaks. Carefully remove the meringues from the baking paper. Place the smooth meringue round on a large flat serving plate, then spread with the cream. Arrange the raspberries on top of the cream, then place the second meringue on top.
5. Sift icing sugar over the top of the gâteau, and sprinkle with finely chopped pistachio nuts. Serve the gâteau as soon as possible.

CHAPTER FIVE

TEABREADS

APRICOT NUT TEABREAD

Serves 6–8

75 g (3 oz) dried apricots, cut into
    small pieces
75 g (3 oz) bran breakfast cereal
    (not flaked)
75 g (3 oz) demerara sugar

300 ml (½ pint) milk
50 g (2 oz) hazelnuts, chopped
1 egg, beaten
175 g (6 oz) self raising flour
5 ml (1 level tsp) baking powder

1. Grease and base-line a 900 g (2 lb) loaf tin. Set aside until required.
2. Put the apricots into a large bowl and add the bran, sugar and the milk. Cover with cling film and leave in a cool place for 3 hours.
3. Stir the hazelnuts, egg, flour and baking powder into the mixture and stir until well blended.

4. Turn the mixture into the prepared tin and bake in the oven at 190°C (375°F) mark 5 for 1–1¼ hours or until firm to the touch. Cover lightly with foil if necessary.
5. Turn out and cool on a wire rack. Store for a few days before eating.

MIXED FRUIT TEABREAD

Serves 6–8

175 g (6 oz) raisins
100 g (4 oz) sultanas
50 g (2 oz) currants
175 g (6 oz) soft brown sugar
300 ml (½ pint) strained cold
    Ridgways Lapsang Souchong tea

1 egg, beaten
225 g (8 oz) plain wholemeal flour
7.5 ml (1½ level tsp) baking powder
2.5 ml (½ level tsp) mixed spice

1. Grease and base-line a 900 g (2 lb) loaf tin. Place the dried fruit and the sugar in a large bowl. Pour over the tea, stir well to mix and leave to soak overnight.
2. The next day, add the egg, flour, baking powder and mixed spice to the fruit and tea mixture. Beat thoroughly with a wooden spoon until all the ingredients are evenly combined.
3. Spoon the cake mixture into the

prepared tin. Level the surface.
4. Bake in the oven at 180°C (350°F) mark 4 for about 1¼ hours until the cake is well risen and a skewer inserted in the centre comes out clean.
5. Turn the cake out of the tin and leave on a wire rack until completely cold. Wrap in cling film and store in an airtight container for 1–2 days before slicing and eating.

APPLE AND WALNUT TEABREAD

Serves 6–8
225 g (8 oz) self raising flour
pinch of salt
5 ml (1 level tsp) mixed spice.
100 g (4 oz) soft tub margarine
100 g (4 oz) caster sugar

2 large eggs
15 ml (1 tbsp) honey or golden syrup
100 g (4 oz) sultanas
50 g (2 oz) walnuts, chopped
1 medium cooking apple, peeled,
*   cored and chopped*

1. Grease and line a 900 g (2 lb) loaf tin.
2. Sift together the flour, salt and mixed spice into a large bowl. Add the remaining ingredients and beat together until well blended.
3. Turn the mixture into the prepared tin and bake in the oven at 180°C (350°F) mark 4 for 1 hour. Reduce the oven temperature to 170°C (325°F) mark 3 and bake for a further 20 minutes.
4. Turn out and leave to cool on a wire rack. Serve thickly sliced and buttered.

BANANA AND HONEY TEABREAD

Serves 6–8
450 g (1 lb) bananas
225 g (8 oz) self raising flour
2.5 ml (½ level tsp) salt
1.25 ml (¼ level tsp) freshly grated
*   nutmeg*
100 g (4 oz) butter or block

margarine
100 g (4 oz) caster sugar
grated rind of 1 lemon
2 large eggs
120 ml (8 tbsp) thick honey
8 sugar cubes (optional)

1. Grease and base-line a 900 g (2 lb) loaf tin.
2. Peel the bananas, then mash the flesh using a fork or potato masher. Mix the flour, salt and nutmeg together. Rub in the fat until the mixture resembles fine breadcrumbs.
3. Stir in the sugar, lemon rind, eggs, 90 ml (6 tbsp) honey and mashed banana. Beat well until evenly mixed. Turn the mixture into the prepared tin.
4. Bake in the oven at 180°C (350°F) mark 4 for about 1¼ hours, covering lightly if necessary. Test with a fine skewer which should come out clean when the teabread is cooked.
5. Cool slightly, then turn out on to a wire rack to cool completely. Gently warm the remaining honey, then brush over the teabread. Roughly crush the sugar lumps, and scatter over the top.

clockwise from back:
Boston Brownies
(page 26), Cherry
Garlands (page 85),
Malted Fruit Loaf
(page 66)

CHOCOLATE, DATE AND NUT LOAF

Serves 6–8
175 ml (6 fl oz) boiling water
175 g (6 oz) stoned dates, sliced
275 g (10 oz) plain flour
50 g (2 oz) caster sugar
7.5 ml (1½ level tsp) salt
5 ml (1 level tsp) baking powder
5 ml (1 level tsp) bicarbonate of soda

175 g (6 oz) plain chocolate
50 g (2 oz) butter
1 egg
175 ml (6 fl oz) milk
5 ml (1 tsp) vanilla essence
175 g (6 oz) shelled walnuts, roughly
*   chopped*

1. Grease a 900 g (2 lb) loaf tin.
2. Pour the boiling water over the dates and leave to stand. Meanwhile, sift the flour, sugar, salt, baking powder and bicarbonate of soda into a large bowl. Melt the chocolate with the butter.
3. Beat the egg with the milk and vanilla essence. Add to the dry ingredients all at once with the walnuts, dates with their soaking water and melted chocolate and stir until just blended.
4. Pour the mixture quickly into the tin. Bake at 180°C (350°F) mark 4 for 1 hour 10 minutes. Cool in the tin on a wire rack for 10 minutes and then turn out on to the rack and leave to cool completely.

MALTED FRUIT LOAF

Serves 6–8
350 g (12 oz) plain flour
2.5 ml (½ level tsp) bicarbonate of
*   soda*
5 ml (1 level tsp) baking powder
250 g (9 oz) sultanas

30 ml (2 level tbsp) demerara sugar
135 ml (9 tbsp) malt extract
2 eggs, beaten
200 ml (7 fl oz) strained cold
*   Ridgways Her Majesty's Blend*
*   (H.M.B.) tea*

1. Grease and base-line a 900 g (2 lb) loaf tin. Grease the underside of a baking sheet.
2. Sift the flour, bicarbonate of soda and baking powder together in a bowl. Stir in the sultanas.
3. Slowly heat together the demerara sugar and malt extract. Do not boil. Pour on to the dry ingredients. Add the eggs and tea and beat well.
4. Turn the mixture into the prepared tin. Cover with the baking sheet, greased side down. Place a weight on top. Bake in the oven at 150°C (300°F) mark 2 for about 1½ hours. Turn out and cool on a wire rack. Wrap and keep for two days before eating.

DATE RIPPLE LOAF

Serves 10–12

225 g (8 oz) cooking apple, peeled and cored
150 g (5 oz) stoned cooking dates
grated rind and juice of 1 lemon
45 ml (3 tbsp) water
125 g (4 oz) butter
125 g (4 oz) dark brown sugar
2 eggs, beaten
125 g (4 oz) self raising flour

1. Grease a non-stick rectangular cake tin that has a top measurement of 26 × 10 cm (10½ × 4 inch).
2. Chop the apple and 100 g (4 oz) of the dates, then place in a saucepan with the lemon rind and juice and water. Cook over a gentle heat until reduced to a soft purée. Beat well and set aside to cool.
3. Cream together butter and sugar until light and fluffy. Gradually beat in the eggs then lightly beat in the flour.

4. Spoon one-third of the cake mixture into the prepared tin. On top of this spread half the date mixture. Repeat the layering, finishing with cake mixture.
5. Cut the remaining dates into thin slivers and arrange in a line down the length of the cake. Bake at 170°C (325°F) mark 3 for about 1 hour 10 minutes. Cover with foil half-way through cooking time.
6. Leave to cool in the tin for 10 minutes, then turn out on to a wire rack to cool.

GINGER MARMALADE TEABREAD

Serves 6–8

200 g (7 oz) plain flour
5 ml (1 level tsp) ground ginger
5 ml (1 level tsp) baking powder
40 g (1½ oz) block margarine
65 g (2½ oz) light soft brown sugar
60 ml (4 tbsp) ginger marmalade
1 egg, beaten
60 ml (4 tbsp) milk
40 g (1½ oz) stem ginger, chopped

1. Grease and base-line a 900 g (2 lb) loaf tin.
2. Put the flour, ginger and baking powder into a bowl and rub in fat until mixture resembles fine breadcrumbs. Stir in sugar.
3. Mix together the marmalade, egg and most of the milk. Stir into the dry ingredients and add the rest of the milk, if necessary, to mix to a soft dough.
4. Turn the mixture into the prepared tin, level the surface and press pieces of ginger on top. Bake in the oven at 170°C (325°F) mark 3 for about 1 hour or until golden. Turn out on to a wire rack to cool.

LEMON ALMOND TEABREAD

Serves 6–8
175 g (6 oz) courgettes
150 g (5 oz) polyunsaturated
  margarine
150 g (5 oz) light soft brown sugar
3 eggs
175 g (6 oz) self raising wholemeal
  flour

5 ml (1 level tsp) baking powder
2.5 ml (½ level tsp) ground allspice
grated rind of 1 lemon
25 g (1 oz) fresh brown breadcrumbs
50 g (2 oz) flaked almonds
30 ml (2 tbsp) runny honey

1. Grease and base-line a 900 g (2 lb) loaf tin. Peel and coarsely grate the courgettes (a food processor fitted with a coarse grating blade is ideal).
2. Beat the margarine and sugar until fluffy, gradually whisk in the lightly beaten eggs. Fold in the flour, baking powder and allspice.
3. Stir in the courgettes, grated lemon rind, breadcrumbs and 40 g (1½ oz) almonds. Spoon the mixture into the prepared tin.

4. Bake at 180°C (350°F) mark 4 for about 50 minutes or until the teabread is just firm to the touch.
5. Brush the teabread with honey and sprinkle over the remaining almonds. Return to the oven and bake for a further 30 minutes or until well browned and quite firm to the touch. A skewer inserted into the teabread should come out clean.
6. Allow the teabread to cool slightly in the tin, then turn out on to a wire rack to cool completely.

BRAN AND CURRANT TEABREAD

Serves 6–8
75 g (3 oz) All Bran type cereal
150 g (5 oz) currants
50 g (2 oz) light soft brown sugar
50 g (2 oz) desiccated coconut

200 ml (7 fl oz) milk
200 ml (7 fl oz) strained cold
    Ridgways China Caravan tea
175 g (6 oz) self raising flour
5 ml (1 level tsp) baking powder

1. Place the cereal, currants, sugar and coconut in a bowl. Pour over the milk and tea, cover and leave to soak overnight.
2. Grease and base-line a 900 g (2 lb) loaf tin.
3. Stir the flour and baking powder into the bran mixture then spoon the mixture into the prepared loaf tin.
4. Bake at 190°C (375°F) mark 5 for about 1¼ hours or until well risen and firm to the touch. Cover lightly with foil if necessary. A skewer inserted into the teabread should come out clean.
5. Allow to cool slightly in the tin, then turn out on to a wire rack to cool completely. Wrap in greaseproof paper and foil and leave for 1–2 days to mature before eating.

DARK HONEY TEABREAD

Serves 4–6
100 g (4 oz) plain flour
5 ml (1 level tsp) ground cinnamon
5 ml (1 level tsp) bicarbonate of soda
pinch of salt
45 ml (3 tbsp) vegetable oil
30 ml (2 tbsp) runny honey
30 ml (2 tbsp) golden syrup
50 g (2 oz) demerara sugar

1 egg
30 ml (2 tbsp) milk
75 g (3 oz) sultanas

Topping
15 g (½ oz) glacé cherries
15 g (½ oz) walnuts
15 ml (1 tbsp) runny honey

1. Lightly grease and line a 450 g (1 lb) loaf tin.
2. Sift together the flour, cinnamon, bicarbonate of soda and salt into a large bowl. Add the remaining ingredients, except the topping ingredients. Mix well, then beat for 2–3 minutes until well blended.
3. Pour the mixture into the prepared tin and bake in the oven at 180°C (350°F) mark 4 for 1 hour. Cool in the tin for a few minutes, then turn out and leave to cool on a wire rack.
4. Roughly chop the cherries and walnuts for the topping. Brush the top of the cake with honey, then sprinkle over the cherries and nuts. Serve sliced and spread with butter.

CHAPTER SIX

PASTRIES

JALOUSIE

Makes 8 slices

368 g (13 oz) packet frozen puff
    pastry, thawed
225 g (8 oz) raspberry conserve

1 small egg, beaten with 10 ml
    (2 level tsp) sifted icing sugar
icing sugar for sifting

1. Roll out the puff pastry on a lightly floured surface to a square a little larger than 30 cm (12 inches). Trim the pastry edges to form an exact 30 cm (12 inch) square. Cut the pastry equally in half. Place the pastry lengths on baking sheets and chill for about 10 minutes. Chilling the pastry at this stage will make it much easier to assemble.

2. Spread the raspberry conserve down the centre of one of the pieces of pastry, leaving a 2.5 cm (1 inch) border all round.

3. Remove the second piece of pastry from the baking sheet and fold in half lengthways, then make cuts all along the folded edge to within 2.5 cm (1 inch) of the edges, spacing the cuts about 1 cm ($\frac{1}{2}$ inch) apart.

4. Without unfolding the pastry, place it on top of the pastry spread with jam so that the edges line up with the bottom piece of pastry, then carefully unfold the pastry to cover the jam completely. Press all the pastry edges well together to seal. Chill for 30 minutes.

5. Remove the chilled jalousie from the refrigerator, then flake the edge with a small knife and mark into flutes. Brush the top with the beaten egg—do not allow the glaze to run down the sides as it will prevent them from rising.

6. Bake at 230°C (450°F) mark 8 for 20–30 minutes until it is well risen, and golden brown. Allow to cool.

7. Sift with icing sugar then place on a doily-lined tray. To serve, cut into slices across the jalousie.

Danish Pastries
(page 74)

DANISH PASTRIES

Makes 16
25 g (1 oz) fresh yeast or 15 ml
    (1 level tbsp) dried yeast and 5 ml
    (1 level tsp) sugar
150 ml (¼ pint) tepid water
450 g (1 lb) plain flour
5 ml (1 level tsp) salt
50 g (2 oz) lard
30 ml (2 level tbsp) sugar
2 eggs, beaten
300 g (11 oz) butter or margarine,
    softened
50 g (2 oz) sultanas
beaten egg, to glaze

Almond paste
15 g (½ oz) butter or margarine
75 g (3 oz) caster sugar
75 g (3 oz) ground almonds
1 egg, beaten

Cinnamon butter
50 g (2 oz) butter
50 g (2 oz) caster sugar
10 ml (2 level tsp) ground cinnamon

Glacé icing
100 g (4 oz) icing sugar
about 15 ml (1 tbsp) warm water
flaked almonds to decorate

1. Blend the fresh yeast with the water. If using dried yeast, sprinkle it into the water with the 5 ml (1 tsp) sugar and leave in a warm place for 15 minutes, until frothy.
2. Mix the flour and salt, rub in the lard and stir in the 30 ml (2 level tbsp) sugar. Add the yeast liquid and beaten eggs and mix to an elastic dough, adding a little more water if necessary. Knead well for 5 minutes on a lightly floured surface, until smooth. Return the dough to the rinsed-out bowl, cover with a clean tea towel and leave the dough to 'rest' in the refrigerator for 10 minutes.
3. Shape the butter into an oblong. Roll out the dough on a floured board to an oblong about three times as wide as the butter. Put the butter in the centre of the dough and fold the sides of the dough over the butter. Press the edges to seal.
4. With the folds at the sides, roll the dough into a strip three times as long as it is wide; fold the bottom third up, and the

top third down, cover and leave to 'rest' for 10 minutes. Turn, repeat, rolling, folding and resting twice more.
5. To make the almond paste, cream the butter and sugar, stir in the almonds and add enough egg to make a soft and pliable consistency.
6. Make the cinnamon butter by creaming the butter and sugar and beating in the cinnamon.
7. Roll out the dough into the required shapes and fill with almond paste or cinnamon butter.
8. After shaping, cover the pastries with a clean tea towel and leave to prove in a warm place for 20–30 minutes. Brush with beaten egg and bake in the oven at 220°C (425°F) mark 7 for about 15 minutes.
9. Meanwhile sift the icing sugar into a basin and add enough water to make a smooth, thin glacé icing.
10. While the pastries are hot brush with the icing and sprinkle with flaked almonds.

Shaping Danish Pastries

Crescents Cut out a 23 cm (9 inch) round. Divide into four segments and put a little almond paste at the base of each. Roll up from the base and curl round to form a crescent.

Imperial stars Cut into 7.5 cm (3 inch) squares and make diagonal cuts from each corner to within 1 cm ($\frac{1}{2}$ inch) of the centre. Put a piece of almond paste in the centre of the square and fold one corner of each cut section down to the centre, securing the tips with beaten egg.

Foldovers and cushions Cut into 7.5 cm (3 inch) squares and put a little almond paste in the centre. Fold over two opposite corners to the centre. Make a cushion by folding over all four corners, securing the tips with beaten egg.

Pinwheels Cut into a rectangle 25.5 × 10 cm (10 × 4 inches). Spread with cinnamon butter and sultanas, roll up like Swiss rolls and cut into 2.5 cm (1 inch) slices. Bake cut side upwards.

Twists Cut into rectangles as for pinwheels. Cut each rectangle lengthways to give four pieces. Spread with cinnamon butter and fold the bottom third of each up and the top third down, seal and cut each across into thin slices. Twist these slices and put on a baking sheet.

ECCLES CAKES

Makes 16–20
368 g (13 oz) packet frozen puff pastry, thawed
40 g (1½ oz) caster sugar
2.5 ml (½ level tsp) mixed spice

100 g (4 oz) currants
40 g (1½ oz) chopped mixed peel
25 g (1 oz) butter, melted
lightly beaten egg white and granulated sugar, for glazing

1. Roll out the pastry to 0.3 cm (⅛ inch) thickness on a lightly floured surface using a floured rolling pin. Cut into circles using a 10 cm (4 inch) plain cutter.

2. Mix the sugar and spice together, then stir in the currants, peel and butter. Place 5 ml (1 tsp) of the fruit mixture on the centre of each circle. Brush the edges with beaten egg white, then draw them up over the filling and pinch them together to seal.

3. Turn the pastries over and roll lightly to flatten them slightly. Cut three parallel slits in the top of each, brush with egg white and sprinkle with sugar.

4. Place on a dampened baking sheet, and bake at 220°C (425°F) mark 7 for about 15 minutes, until puffed and golden brown.

5. Transfer to a wire rack to cool slightly before serving.

*Mille Feuilles
(below)*

MILLE FEUILLES

Makes 6
212 g (7½ oz) packet frozen puff
.pastry, thawed
100 g (4 oz) raspberry jam
300 ml (½ pint) double cream,
    whipped

Glacé icing
175 g (6 oz) icing sugar
15–30 ml (1–2 tbsp) warm water
red food colouring

1. Dampen a baking sheet. Roll out the pastry on a lightly floured working surface into a rectangle measuring 25 × 23 cm (10 × 9 inches) and place on the baking sheet. Prick all over with a fork.
2. Bake in the oven at 220°C (425°F) mark 7 for 10 minutes, until well risen and golden brown. Transfer to a wire rack and leave for 30 minutes to cool.
3. When cold, trim the pastry edges, cut in half lengthways and cut each half across into six slices. Spread half with raspberry jam, then cover with the cream.
4. Spread jam on the bases of the remaining pastry pieces and place on top of the first layers.

5. Sift the icing sugar into a basin. Gradually add the water to make a smooth, thick icing.
6. Mix 15 ml (1 tbsp) icing with a few drops of red colouring. Set aside. Spread remaining white icing over pastries.
7. Pour the pink icing into a greaseproof paper piping bag. Cut off the tip and carefully pipe fine pink lines 1 cm (½ inch) apart on top of the white icing, across each pastry.
8. Draw a skewer down the length of the mille feuilles at 1 cm (½ inch) intervals to make a 'feathering' design. Leave for 1 hour to set.

PALMIERS

Makes 12
*368 g (13 oz) packet frozen puff
pastry, thawed*

caster sugar, for sprinkling
150 ml (¼ pint) double cream
75 ml (3 fl oz) single cream

1. Roll out the pastry on a lightly floured working surface to a rectangle measuring 30 × 25 cm (12 × 10 inches).
2. Dredge with caster sugar. Fold the long sides of the puff pastry halfway towards the centre.
3. Dredge with more caster sugar and fold again, taking the sides right to the centre.
4. Dredge with sugar again and fold in half lengthways, hiding the first folds and pressing lightly.
5. Cut across the pastry length into 24 equal-sized slices. Dampen a baking sheet

and place the palmiers on it, cut-side down. Flatten them slightly with a palette knife or the palm of your hand.
6. Bake in the oven at 220°C (425°F) mark 7 for 8 minutes until golden brown. Turn each over and bake for a further 4 minutes. Transfer to a wire rack and leave for about 20 minutes to cool.
7. Whip the creams together with a little caster sugar, until lightly peaked. Sandwich the palmiers together with the cream before serving. Sprinkle with caster sugar.

*Chocolate Eclairs
(page 78)*

CHOCOLATE ECLAIRS

Makes 12

Choux pastry
90 g (3½ oz) plain flour
pinch of salt
185 ml (6 fl oz) water
65 g (2½ oz) butter
3 large eggs, beaten

Filling
300 ml (½ pint) whipping cream
15 ml (1 level tbsp) icing sugar,
 sifted
few drops of vanilla flavouring

Icing
100 g (4 oz) plain chocolate
40 ml (2½ tbsp) water
25 g (1 oz) butter

1. Dampen a baking sheet. Sift the flour with the salt on to a piece of paper or a plate. Put the water and butter in a saucepan, and heat, allowing the butter to melt before boiling point is reached. Bring to a fast boil, and immediately pour in the flour.
2. Remove the pan from the heat. Beat the mixture until it is smooth and leaves the sides of the pan. Cool, then gradually beat in the eggs. You may not need to add all of the eggs. Add just enough eggs to make the mixture glossy and smooth, and of a dropping consistency.
3. Spoon the choux pastry into a large piping bag fitted with a large star nozzle. Pipe into about 12 × 12.5 cm (5 inch) lengths on the prepared baking sheet. Leave space for the mixture to puff up.
4. Bake at 200°C (400°F) mark 6 for 35–40 minutes, until crisp and golden. Remove from the oven and pierce each eclair to allow the steam to escape. Return to the oven for 5 minutes to dry, then cool on a wire rack.
5. Whip the cream with the sugar and vanilla until stiff. Spoon into a piping bag fitted with a small star nozzle and fill the eclairs.
6. Melt the chocolate with the water in a bowl set over a pan of simmering water. Stir in the butter. Dip the tops of the eclairs in chocolate and leave on a wire rack to set.

APRICOT FLAN

Serves 6–8
about 17 fresh apricots, halved,
   stoned and poached or use 34
   canned or bottled apricot halves
30 ml (2 tbsp) kirsch

Pâte sucrée
150 g (5 oz) plain flour
pinch of salt
25 g (1 oz) icing sugar
75 g (3 oz) butter, cubed
2 egg yolks

Filling
100 ml (4 fl oz) single cream
1 egg
10 ml (2 tsp) caster sugar
15 ml (1 tbsp) apricot jam

Decoration
150 ml ($\frac{1}{4}$ pint) double cream
25 g (1 oz) plain chocolate, melted

1. Put the apricot halves into a bowl, sprinkle with the kirsch, cover and leave to stand for about 1 hour.
2. For the pâte sucrée, sift the flour, salt and icing sugar into a bowl. Rub in the butter until the mixture resembles fine breadcrumbs. Add the egg yolks and mix with a round-bladed knife to form a dough. Turn on to a lightly floured surface and knead for a few seconds until smooth.
3. Roll out the pâte sucrée on a lightly floured surface to a round, 2.5 cm (1 inch) larger than a 23 cm (9 inch) fluted flan tin. Line the tin with the pastry, pressing it well into the flutes. Trim the edge, and prick the pastry all over with a fork. Chill for 30 minutes, then partially bake at 220°C (425°F) mark 7 for 20 minutes.
4. Meanwhile, drain the apricots, reserving any kirsch. Lightly whisk the cream with the egg, caster sugar and remaining kirsch.

5. Remove the partially baked flan case from the oven. Reduce the oven temperature to 190°C (375°F) mark 5. Leaving the pastry case in the flan tin, spread the apricot jam over the bottom of the flan. Reserve six apricot halves for decoration, then arrange the rest on top of the jam. Pour in the custard mixture. Bake for 30–40 minutes until the custard is set. Cool.
6. Whip the double cream for the decoration until it will hold soft peaks. Transfer the flan to a serving plate and spread the cream evenly over the top.
7. Put the melted chocolate into a small paper piping bag, then cut a small hole in the bottom of the bag. Pipe the chocolate, in criss-cross lines, across the cream. Cut each of the reserved apricot halves in half and arrange neatly around the edge of the flan on the cream to decorate.

Apricot Flan
(page 79)

MAIDS OF HONOUR

Makes 12
568 ml (1 pint) pasteurised milk
15 ml (1 tbsp) rennet
212 g (7½ oz) packet frozen puff
* pastry, thawed*

1 egg, beaten
15 g (½ oz) butter or margarine,
* melted*
50 g (2 oz) caster sugar

1. Gently heat the milk in a saucepan until just warm to the finger. Remove from the heat and stir in the rennet. Leave for 1½–2 hours until set.
2. When set, put the junket into a muslin bag and leave to drain overnight. Next day, refrigerate the curd for several hours or until very firm.
3. Grease 12 × 6.5 cm (2½ inch) patty tins. On a lightly floured surface, roll out the

pastry very thinly and using a 7.5 cm (3 inch) plain cutter, cut out 12 rounds. Line the patty tins with the pastry rounds and prick well.
4. Stir the egg, butter and sugar into the drained curd. Divide the mixture between the pastry cases and bake in the oven at 200°C (400°F) mark 6 for 30 minutes, until well risen and just firm to the touch. Serve warm.

ALMOND CUSTARD TARTS

Makes 10
125 g (4 oz) butter or block
  margarine
225 g (8 oz) plain flour
about 45 ml (3 tbsp) water
200 ml (7 fl oz) milk

2 eggs
50 g (2 oz) caster sugar
1.25 ml ($\frac{1}{4}$ tsp) ratafia essence or
  almond flavouring
flaked almonds, toasted

1. Grease ten 7.5 cm (3 inch), top measurement, fluted brioche tins. Rub the fat into the flour, then bind to a firm dough with the water.
2. Roll out the pastry thinly and cut out 10 circles large enough to line the prepared tins. Press the pastry into the tins and place on a baking sheet. Bake blind (see note on page 83) at 200°C (400°F) mark 6 for

15 minutes. Reduce oven to 180°C (350°F) mark 4.
3. Whisk together the milk, eggs, caster sugar and ratafia essence or almond flavouring. Pour into the pastry cases. Scatter toasted almonds on top. Bake the custards in the oven for about 15–20 minutes or until just set. Leave to cool before serving.

*Fresh Fruit Tartlets
(page 82)*

FRESH FRUIT TARTLETS

Makes 12

Crème pâtissière

2 small egg yolks
25 g (1 oz) caster sugar
30 ml (2 tbsp) plain flour, sifted
150 ml (¼ pint) milk
5 ml (1 tsp) vanilla flavouring
1 small egg white
50 ml (2 fl oz) double cream

Almond pastry

150 g (5 oz) plain flour
pinch of salt

40 g (1½ oz) caster sugar
50 g (2 oz) ground almonds
90 g (3½ oz) butter, cubed
few drops of vanilla flavouring
1 egg, beaten

Apricot glaze

325 g (12 oz) apricot conserve
30 ml (2 tbsp) kirsch

Filling

a selection of fresh fruit, prepared as
necessary

1. Whisk the egg yolks and a quarter of the caster sugar in a bowl until pale and thick. Fold in the flour.
2. Put the milk and the vanilla into a saucepan and bring almost to the boil. Gently whisk the hot milk into the egg and flour mixture. Strain the mixture, through a nylon sieve, back into the pan.
3. Cook the custard over a gentle heat, stirring, until thickened. Pour into a clean bowl, then cover the surface closely with greaseproof paper to prevent a skin forming. Allow to cool, but not to set too firmly.
4. Whisk the egg white until stiff, then gradually whisk in the remaining caster sugar. Whip the cream until thick.
5. Whisk the cooled custard until smooth, gradually fold in the egg white then the cream. Cover the crème pâtissière with cling film and chill thoroughly.
6. Make the almond pastry: sift the flour, salt and sugar into a bowl, then mix in the ground almonds. Rub in the butter until the mixture resembles fine breadcrumbs.

Make a well in the centre, add the vanilla and the beaten egg. Mix together with a round-bladed knife to form a dough. Turn on to a lightly floured surface and knead for a few seconds until smooth. Wrap the pastry in cling film and chill for 30–40 minutes until firm, before using.
7. Roll out the pastry on a lightly floured surface and cut out 12 × 12.5 cm (5 inch) circles with a round cutter and use to line 10 cm (4 inch) tartlet tins. Trim the edges and prick the base of each tartlet with a fork, then place the lined tins on baking sheets and chill for at least 30 minutes.
8. Bake blind at 220°C (425°F) mark 7 for 20–25 minutes until very lightly browned. Allow the cases to cool a little in their tins, then carefully transfer to a wire rack.
9. Make the apricot glaze: heat the apricot conserve gently until melted, then press through a sieve and mix with the kirsch. Brush it evenly over the inside of each pastry case. Reserve the remaining glaze.
10. Divide the crème pâtissière equally between the pastry cases. Arrange the fruit

attractively in the cases.

11. Reheat the remaining apricot glaze until boiling, adding a little water if necessary. Carefully brush it over the fruit to glaze evenly. If liked, sprinkle raspberries with icing sugar instead of glazing them. Serve as soon as possible.

Note
To bake blind, line the pastry cases with greaseproof paper, then weight down with baking beans or dried peas. Remove the paper and beans or peas as soon as the pastry is taken out of the oven.

FIG AND ALMOND TART

Serves 4–6
75 g (3 oz) plain flour
40 g (1½ oz) plus 30 ml (2 level tbsp) ground almonds
40 g (1½ oz) caster sugar
125 g (4 oz) butter or polyunsaturated margarine
1 egg yolk

1–2 drops vanilla flavouring
6–8 ripe figs
30 ml (2 tbsp) brandy
30 ml (2 level tbsp) semolina
30 ml (2 level tbsp) soft brown sugar
45 ml (3 level tbsp) apricot jam
15 ml (1 tbsp) lemon juice
single cream or Greek yogurt to serve

1. Place the flour on a clean work surface and form a large well in the centre. Sift 40 g (1½ oz) ground almonds on to the flour.
2. In the well, place the caster sugar, softened butter or margarine, egg yolk and vanilla flavouring. Using the fingertips of one hand, pinch these ingredients together until evenly blended. Gradually draw in the flour and ground almonds with the help of a palette knife and form the mixture, with your hand, into a smooth, pliable dough. Wrap and chill well for at least 30 minutes.
3. Meanwhile, peel the figs, slice thinly and place them in layers in a shallow dish. Pour over the brandy and leave to soak.

4. Roll out the pastry and use to line an 18 cm (7 inch) fluted loose-based flan tin. Prick the base and bake blind at 190°C (375°F) mark 5 for about 10–15 minutes, or until dry and beginning to colour.
5. Mix together 30 ml (2 level tbsp) ground almonds, the semolina and brown sugar. Spoon evenly over the base of the flan. Arrange the figs on top and place back into the oven for 15–20 minutes.
6. Meanwhile, sieve the jam into a small pan; add the lemon juice and heat until the jam has melted. Brush over the baked fig tart to glaze. Allow to cool *slightly* before serving with single cream or Greek yogurt.

CHAPTER SEVEN

BISCUITS

CHERRY GARLANDS

Makes 24
225 g (8 oz) soft tub margarine
50 g (2 oz) icing sugar
200 g (7 oz) plain flour
150 g (5 oz) cornflour
vanilla flavouring

50 g (2 oz) glacé cherries, very finely
  chopped
whole cherries and angelica, to
  decorate
icing sugar

1. Lightly grease two baking sheets. Cream the margarine and sugar together until pale and fluffy.
2. Beat in the flours, a few drops of vanilla flavouring and the chopped cherries. (If using an electric handmixer, beat for 3–4 minutes; by hand, beat until the mixture is very soft.)
3. Spoon half the mixture into a piping bag fitted with a 1 cm (½ inch) star nozzle. Pipe 5 cm (2 inch) rings on the baking

sheets allowing room for spreading.
4. Decorate with a quartered cherry and pieces of angelica. Repeat with the remaining mixture.
5. Bake in the oven at 190°C (375°F) mark 5 for about 20 minutes until pale golden. Allow to firm up slightly on the baking sheets for about 30 seconds before sliding on to a wire rack to cool. Dredge with icing sugar.

Chocolate Viennese Fingers (page 86)

CHOCOLATE VIENNESE FINGERS

Makes about 18
125 g (4 oz) butter or block
   margarine
25 g (1 oz) icing sugar
75 g (3 oz) plain chocolate

125 g (4 oz) plain flour
1.25 ml (¼ level tsp) baking powder
15 ml (1 level tbsp) drinking
   chocolate powder (optional)
few drops of vanilla flavouring

1. Grease two baking sheets. Put the butter into a bowl and beat until pale and soft, then beat in the icing sugar.
2. Break 25 g (1 oz) chocolate into a heatproof bowl and place over simmering water. Stir until the chocolate is melted, then remove from heat and leave to cool for 10 minutes.
3. When the chocolate is cool, but not thick, beat it into the creamed mixture.
4. Sift in the flour, baking powder and drinking chocolate, if using. Beat well, adding a few drops of vanilla flavouring.
5. Spoon into a piping bag fitted with a medium star vegetable nozzle and pipe finger shapes about 7.5 cm (3 inches) long on to the prepared baking sheets, allowing room between each for the mixture to spread. Bake at 190°C (375°F) mark 5 for 15–20 minutes until crisp and pale golden. Cool on a wire rack for 30 minutes.
6. When the fingers are cold, break the remaining 50 g (2 oz) chocolate into a heatproof bowl. Stand the bowl over a pan of simmering water and stir until the chocolate has melted. Remove from the heat and dip both ends of the fingers into the melted chocolate. Leave on a wire rack for 30 minutes to set.

GRANTHAM GINGERBREADS

Makes 30
100 g (4 oz) butter or block
   margarine
350 g (12 oz) caster sugar

1 egg, beaten
250 g (9 oz) self raising flour
5 ml (1 level tsp) ground ginger

1. Grease two or three baking sheets.
2. Cream the butter and sugar together in a bowl until pale and fluffy. Gradually beat in the egg.
3. Sift the flour and ginger into the mixture and work in with a fork until a fairly firm dough is obtained.
4. Roll the dough into small balls about the size of a walnut and put them on the baking sheets, spaced apart.
5. Bake in the oven at 150°C (300°F) mark 2 for 40–45 minutes, until crisp, well risen, hollow and very lightly browned.

SHORTBREAD ROUNDS

Makes about 20
125 g (4 oz) butter or block
    margarine
50 g (2 oz) caster sugar

125 g (4 oz) plain flour
50 g (2 oz) ground rice
caster sugar to sprinkle

1. Grease two baking sheets. Cream the fat until soft. Add the caster sugar and beat until very light and fluffy.
2. Stir in the flour and ground rice, until the mixture comes together. Knead well to form a smooth dough.
3. On a lightly floured surface thinly roll out the dough. Using a 7 cm (2¾ inch) fluted cutter stamp out 20 rounds, re-rolling the dough as necessary.
4. Place the rounds on greased baking sheets, prick the surface with a fork. Bake at 180°C (350°F) mark 4 for about

15 minutes or until pale golden and just firm to the touch.
5. Cool on wire racks, then sprinkle with caster sugar.

Variation
Complete as above to the end of stage 3. Using a 2.5 cm (1 inch) fluted cutter, stamp out the centre of half the biscuits to form rings. Bake as above; when cold sandwich a complete round and ring together with jam. Dredge with caster sugar before serving.

SPICE BISCUITS

Makes 36
100 g (4 oz) butter
200 g (7 oz) caster sugar
1 egg, beaten
10 ml (2 tsp) milk
225 g (8 oz) plain flour

5 ml (1 level tsp) bicarbonate of soda
5 ml (1 level tsp) ground cinnamon
1.25 ml (¼ level tsp) ground nutmeg
pinch of ground cloves
75 g (3 oz) currants

1. Grease three baking sheets. Cream the butter with 175 g (6 oz) of the sugar until light and fluffy and then beat in the egg and milk.
2. Stir in the remaining ingredients and mix well until smooth. Cover and refrigerate the mixture until it is firm enough to handle.

3. On a lightly floured surface roll out the mixture as thinly as possible. Sprinkle evenly with the remaining sugar and cut into star or diamond shapes about 5 cm (2 inches) in length.
4. Place on the baking sheets. Bake at 190°C (375°F) mark 5 for 8 minutes or until lightly browned. Cool on a wire rack.

clockwise from back:
Spice Biscuits
(page 87), Black
Forest Gâteau
(page 50), Ginger
Whirls (page 31),
Coconut Macaroons
(page 92)

LEMON AND NUTMEG SHORTIES

Makes 24
125 g (4 oz) butter or block
     margarine, softened
50 g (2 oz) caster sugar
175 g (6 oz) plain flour

25 g (1 oz) ground rice
1.25 ml (¼ level tsp) ground nutmeg
grated rind of 1 lemon
5 ml (1 tsp) lemon juice
caster sugar and nutmeg, to sprinkle

1. Lightly grease two baking sheets. Cream together the butter and sugar until very pale. Stir in the flour, ground rice, nutmeg, lemon rind and juice. Knead very well to form a smooth, workable paste.
2. On a lightly sugared surface, roll out the biscuit dough to slightly more than 0.5 cm (¼ inch) thick.
3. With a sharp knife, cut into 7.5 × 2 cm (3 × ¾ inch) fingers. Place on the baking sheets and chill for 30 minutes.
4. Bake in the oven at 190°C (375°F) mark 5 for about 25 minutes until just changing colour.
5. Sprinkle with caster sugar and ground nutmeg while still warm. Leave to cool completely on a wire rack.

DEVON FLATS

Makes about 24
225 g (8 oz) self raising flour
pinch of salt
100 g (4 oz) caster sugar

100 ml (4 fl oz) clotted cream
1 egg, beaten
about 15 ml (1 tbsp) milk, to mix

1. Grease two baking sheets. Mix the flour and salt together then stir in the sugar. Lightly bind together with the cream, egg and sufficient milk to give a fairly stiff dough. If the dough feels at all sticky, cover it and place in the refrigerator to firm up.
2. Roll out the dough on a lightly floured surface to about 0.75 cm (⅓ inch) thick and cut into circles with a 7.5 cm (3 inch) cutter.
3. Transfer to a greased baking tray and bake at 220°C (425°F) mark 7 for 8–10 minutes, until a light golden brown. Carefully transfer to a wire rack and leave to cool.
4. The biscuits can be stored in an airtight container in a cool place for up to 3 days.

CHOCOLATE NUT SNAPS

Makes 24
1 egg, separated
100 g (4 oz) caster sugar
150 g (5 oz) plain chocolate
125 g (4 oz) hazelnuts, finely
*   chopped*

40 g (1½ oz) plain flour
200 g (7 oz) icing sugar
about 30 ml (2 tbsp) water

1. Grease two baking sheets. Whisk the egg white until stiff. Fold in the caster sugar.
2. Coarsely grate 75 g (3 oz) plain chocolate into the mixture and stir in with the hazelnuts, flour and egg yolk.
3. Turn out on a well floured surface and knead lightly. Cover and refrigerate for about 30 minutes.
4. Roll the dough out to 5 mm (¾ inch) thickness. Using a 5 cm (2 inch) plain cutter, cut out 24 shapes. Knead lightly and place on the prepared baking sheets. Cover and refrigerate the biscuits again for 30 minutes.

5. Bake in the oven at 190°C (375°F) mark 5 for about 20 minutes until crisp. Immediately ease off the baking sheet on to a wire rack to cool for 30 minutes.
6. Break the remaining chocolate into a heatproof bowl and place over simmering water. Stir until the chocolate is melted, then remove from heat.
7. Cut the tip off a paper icing bag and spoon in the melted chocolate. Pipe lines of chocolate across the biscuits. Leave to set for 30 minutes. The biscuits can be stored, un-iced, in airtight containers for 2–3 weeks.

ORANGE AND RAISIN COOKIES

Makes 25
150 g (5 oz) plain flour
100 g (4 oz) sugar
100 g (4 oz) butter, softened
1 egg, beaten

2.5 ml (½ level tsp) baking powder
2.5 ml (½ level tsp) salt
2.5 ml (½ tsp) vanilla flavouring
100 g (4 oz) seedless raisins
15 ml (1 tbsp) grated orange rind

1. Grease three baking sheets. Place all the ingredients except for the raisins and grated orange rind in a large bowl and beat lightly until just mixed. Stir in the raisins and orange rind.
2. Drop heaped dessertspoonfuls of the mixture about 5 cm (2 inches) apart on to the baking sheets.
3. Bake at 190°C (375°F) mark 5 for 15 minutes or until the cookies are golden brown. Remove from the baking sheets and cool on a wire rack.

BRANDY SNAPS

Makes about 12
50 g (2 oz) butter, cubed
50 g (2 oz) caster sugar
30 ml (2 tbsp) golden syrup
50 g (2 oz) plain flour
2.5 ml (½ level tsp) ground ginger

5 ml (1 tsp) brandy
finely grated rind of ½ a lemon

Filling
175 ml (6 fl oz) double cream

1. Line two or three large baking sheets with non-stick baking paper. Gently heat the butter, sugar and syrup until the butter has melted and the sugar dissolved. Remove from the heat.
2. Sift the flour and ginger together, then stir into the melted mixture with the brandy and lemon rind. Drop teaspoonfuls of the mixture on to a prepared baking sheet, leaving about 10 cm (4 inches) in between them.
3. Bake towards the hottest part of the oven at 180°C (350°F) mark 4 for about 7 minutes until the biscuits are bubbling and lacy in appearance.
4. Meanwhile, prepare another tray of the mixture ready for baking. As soon as the baked biscuits are cooked, remove them from the baking sheet using a palette knife and roll each one around the buttered handle of a wooden spoon. Leave on the handles until set, then gently twist each one, remove it and leave to cool completely.
5. If the biscuits set before they have been shaped, return them to the oven for a few minutes to soften. Store in an airtight container until required.
6. Just before serving, whip the cream until it stands in soft peaks. Spoon into a piping bag fitted with a star nozzle and pipe the cream into the snaps.

COCONUT MACAROONS

Makes 18
2 egg whites
100 g (4 oz) icing sugar, sifted

100 g (4 oz) ground almonds
few drops of almond flavouring
100 g (4 oz) desiccated coconut

1. Line two baking sheets with non-stick paper.
2. Whisk the egg whites until stiff but not dry. Lightly fold in the sugar.
3. Gently stir in the almonds, almond flavouring and desiccated coconut until the mixture forms a sticky dough.
4. Spoon walnut-sized pieces of mixture on to the baking sheets.
5. Bake in the oven at 150°C (300°F) mark 2 for about 25 minutes. The outer crust should be golden and the inside soft. Cool on a wire rack.

Eccles Cakes (page 75), Brandy Snaps (opposite)

CINNAMON BISCUITS

Makes 36
50 g (2 oz) butter
100 g (4 oz) caster sugar
1 egg yolk, beaten
100 g (4 oz) plain flour

5 ml (1 level tsp) ground cinnamon
1.25 ml (¼ level tsp) baking powder
1.25 ml (¼ level tsp) salt
15 ml (1 tbsp) milk

1. Cream the butter, beat in the sugar and egg yolk and stir in the remaining ingredients. Refrigerate for 2–3 hours to make the mixture easier to roll.
2. Divide the mixture in half and with a lightly floured rolling pin roll out each piece on a cold baking sheet to an even 0.3 cm (⅛ inch) thickness.
3. Use a floured 6 cm (2¼ inch) plain cutter to stamp out rounds, spaced about 2.5 cm (1 inch) apart. Refrigerate for a further

1 hour.
4. Remove the mixture between the rounds from the baking sheet. Knead lightly and re-roll to 0.3 cm (⅛ inch) thickness on another cold baking sheet. Cut out more rounds.
5. Bake at 180°C (350°F) mark 4 for 15 minutes, transfer the biscuits immediately to a wire rack and leave to cool completely.

INDEX